P9-DMF-904

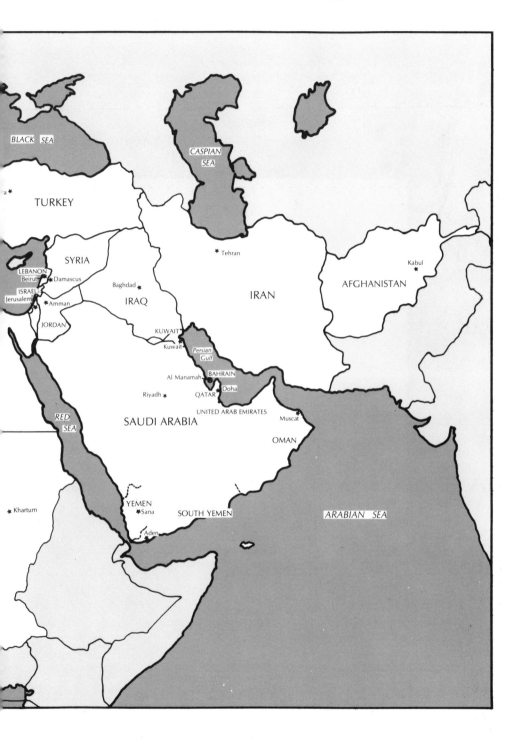

BLACK SEA

CASPIAN SEA

TURKEY

SYRIA

LEBANON
Beirut
Damascus

ISRAEL
Jerusalem

Amman

JORDAN

Baghdad

IRAQ

KUWAIT

Kuwait

Tehran

IRAN

Kabul

AFGHANISTAN

Persian
Gulf

Al Manamah

BAHRAIN

Doha

Riyadh

QATAR

UNITED ARAB EMIRATES

Muscat

SAUDI ARABIA

OMAN

RED
SEA

Khartum

YEMEN

Sana

SOUTH YEMEN

ARABIAN SEA

Aden

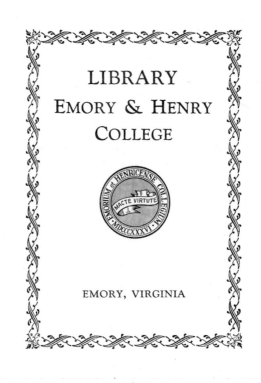

The
Middle
East
Annual

A Reference Publication in Middle Eastern Studies
David H. Partington, Series Editor

The Middle East Annual

Issues and Events
Volume 4—1984

Edited by
David H. Partington

G. K. Hall & Co.
70 Lincoln Street, Boston, Mass.

Copyright © 1985 by G. K. Hall & Co.

ISBN 0-8161-8718-5

ISSN 0733-5350

This publication is printed on permanent/durable acid-free paper
MANUFACTURED IN THE UNITED STATES OF AMERICA

Contents

Foreword

History may teach. But we don't always learn.

The annals of preceding centuries—or even millennia—in the Middle East have not often brought wisdom to those outside the area who have business with it. Those annals have not even bequeathed sensible policies to those inside the Mideast, however well they may feel they know each other's political and ethnic intricacies.

Napoleon, for example, resisted temptation and stayed out of Lebanon after his famous Egyptian excursion. But few, in or out of the region, have repeated his wisdom lately. Neither Israel, nor the United States, nor Syria (with, admittedly, a historic claim) has held back from that morass.

The Soviet defense ministry had available to it the history of Britain's Pyrrhic victories at Kandahar and Kabul and eventual retreat to the Khyber Pass, but still rides the same see-saw in Afghanistan. Messrs. Carter and Brzezinski might have hesitated over the supposed permanence of the shah's new Persian empire had they read *The Adventures of Hadjji Baba of Ispahan*. And on and on: Nasser in Yemen; Haig, Sharon, Shultz in Lebanon; Saddam Hussein in Iran; Numayri in Juba; Amin Gemayel in his own suburbs; Qaddafi in Chad.

War and suzerainty have ebbed and flowed across this crucial region— one of few on the globe that really deserves to be called a crossroads—since the dawn of written history.

It's tempting to see today's inhabitants as carrying on dramas that bear more than a passing resemblance to the wars, treaties, trade alliances, water acquisitiveness, and feuding vengeance, of Hittites, Babylonians, Israelites, Assyrians, Trojans, Greeks, Carthaginians, Crusaders, Moguls, Berbers, Persians, Osmans, and Mamelukes. Those quaintly costumed casts lacked the supertankers, hijackable jets (though not the hostages), antipersonnel bombs, and press spokesmen of today. The play is never performed the same way in revival. But the modern reruns strike chords in memory.

If we haven't profited from ancient history, or from more recent pillars of wisdom, is it likely that we will learn from this volume's careful scrutiny of the preceding year—plus its analyses of of five key areas? Odd though it may seem in the face of the record sketched above, the answer may be "yes."

Why? Because the Near East has increasingly seized the attention of the leaders and citizens of the outer world—from Japan to Europe to America. The accumulated residue of Israeli-Arab quick-wars of 1956, 1967, 1973, and 1982, plus subsequent oil crises, tanker sinkings, and hostage-holding have educated and focused political minds in all those capitals. Complacency may creep back with the level of oil storage tanks. But not for long.

Foreign ministry specialists and businessmen realize that issues of fundamental importance are coming to a head—between Palestinians and Israelis over West Bank land ownership; between the Saudi petrochemical industry and its older competitors on other continents; between Saudi oil production and that of OPEC partners; in hints that Iran may seek a gradual rapprochement with the U.S.; in decisions by the new Gorbachev team in Moscow on whether to escalate or seek compromise in Afghanistan; between Libya and France in Chad, between Khartum and its distant black minority in southern Sudan.

The Middle East Annual, now in its fourth year, does a clear, precise job of assisting policymaker, scholar, businessman, journalist, or interested amateur in understanding the meaning of events from Afghanistan to the Spanish Sahara. It carefully documents what actually happened during the year so that fickle memories may find accurate compass readings.

Modern man's attention span is influenced more than any of us like to believe by the moving spotlight of broadcast and print media. That restless light deluges us with brief scenes and headlines, then moves on, leaving disconnected afterimages on our retinas: After 1967, of omnipotent Israel. After 1973, of omnipotent OPEC. In President Numayri's heyday, of a Sudan destined to become the breadbasket of northeast Africa. Before the Iran-Iraq war, of Iraq as a future world power, with an extraordinary asset base—oil, water, arable land, population. Of petrodollars rampant, then boomeranging third-world debt. And always of rival Israeli and Arab claims to be America's and the West's chief asset at a crossroads of world fuel and transport.

Both the undersigned and the more knowledgeable specialists who have written the five perceptive essays that make up the heart of this volume have the advantage of looking back over 1984 with some extra months of denouement in 1985 to help with Monday morning quarterbacking.

We know, for example, that Israel's coalition government finally followed the advice its military chiefs put forward privately in the spring of 1984: to withdraw from Lebanon as soon after the July Israeli elections as feasible. To delay, said the generals, would mean turning Shiite acceptance into enmity. It would mean piling up bills for a government already beset by overspending and hyperinflation.

We know that the Reagan administration has finally—after 1984's election—decided that 1985 is a crucial year for its own at times fatherless Middle East peace plan of September 1982. But we are still in suspense over the degree to which that plan will woo the Palestinians' Yasir Arafat, Jordan's King Hussein, and the Siamese-twin Israeli government of Shimon Peres and Yitzhak Shamir toward bargaining instead of feinting. That, and the long-term outcome of the population shift from Ashkenazis (Europeans) to Sephardim (Orientals) among Jews in Israel, as well as the growth of the Israeli Arab population, remain key issues for the future peace of the Middle Eastern core.

We know also that Hashemi Rafsanjani, speaker of the Iranian parliament, has cast out hints about improving relations with "satan" America. Furthermore, Rafsanjani's leader, the Ayatollah Khomeini, has spoken in terms of a defensive continuation of his fundamentalist holy war. But we don't yet know the degree to which this, or the eventual demise of Khomeini, will mean the end of the Jacobin period of the Iranian revolution.

In the five chapters covering Saudi Arabia, the Gulf war and the hanseatic league of Gulf states, Israeli politics, Libyan dynamics, and terrorism in the region, readers will find a great deal of added insight. Instead of the thin outer layer of onionskin that is examined before the TV cameras, they will find the complex inner layers made clear. Let us hope that some of the eyes skimming this page and about to turn to the meat within are those of government officials.

Arnold Toynbee's majestic thesis that civilizations progress by responding to challenge is not unvaryingly accurate. If it were, we would have to conclude that much of the Middle East, under persistent challenge, should be on the brink of a new renaissance. Instead we often find parts of it merely close to the brink of an abyss.

But cynicism is not in order. Saudi Arabia's technical education system, its state-of-the-art petrochemical industry, as well as its proven oil reserves may yet stimulate a creative era. Ditto Israel's high-technology entrepreneurs. Iraq, despite the albatross of a long trench war, has continued to build new industries and increase pipeline flow. Lebanon's political realignment holds some promise of ending internal carnage. The Maghreb countries still have a significant agricultural advantage over southern European farmers in supplying specialty fruits and vegetables early to European buyers.

Toynbee's idea of challenge and response may not have counted on terrorism and endless retaliatory strikes as challenges. But if sensible negotiators can find a way to reduce those plagues, the Toynbeean equation may yet bear more fruit than weary diplomats expect.

Earl W. Foell
Editor in chief, *The Christian Science Monitor*

Introduction

David H. Partington

With this fourth volume of *The Middle East Annual: Issues and Events*, the editor and publisher continue their effort to provide the general reader and scholar with unbiased analyses of major issues or problems. As in previous volumes, we have invited prominent scholars to address issues that are of current concern to the United States.

In addition to authoritative essays, this publication contains a detailed chronicle of events of 1984, an annotated bibliography of the principal monographs on the contemporary Middle East that appeared this year, and also an annotated bibliography of selected serial articles—all presented to enhance the value of this volume as a reference work.

The Middle East in 1984 maintained its reputation as the major trouble spot of the world. The American press however, perhaps because of the long presidential election campaign and the increasingly troublesome events in Central America, seemed to provide less effective coverage of the area than in previous years.

Although internal events in Iran were virtually ignored, the Iran-Iraq war drew American interest as the United States began to perceptibly favor Iraq, despite our official policy of neutrality. The possibility that a militant, Shiite Iran avowedly hostile to the United States might overwhelm Iraq and pose a threat to the Arab Gulf states clearly worried our policy makers, for the security of the Saudi Arabian oil fields is one of the few constant and clear aims of the country.

During the year, the Iran-Iraq war seemed fairly deadlocked on land, and although major battles were fought, the Iranian forces did not achieve a major breakthrough. Both combatants, however, initiated serious attacks on oil tankers in the Gulf, thereby raising the possibility of a great-power confrontation. In this issue of the *Annual*, Professor R. Hrair Dekmejian discusses the politics of the Gulf states, their quest for mutual security, and the policy of the United States in the Gulf.

Although Saudi Arabia is the largest and most important of the Gulf states, few people understand the extent of American-Saudi involvement. Dr. J. E. Peterson details this special relationship, presents an in-depth study of the internal situation in the oil-rich desert kingdom, outlines the effect of the Iran-Iraq war on Riyadh, and ventures to predict the future course of American-Saudi relations.

One anticipated consequence of an Iranian victory over Iraq is an increase in terrorism directed against the Gulf states, which generally represent the moderate stratum of Arab governments. The American news media favor crisis reporting, and it is unfortunate that terrorists provided another major disaster for the United States with the destruction of the U.S. embassy annex in Beirut in September.

Terrorism is a recognized feature of the contemporary Middle Eastern political landscape, and in this issue of the *Annual* we include an essay on the subject by Dr. John W. Amos, II, that provides historical background on the development of the use of terror and elucidates the changing nature of terrorism.

One of the more visible actors on the Middle Eastern stage is Colonel Qaddafi, leader of Libya and proponent of the "rejectionist front." Qaddafi has authorized his agents to strike Libyan dissidents and exiles, and a bungled situation at the Libyan embassy in London resulted this year in the breaking of diplomatic relations with Great Britain. The oil wealth of Libya has enabled Qaddafi to exert influence from Belfast to Tehran, and he has been a principal irritant to the United States, backing the Polisario against Morocco in the Western Sahara, threatening Sudan and Egypt, invading Chad, and funding those who oppose the so-called moderate governments of the Arab world. To assist readers of the *Annual* in gaining insight into Qaddafi and his policies we present an essay prepared by Dr. Marius and Mary-Jane Deeb on the current political and social situation in Libya.

For four decades, the American perception of the Middle East as a problem in international relations has been constructed with Israel as the keystone, the only sure ally in the strategic confrontation with the Soviet Union. Assured of virtually unconditional American support, and receiving financial assistance without parallel, Israel as a major military power has long pursued a policy of aggressive expansion and bellicose reaction to actual and potential threats from the Arab states.

It is now clear that the Israeli invasion of Lebanon in 1983, the campaign sometimes called "Sharon's War," marked a turning point in the history of Israel. New movements and pressures within Israeli society, and severe doubts on the part of significant numbers of Israeli citizens about the war make the parliamentary elections of 1984 especially interesting and revealing. Professor Don Peretz, a long-time observer of Israeli politics, clarifies the many issues of the 1984 elections in his essay.

I wish to thank John W. Amos, II, Marius and Mary-Jane Deeb, R. Hrair Dekmejian, Don Peretz, and John Peterson for their contributions to this volume. My special thanks go to Mark T. Day for his persistence in compiling and annotating the monograph bibliography, and to Ara Salibian, manuscript editor at G. K. Hall & Co. for painstaking attention to the production of this work.

Middle Eastern Chronicle:
The Events of 1984

David H. Partington

This chronicle is limited to political events, or happenings of political import, in that area of the world stretching from Morocco through India. It also includes pertinent events in the Western capitals. All citations in this chronicle are taken from the *New York Times*, and they are arranged in chronological order. Readers seeking a chronicle that is subdivided by topic and draws upon multiple sources are referred to the quarterly issues of the *Middle East Journal*. Another chronicle of unusual depth, and one that is especially useful for the events of Lebanon, can be found in the trilingual *Hāliyāt/Panorama de l'actualité/Panorama of Events*, which is issued quarterly by the Lebanese Center for Documentation and Research in Beirut.

1 January	The French cultural center in Tripoli, Lebanon, is destroyed by a bomb.
	The Reverend Mr. Jesse Jackson, who is in Damascus to secure the release of the captured U.S. airman Lt. Robert O. Goodman, Jr., plans to extend his stay in Syria to visit President Hafiz al-Assad.
	The Polisario Front says its forces in the Western Sahara have killed 154 Moroccan soldiers in a new offensive.
	Maj. Gen. Mohammed Buhari assumes power in Nigeria after a coup by the military forces.
2 January	France announces it will move about 25 percent of its troops in the multinational force in Beirut to southern Lebanon.
	Democratic and Republican leaders in the House of Representatives call for a reassessment of U.S. policy in Lebanon.
	Maj. Sa'd Haddad, commander of an Israeli-supported militia in southern Lebanon, is hospitalized in Haifa.
	King Hussein of Jordan calls for Jordanian–Palestine Libera-

tion Organization (PLO) talks on strategy to recover the West Bank.

Tunisian government forces quell riots caused by a recent increase in the price of bread.

3 January   The Syrian government releases Lt. Robert O. Goodman, Jr., in response to the appeal made by the Reverend Mr. Jesse Jackson; President Reagan expresses his thanks for the Syrian action and calls on President Assad to cooperate with the United States to bring stability to Lebanon and the withdrawal of foreign troops.

Israeli warplanes attack targets in Bhamdun, Lebanon, in apparent retaliation for guerrilla attacks on Israeli forces in southern Lebanon.

The Tunisian government imposes a state of emergency to secure order after widespread riots over a rise in the price of bread.

Civil servants in Israel protest new government-introduced austerity measures.

Turkey announces it will reduce its armed forces stationed on Cyprus by 1,500 troops as a goodwill gesture.

4 January   Israeli warplanes bomb targets in eastern Lebanon: casualties reach almost one hundred dead and four hundred wounded. Baalbak, the center of activity by the Amal, is the principal target.

The Egyptian government says it is ready to join Jordan and the PLO in any new talks on a general peace settlement.

In New Delhi anonymous diplomatic sources say that battles occur daily in Kandahar, Afghanistan, between insurgents and government troops.

Hampig Sassounian, an Armenian immigrant, is convicted of first-degree murder in the assassination of Turkish consul general Kemal Arikan.

5 January   Lebanon requests that a force of American Marines be deployed southward from Beirut to assist the Lebanese army.

Lebanon announces that various warring factions have approved in principle a plan for separating their forces. If accepted, the plan foresees the extension of central authority to about twenty miles south of Beirut.

6 January   President Bourguiba of Tunisia announces that the price of bread will be reduced; a government-decreed price increase had caused widespread rioting in Tunisia.

7 January   President Bourguiba of Tunisia dismisses the minister of the interior in the aftermath of recent riots.

Iran claims successes against the Kurds: thirty villages taken and 230 rebels killed after a week's campaign.

The foreign minister of Chad, Idriss Miskine, dies of malaria shortly before the opening of a conference in Addis Ababa on ways to achieve peace in Chad.

8 January An American Marine is killed in a Beirut ambush; this death brings to 262 the number of U.S. military personnel killed in Lebanon.

The British foreign secretary, Sir Geoffrey Howe, starts a five-day tour of Egypt, Saudi Arabia, and Syria.

The Islamic Tendency Movement claims credit for organizing the antigovernment riots that broke out in Tunisia last week over a rise in food prices.

9 January Palestinians and Jewish settlers clash in Ramallah in the West Bank.

The secretary of the navy recommends that officers be reprimanded for security failures associated with the 23 October 1983 bomb attack on the Marine compound in Beirut.

Chad peace talks scheduled to begin in Addis Ababa are called off by Hissen Habré, who was annoyed at the warm welcome given in Ethiopia to his rival, Goukouni Oueddei.

Libyan commandos destroy a section of an oil pipeline in southern Tunisia.

10 January Druze and Christian forces exchange heavy shelling south of the Beirut airport; the French embassy is attacked by unidentified gunmen.

U.S. officials publicly state that the defeat of Iraq by Iran would be contrary to American interests in the Middle East.

11 January Lebanese government troops and Muslim militiamen fight in the southern suburbs of Beirut.

Several senators attack President Reagan's Lebanese policy and call for the withdrawal of the Marines from Beirut.

Israeli opens the bridges over the Awali River to civilian traffic.

Moshe Arens, defense minister of Israel, invites the United States to stockpile American military supplies in Israel for future use in emergency situations.

Britain's foreign minister, Sir Geoffrey Howe, arrives in Damascus for talks after completing a visit to Saudi Arabia.

Muhammad Husayn Rashid is acquitted in Portugal of the murder of PLO moderate Dr. 'Isam Sartawi.

12 January Artillery battles rage between Druze units and the Lebanese army.

Special envoy Donald Rumsfeld begins talks in Damascus on ways to settle hostilities among the various factions in Lebanon.

13 January   The Marines' base in Lebanon comes under heavy rifle fire; the Lebanese army engages Shiite militiamen in extensive street fighting in Beirut.

The Organization of African Unity (OAU) suspends efforts in Addis Ababa to bring together the factions warring in Chad.

Mauritius expels Libyan diplomats on the charge of interfering in the island's affairs.

14 January   Syrian president Hafiz al-Assad tells Donald Rumsfeld, the special U.S. envoy, that he will not withdraw Syrian troops from Lebanon until American and other foreign forces leave; this represents a hardening of Syria's position.

Maj. Sa'd Haddad, leader of an Israeli-supported militia in southern Lebanon, dies after a long illness.

15 January   The U.S. battleship *New Jersey* and a destroyer fire upon Druze military areas after Marines at the Beirut airport come under attack.

16 January   Secretary of State George Shultz admits U.S. attempts to find a political settlement with Syria have failed.

King Hussein, in addressing the Jordanian parliament reconvened after a ten-year suspension, asks the PLO to join him in peaceful efforts to free the West Bank and Gaza; Hussein also says Egypt should be welcomed back into the Arab world.

France and Saudi Arabia announce the conclusion of an arms sale agreement for a system of mobile antiaircraft missiles; the system is to cost $4.5 billion.

17 January   Iraqi aircraft strike Iranian troop concentrations in the central sector of the war front; this is the first use of Iraqi airplanes since 15 December 1983.

The Saudi Arabian consul general is kidnapped in Beirut.

At the Islamic Conference Organization, which is meeting in Casablanca, several non-Arab representatives urge that Egypt be brought back into the organization.

18 January   Dr. Malcolm H. Kerr, the president of the American University of Beirut, is assassinated in his office; the Islamic Jihad claims responsibility for the killing.

Prime Minister Yitzhak Shamir of Israel criticizes Jordan's King Hussein for proposing that Jordan and the PLO join in negotiations for a peaceful solution of the West Bank and Gaza questions.

19 January	The Islamic Conference votes to readmit Egypt. Egyptian membership had been suspended in 1979 when Egypt signed a peace treaty with Israel.
	The State Department accuses Iran of persecuting members of the Bahai faith.
20 January	Egypt announces its intention of meeting soon with Jordan and the PLO to find a new approach to the West Bank problem.
	Prime Minister Thatcher of Great Britain confers with U.S. special envoy Donald Rumsfeld on alternatives to keeping military forces in Lebanon.
21 January	Druze insurgents shell the governmental palace in Lebanon.
	Riots occur in Wujda, Morocco, over increases in the costs of education and food.
22 January	Walid Jumblat, leader of the Lebanese Druze, says his forces will not stop their military actions until the Lebanese cabinet resigns.
	King Hassan II of Morocco blames Zionists, communists, and Khomeini's followers for recent riots in six Moroccan cities.
24 January	Scattered disturbances continue in northern Morocco, with several demonstrators killed; sixty persons are estimated to have perished in the riots that began a week ago when the government decreed a rise in food prices.
	Helmut Kohl, chancellor of West Germany, visits Israel. The visit causes widespread protests by Israelis, partly because of German plans to sell weapons to Saudi Arabia.
	Shake-ups in the top command of the Afghan army are reported in New Delhi; these follow a series of recent assassinations of party loyalists in Kabul. Afghan insurgent leaders in Iran report they have attacked Soviet forces inside the Soviet Union as part of their "holy war."
25 January	Antigovernment forces in Chad shoot down a French warplane engaged in reconnaissance.
26 January	The Reagan administration informs Israel that it intends to pursue plans for a Jordanian rapid deployment force; similar plans were dropped last year because of Israeli objections.
	The Lebanese government offers to promote a group of Druze officers as a gesture to improve internal relations.
	Iraqi warplanes fly over Tehran.
27 January	Druze leader Walid Jumblat rejects the Gemayel government's offer to reinstate a number of Druze officers in the Lebanese army.

In Sidon, Lebanon, an explosion damages an Israeli army post.

Jewish right-wing religious conservatives attempt to plant bombs in the Muslim shrines of the Dome of the Rock and the Masjid al-Aqsa.

French troops in Chad are ordered to increase their zone of control.

28 January   King Hussein of Jordan announces that any special American military aid for an eight-thousand-member strike force would be used only to create a force to respond to requests for help from Arab states.

Pakistan reports that a recent raid on one of its border villages by Afghan aircraft killed forty civilians.

29 January   Mordachai Ben Porat, an Israeli cabinet minister, resigns from the Shamir government because of differences over policies on Lebanon.

30 January   U.S. Marine forces in Beirut are attacked by Druze and Shiite militiamen; one Marine is killed.

Egypt accepts an invitation to rejoin the Islamic Conference Organization.

Colonel Qaddafi warns that the French decision to move its defense line in Chad sixty miles to the north could lead to renewed fighting.

31 January   Iraq claims successful attacks on five Iranian ships.

Reports in New Delhi indicate that government forces in Afghanistan have killed hundreds of civilians in bombing raids north of Kabul.

1 February   Chad officials claim victory over insurgents who had penetrated southern Chad; several hundred rebels are reported killed.

2 February   Extremely intense artillery battles are fought between the Lebanese army and Druze and Shiite groups.

The Reagan administration cautions Congress that the withdrawal of U.S. troops from Lebanon would aid radicalism.

Israeli military authorities shut the downtown campus of Bir Zeit University in Ramallah after violent demonstrations on campus.

French and government forces in Chad expand their control north of the defensive line at the sixteenth parallel.

Guerrillas in southern Sudan seize an American-operated oil installation at Bentiu.

4 February	Nabih Berri, Lebanese Shiite leader, asks Muslim members of President Gemayel's cabinet to resign.
	In Jerusalem, thirty thousand Israelis march in a "Peace Now" demonstration in support of the immediate withdrawal of Israeli forces from Lebanon.
5 February	The Lebanese cabinet resigns; President Gemayel announces an eight-point program for national reconciliation, while the army battles Shiite militiamen in the fourth day of intense fighting in the southern suburbs of Beirut.
	The Israeli cabinet declares that all residents of the West Bank and the Gaza Strip are enjoined to obey the law; this is seen as a warning that armed Jewish terrorists or vigilantes will be punished for attacking Arab residents.
6 February	Shiite and Druze forces seize most of West Beirut; U.S. naval and air forces attack an antigovernment position near Beirut. Both the French and American positions in Beirut come under attack.
7 February	President Reagan orders the Marines in Beirut to begin a phased redeployment to U.S. warships off the coast of Lebanon; naval and air forces are ordered to intensify their attacks on antigovernment positions. The U.S. embassy staff is evacuated.
	Shiite Amal and Druze forces assume control of West Beirut as the Lebanese army suffers defections of up to 40 percent of its personnel to the Muslim militias.
	Exiled Iranian general Ghulam 'Ali Oveissi is assassinated in Paris. The Islamic Jihad claims responsibility for the death of the general and his brother. Both men were shah loyalists.
8 February	U.S. warships, including the battleship *New Jersey* bombard Syrian and Druze positions in the heaviest American action since the Marines landed in Beirut. The Phalangist radio reports that the nine-hour barrage destroyed thirty antigovernment gun batteries.
	The ambassador of the UAE is assassinated in Paris.
	The 115-man British contingent in the multinational force in Beirut is withdrawn to a naval vessel; Italy orders a gradual pullback of its contingent but continues to protect refugee camps in its area.
9 February	American naval forces continue to bombard antigoverment positions in Lebanon.
10 February	More than four hundred American citizens and other Western foreigners are evacuated from Beirut.
	Israeli jets attack Palestinian guerrilla positions at Bhamdun, east of Beirut, in retaliation for the launching yesterday of rockets into northern Israel.

The president of Iran threatens to cut off oil deliveries to the West if the United States becomes involved in the Iran-Iraq war.

11 February   President Hosni Mubarak of Egypt confers with President Mitterrand on a joint peace plan.

12 February   President Gemayel of Lebanon informs his opponents that if they agree to participate in another Geneva conference he will reconsider the Lebanese-Israeli withdrawal agreement.

Syria declares that the shelling of targets by the U.S. fleet is a sign of the bankruptcy of American foreign policy.

Iran shells three towns in Iraq in retaliation for an Iraqi attack on an Iranian town; these are the first occurrences of deliberate attacks on civilian targets in the Iran-Iraq war.

13 February   In Washington, President Reagan assures King Hussein that the recent decision to pull the Marines out of Lebanon does not mean the United States is decreasing its support for Jordan and Lebanon in their conflicts with Syria.

14 February   Druze forces inflict a major defeat on the Lebanese army southeast of Beirut; Druze leaders report they have received large quantities of military aid from Syria.

President Reagan, King Hussein of Jordan, and President Hosni Mubarak of Egypt confer in Washington. Both Arab leaders urge the president to bring the PLO into the peace process between Israel and the Arab states.

15 February   Druze forces continue their drive against the Lebanese army and link up with Shiite Amal positions; Walid Jumblat, in Damascus, calls for President Gemayel's resignation.

France calls upon the Security Council to create an international peacekeeping force to replace the present multinational force in the Beirut area.

A Sudanese guerrilla group reports it recently attacked a Nile steamer and captured 222 soldiers.

16 February   President Gemayel of Lebanon informs his opponents that he will cancel the 1983 agreement with Israel.

Israeli defense minister Moshe Arens, speaking to Christian leaders in Jezzin, Lebanon, avers that Israel will remain in Lebanon as long as the security of northern Israel is threatened.

Iran launches a fresh drive against Iraq in the Mehran area, ninety miles east of Baghdad; American officials predict that a huge World War I–type battle is evolving.

17 February   Opposition leaders in Lebanon reject President Gemayel's eight-point reconciliation proposal.

Syrian foreign minister Khaddam rejects the Gemayel plan, which had been drafted by the Saudis, because it contradicts the agreements reached at the earlier Geneva reconciliation conference.

18 February   Syrian officials say there will be no reconciliation until the Lebanese-Israeli accord of 1983 is abrogated.

Jordan accuses Libya of destroying the Jordanian embassy in Tripoli, Libya.

Sudanese troops seize thirty rebels who attacked a Nile steamer earlier this week.

19 February   Israeli airplanes attack Palestinian bases in Lebanon.

The Italian contingent of the multinational force begins to withdraw from Beirut.

20 February   Italian troops leave Beirut; the U.S. Marines begin preparations for the final phase of their pullout.

The chairman of the Organization for African Unity initiates new efforts to solve the deadlock between Morocco and the Polisario Front.

21 February   Israeli airplanes bomb four sites in the Shuf Mountains, while an armored column advances to Damur.

Iran claims it has stopped an Iraqi counterattack.

22 February   Jordan cuts diplomatic relations with Libya.

Iran launches a major attack in the direction of Basrah.

23 February   Israeli airplanes attack Palestinian bases east of Beirut.

24 February   One day after the cease-fire agreement was announced by its mediator, Prince Bandar of Saudi Arabia, heavy artillery exchanges break out between the Lebanese army and Shiite militia forces in the Galerie Sama'an area along the Green Line in Beirut.

25 February   Heavy fighting continues between Iranian and Iraqi forces in the Misan region; Iraq claims it has killed seven thousand Iranian troops during the past twenty-four hours.

26 February   The U.S. Marine contingent completes its withdrawal from Beirut; American ships bombard Syrian positions east of Beirut.

Increased fighting occurs along the Green Line in Beirut between the Lebanese army and Muslim militias.

Yasir Arafat and King Hussein meet in Amman, Jordan.

27 February   Severe fighting continues along the Green Line in Beirut.

The Reagan administration admits it no longer seeks a formula for a settlement in Lebanon.

The Israeli government warns West Bank Arabs that it is illegal for them to meet Yasir Arafat in Jordan.

Iraq says it is beginning a blockade of Iran's main oil terminal, Kharg Island.

In Yola, Nigeria, more than thirty persons are killed in clashes between police and Muslim fundamentalists.

28 February The Reagan administration rejects the request from President Gemayel to support his government through increased U.S. naval and air power.

Two hand grenades explode in Jerusalem; the Democratic Front for the Liberation of Palestine claims credit for the attack.

Iraq warns maritime nations that it will attack any ship approaching Iran's oil terminal at Kharg Island.

29 February The United States affirms its support of the Israeli-Lebanese agreement of May 1983 in the face of Saudi arguments that the accord be scrapped.

Amin Gemayel, president of Lebanon, confers with Syrian president Assad in Damascus.

In the Security Council, the Soviet Union vetoes the plan advanced by France for an international peacekeeping body in Beirut.

Iran, in reacting to recent encounters with U.S. naval forces in the Persian Gulf, claims that American naval forces represent an act of aggression.

1 March The French government, reacting to the withdrawal from Beirut of the other members of the multinational force, declares it cannot keep its 1,250-member force in Beirut.

The Defense Department gives Congress a thirty-day notice that it intends to sell 1,613 Stinger missiles to Jordan and 1,200 to Saudi Arabia.

Iraq claims its forces sank seven Iranian ships in the Persian Gulf.

The Turkish government lifts martial law in thirteen of the country's sixty-seven provinces.

2 March Lebanese officials say Amin Gemayel and Hafiz al-Assad reached an agreement on the Lebanese political crisis during their recent talks in Damascus.

The major allies of Syria in Lebanon drop their demands that Amin Gemayel resign from the presidency of Lebanon.

U.S. military analysts report that Iran is preparing a large offensive against Iraq; Iraq claims victories over Iranian forces near Basrah.

3 March Intense fighting breaks out in Beirut between the army and various antigovernment militias, as President Gemayel holds talks with factional leaders to win support for his supposed agreement with Syria.

In a television speech, President Numayri of Sudan threatens to wage war against Libya and Ethiopia if they continue support to rebel factions in southern Sudan.

King Hassan II of Morocco decrees that farmers will be exempted from taxes until the year 2000.

The Afghan government claims a victory over insurgents in a battle near Kabul.

4 March The foreign minister of Lebanon, Elie Salem, says Amin Gemayel will soon cancel the 17 May 1983 agreement with Israel for security and troop withdrawal; Maronite Christians still favor the accords.

The Lebanese army and antigovernment militias battle along the Green Line in Beirut.

Eleven Israeli soldiers are wounded in a bomb attack in Sidon.

In Jerusalem masked gunmen fire automatic weapons at a bus in the West Bank; six Arabs are wounded.

Iran claims that four hundred of its troops were killed recently by Iraqi chemical attacks.

Government sources in Nigeria report that as many as one thousand persons perished last week in civil violence caused by Muslim fundamentalists.

5 March Lebanon unilaterally cancels the 17 May 1983 withdrawal accord. Israeli prime minister Yitzhak Shamir strongly condemns the move, which is seen as a victory for Syria, while the Phalangist party—acting in opposition to the desire of the Phalangist militia—supports the action of the Lebanese cabinet.

The Department of State accuses Iraq of using poison gas against Iranian troops.

Seven American Jews who have settled in Israel are arrested in connection with a terrorist attack on an Arab bus near Ramallah.

6 March President Amin Gemayel of Lebanon invites Lebanese political leaders to a reconciliation conference in Lausanne, Switzerland.

7 March A bus is bombed in Ashdod, Israel. The Abu Nidal guerrilla group claims responsibility.

Iran claims it has repulsed Iraqi efforts to recapture the artificial island Majnun.

The International Committee of the Red Cross issues a report that presumes "the recent use of substances prohibited by international law" by Iraq against Iranian invaders.

The Soviet press agency, Tass, cautions the United States against implementing a proposed restriction on air and sea traffic in the Persian Gulf.

8 March   Greece, claiming that Turkish naval ships have fired on one of its warships, recalls its ambassador from Istanbul; Turkey says its ships were engaged in a previously announced artillery exercise.

9 March   Heavy fighting erupts in Beirut along the Green Line between the Lebanese army and Muslim militias.

The U.S.S.R. agrees to a major military weapons sale with India.

10 March   A high-level Soviet delegation headed by Geidar A. Aliyev, a first deputy prime minister, arrives in Damascus.

Secretary of State Shultz warns Congress against passage of a bill to move the U.S. embassy from Tel Aviv to Jerusalem.

London police trace five bombs, two of which had exploded and injured twenty-four persons, to Libyan terrorists.

In Chad, a French airliner is damaged by two bomb blasts.

11 March   The president of Syria, Hafiz al-Assad, re-forms his cabinet, naming three new vice presidents, among which is his younger brother Rif'at.

Bombs explode in Manchester, England, close to houses occupied by anti-Qaddafi Libyans.

12 March   The Lebanese reconciliation conference opens in Lausanne, Switzerland; all major Lebanese political factions are represented.

Heavy fighting continues in the southern border marshes of Iraq around Majnun Island, and Iran stages a new attack near Basrah.

13 March   The conferees of the Lebanese unity conference in Lausanne agree to impose a cease-fire in Beirut; meanwhile, heavy shelling in Beirut kills twenty-five persons and wounds forty.

14 March   King Hussein of Jordan, in an extensive interview, repudiates American efforts to broker a peace settlement because of what he perceives to be total U.S. submission to Israel's dictates.

The foreign ministers of Arab League countries, meeting in Baghdad, condemn Iran for refusing to negotiate with Iraq and call upon all other nations not to assist the Khomeini government.

15 March The United States, in reacting to King Hussein's position expressed yesterday that it is impossible for an Arab country to negotiate with Israel because of Israeli influence on U.S. policies, maintains that Arab countries themselves must commence talks with Israel.

Iraq reports it has established a bridgehead on Majnun Island.

The meeting of the Lebanese reconciliation conference in Lausanne is interrupted by arguments concerning relations with Israel and Syrian hegemony.

16 March William F. Buckley, an American diplomat, is kidnapped in Beirut.

The city of Omdurman in Sudan is attacked by a single warplane that drops five bombs; President Numayri accuses Libya of the attack.

17 March The United States and Sudan confer on responses to the bombing yesterday of Omdurman; an emergency airlift of military equipment is under consideration.

The U.S.S.R. warns Turkey that its increasing cooperation with the United States is regarded as threatening.

18 March The United States sends two AWACS planes to Egypt to assist in the air defense of Sudan. The United States also reiterates its position of neutrality in the civil conflict in southern Sudan in which Libya and Ethiopia are assisting certain (Christian) tribes against the central government.

19 March The United States warns Libya not to interfere with the AWACS planes sent yesterday to assist Sudan.

20 March After meeting for nine days, the delegates to the Lebanese national unity conference in Lausanne terminate talks and return to Lebanon, having failed to seriously consider changes in Lebanon's political system that would give more political power to the Muslims. The final communiqué calls for a continuation of the (noneffective) cease-fire in Beirut and the formation of a committee to draft a new constitution.

Reports in New Delhi say that Afghan troops have mutinied around Kabul and defected to the ranks of Muslim insurgents.

21 March The Reagan administration cancels plans to sell antiaircraft missiles to Jordan; this is contrary to the desire of the State Department.

22 March Officials in Iran say 1 million Iranians are on standby along the Iraqi front.

The Israeli parliament approves three motions for elections

in May or June; this major defeat for Yitzhak Shamir's government was caused by the defection of five members of the Likud bloc.

Druze forces overwhelm the Sunni Muslim Murabitun militia in Beirut.

23 March   Severe fighting continues in West Beirut between the Libyan-backed Sunni Muslim Murabitun and the Druze Progressive Socialist party militia.

24 March   France announces its 1,250-man force in Beirut will be withdrawn within a week.

Iraq claims it destroyed four oil tankers near Iran's Kharg Island depot.

25 March   The Motherland party of Prime Minister Turgut Özal takes the lead in local elections in Turkey.

26 March   Queen Elizabeth of Great Britain arrives in Jordan for a state visit.

U.S. envoy Donald Rumsfeld confers in Baghdad with Tariq 'Aziz, Iraq's foreign minister, on bilateral relations.

Four American immigrants in Israel are charged with attacks on Palestinians.

27 March   The United States decreases the numbers of advisers who are training the Lebanese army, leaving about fifty persons actively involved in training.

A French cultural attaché is seriously wounded in Beirut by unidentified gunmen.

Iraq for the first time announces that its Super-Etendard aircraft, obtained last fall from France, destroyed two major Iranian naval targets.

Sudan requests the Security Council to condemn Libya for the 16 March bombing of Omdurman; Libya denies the charge.

In New Delhi diplomats report that fifteen Communist party officials were assassinated during the past two days in Kabul.

28 March   President Gemayel of Lebanon convenes the first meeting of the Lebanese Higher Security Committee.

Unusually heavy shelling disrupts Beirut; clashes between Christian and Muslim militias result in eighteen deaths and over one hundred wounded.

In Israel, the Likud bloc and the Labor party agree that national elections will be held on 23 July.

The Turkish embassy in Tehran reports that Armenian terrorists have launched a series of attacks on embassy personnel during the past two days.

The Reagan administration urges Congress to increase economic and military aid to Sudan.

29 March American experts say Iraq has been manufacturing and using nerve gas in the war against Iran.

30 March The American contingent of the multinational force in Lebanon is withdrawn; French troops begin their final withdrawal from Beirut.

31 March The last French troops depart from Beirut; during their participation in the multinational force 89 soldiers were killed and 110 wounded.

U.S. Secretary of Defense Weinberger meets senior Greek officials in Athens to discuss American military bases in Greece.

Turkey announces it will eliminate restrictions on visas for Greeks.

1 April Secretary of State Shultz says the withdrawal of American Marines from Lebanon causes a loss of credibility for the United States.

Egyptian president Hosni Mubarak says he hopes to restore full diplomatic relations between the Soviet Union and Egypt.

Iraq claims its aircraft, in unusually heavy action, inflict severe damage to Iranian positions.

2 April An official delegation from the Soviet Union visits Lebanon and holds meetings with Foreign Minister Elie Salem.

Three Arab terrorists attack civilians in Jerusalem and wound forty-eight persons; the Democratic Front for the Liberation of Palestine claims responsibility.

3 April Palestinian guerrillas attack Israeli army units in southern Lebanon.

4 April Antoine Lahud assumes command of the Israeli-backed South Lebanon Army, succeeding the late major Sa'd Haddad.

5 April Heavy shelling occurs in Beirut.

Israeli troops in Sidon, Lebanon, wound seven civilians after an Israeli patrol is attacked.

Shimon Peres, head of Israel's Labor party, declares he would withdraw Israeli troops from Lebanon were he to be elected.

6 April An independent study conducted by Meron Benvenisti, head of the West Bank Data Base Project, concludes that Israel has redirected a significant portion of U.S. government aid that was intended to assist Palestinians living under Israeli occupation.

7 April	Israeli planes bomb Palestinian guerrilla sites in the mountains east of Beirut.
8 April	A subcommission of representatives from various warring militias reaches an accord on disengagement in Beirut; nevertheless, fighting continues in the city.
9 April	Israeli police arrest four Orthodox Jews on charges of perpetrating grenade attacks in Jerusalem and the West Bank.
	Iran claims to have repulsed Iraqi forces that have been attacking the Majnun Island complex.
10 April	Muslim and Christian residential areas in Beirut are subjected to heavy shelling.
11 April	In Kabul, Afghanistan, an American diplomat is accused of spying and is ordered to leave.
12 April	Druze leader Walid Jumblat joins other opposition figures, such as Maronite Suleiman Franjieh, in recommending that Syria intervene to stop the factional fighting in Lebanon.
	A bus is seized by Arabs south of Tel Aviv; Israeli troops retake it in the Gaza Strip.
	Yitzhak Shamir is nominated by the Likud bloc in preference to former defense minister Ariel Sharon (407–306) to run for prime minister of Israel in the 23 July election.
	Assistant Secretary of State Richard W. Murphy confers in Cairo with top Egyptian officials on Egypt's effort to end the Iran-Iraq war.
	The Mubarak government in Egypt seizes the newspaper of the New Wafd party.
	Pakistan frees three hundred political prisoners.
13 April	In Cairo, the New Wafd party successfully appeals in the civil courts the government's action to impound the newspaper *al-Wafd*.
14 April	The Israeli army demolishes four houses in Gaza belonging to the families of the Palestinian gunmen who hijacked a bus on 12 April.
	Israel asks the United States to take back those former Americans who renounced their citizenship and emigrated to Israel as "Black Hebrews."
	Rocket fire strikes the residential quarters of the presidential palace in Lebanon.
15 April	Iran holds parliamentary elections.
16 April	The East-West crossing in Beirut, known as the Museum

crossing, is closed because of gunfire from Christian and Muslim militiamen.

Druze leader Walid Jumblat confers with Syrian foreign minister 'Abd al-Halim Khaddam, detailing the conditions that President Gemayel must accept before Jumblat is willing to join a new Lebanese government.

17 April In Lebanon Christian and Muslim groups clash in heavy gun battles; a cease-fire is put into effect afterward.

Turkey and the Turkish Cypriot government on Cyprus extend mutual diplomatic recognition.

Machine-gun fire from inside the Libyan embassy in London hits a crowd of Libyans who are demonstrating against Colonel Qaddafi; a British police constable is killed and ten Libyans wounded; police besiege the embassy. In Tripoli, Libyan troops surround the British embassy in retaliation.

18 April The Libyan government allows British citizens who were detained in the British embassy to return home.

19 April In Beirut, the various militia groups initiate the first step of a plan for disengagement: cease-fire observers are posted along the Green Line dividing East and West Beirut.

Amin Gemayel, president of Lebanon, and Hafiz al-Assad, president of Syria, meet in Damascus to seek solutions to the Lebanese civil crisis.

20 April Soviet forces begin large-scale attacks into the Panjshir Valley, fifty miles north of Kabul.

22 April Great Britain cuts diplomatic relations with Libya.

Rauf Denktash, Turkish Cypriot leader, warns Greece not to send troops to Greek Cyprus.

Reports in Paris say the Saharan Arab Democratic Republic won an engagement with the Moroccan army.

24 April Great Britain deports the chief representative of Colonel Qaddafi.

Armenians in Greece demonstrate at the Turkish embassy.

Reports from Afghanistan indicate that Soviet and Afghan forces have secured the Panjshir Valley.

25 April The State Department urges a worldwide ban on sales of nuclear equipment or technology to Iran.

The Israeli government charges that *New York Times* correspondent David K. Shipler violated military censorship when he reported that an Arab bus hijacker was killed during captivity.

Anti-Khomeini Iranians carry out coordinated protests in five European cities.

26 April   President Gemayel of Lebanon asks Rashid Karami to form a government of national unity. Karami, a sixty-two-year-old lawyer from Tripoli, is a Sunni Muslim and pro-Syrian politician.

27 April   In Israel a commission is formed to investigate the deaths of four Palestinians who hijacked a bus in April.

Iraq claims it has sunk three naval targets in the Persian Gulf.

British diplomats leave Tripoli, completing the diplomatic break with Libya.

28 April   Heavy fighting closes the crossing between East and West Beirut.

Lebanon reestablishes diplomatic relations with Libya.

West Bank Israelis are arrested for placing bombs on seven Arab buses.

In Israel, the military censor orders the printing plant of the Hebrew newspaper *Hadashot* closed for four days because it disclosed the existence of a military commission charged with investigating the deaths of four Palestinian hijackers.

Armenian terrorists critically wound a Turkish businessman in Tehran.

29 April   Sudan declares a state of emergency.

30 April   Yasir Arafat appeals to Egypt for permission to base the PLO there.

Israeli radio reports that former prime minister Begin has decided not to run for president.

Israel detains twenty Jewish suspects for questioning about an apparent plot to bomb Arab buses.

President Numayri of Sudan issues decrees giving greater power to his government during the state of emergency.

1 May   Three Israeli military personnel are captured north of Beirut by Syrian forces and taken to Damascus.

Construction begins on the first university to be built in Bahrain.

Reports are circulated in New Delhi saying that Soviet troops have captured about half of the Panjshir Valley north of Kabul.

2 May   In Jerusalem two Israelis who were arrested recently for planting bombs on Arab buses confess to last summer's attack on the Islamic College in Hebron in which three Arabs were killed and thirty-three wounded.

Colonel Qaddafi of Libya claims that British agents planted weapons and shell casings in the Libyan embassy in London.

President Numayri of Sudan dismisses six of twenty-one cabinet members; Washington says Assistant Secretary of State for African Affairs Crocker A. Snow will go to Sudan for conferences.

3 May   In a Paris suburb three bomb explosions damage a monument to Armenian victims of the 1915 massacre in Turkey.

5 May   Heavy shelling between East and West Beirut takes place; up to ten persons are killed and seventy-five wounded. Druze and Sunni militias also battle each other in Beirut.

UN officials reveal that forty thousand persons have fled from southern Sudan to Ethiopia during the last six months to escape famine and civil war.

6 May   The International Press Institute protests to Prime Minister Shamir Israel's decision to close the newspaper *Hadashot* for four days for transgressing military censorship.

7 May   Nabih Berri, leader of Lebanese Shiites, agrees to join the new ten-member coalition government of Rashid Karami, after a new post (minister of state for southern Lebanese affairs) is created for him.

8 May   Benjamin Thomas Weir, an American Presbyterian minister, is kidnapped in West Beirut by unknown persons; he is the fourth American to be seized during the past three months.

Gunmen attack the barracks used as a residence by Colonel Qaddafi in Tripoli, Libya.

The FBI reveals it has kept the Libyan UN mission under surveillance since 1981 to determine if Libya is funding black activists in this country.

9 May   The administration's request for military aid to Turkey is cut by the House of Representatives from $755 million to $670 million.

An explosion kills five Libyans in Addis Ababa. The explosion. possibly a bomb, destroyed a house used to store munitions that possibly were intended for guerrilla operations in Africa.

10 May   The Lebanese cabinet meets: nine of its ten members are present.

Major rallies in support of Colonel Qaddafi take place in the major cities of Libya.

11 May   The State Department reacts strongly to remarks by Prime Minister Papandreou of Greece that praised the Soviet

Union's desire for détente and condemned the United States for imperialism.

12 May   Rabbi Moshe Levinger, a leader of the Gush Emunim, criticizes the Israeli government for arresting Jews in connection with three major terrorist attacks against Arabs in Nablus and Hebron.

The Security Council votes 13 to 1 to condemn Turkish "secessionist action" on Cyprus.

Vice-President Bush in New Delhi criticizes Soviet intervention in Afghanistan.

13 May   Israeli authorities exhume the bodies of two Arabs who were killed during an attack on an Israeli bus in April; the Defense Ministry has ordered new autopsies on the bodies in an effort to decide how the Arabs were killed.

Rabbi Moshe Levinger, a leader of the Jewish settlement movement in the occupied West Bank, is arrested on suspicion of complicity in the planning of terrorist attacks on Arabs.

Security forces in Libya locate and kill the leader of an attack on Colonel Qaddafi last month.

14 May   A Kuwaiti tanker is attacked in the Persian Gulf.

Prime Minister Indira Gandhi of India informs Vice-President Bush that U.S. arms sales to Pakistan could lead to a regional arms race.

15 May   Syria recalls its ambassador to Morocco to protest high-level Moroccan participation, including the presence of Crown Prince Muhammad, in a conference of Moroccan Jews that included an official delegation from Israel.

Turkish authorities refuse to permit the publication of a petition by intellectuals denouncing press censorship.

Vice-President Bush, speaking in India, says the United States will continue to strengthen Pakistan while Soviet forces occupy Afghanistan.

16 May   Israeli troops storm the 'Ayn al-Hilwah refugee camp at Sidon because of an anti-Israel demonstration there.

Most of the one thousand Iranians stationed at Baalbak, Lebanon, have been removed from the country at the request of Syria.

Shaykh Sa'd al-Din 'Alami, chairman of the Supreme Muslim Council in Israel, urges Israeli authorities to remove the armed guards stationed at the Masjid al-Aqsa and the Dome of the Rock.

Tunisia recalls its ambassador to Libya in response to Libyan complaints of anti-Qaddafi propaganda.

A Saudi oil tanker is attacked by unidentified aircraft in the Persian Gulf; the attack causes ship insurers to raise their rates.

The United States offers air cover to Arab countries on the Persian Gulf if those countries offer adequate bases for land-based aircraft.

17 May

Saudi Arabia, worried over recent Iranian attacks on its oil tankers, seeks a recommitment of American support. American officials take the position that a direct request for U.S. assistance would have to provide for the use of land bases in the Persian Gulf.

The Libyan Press Agency reports that "suicide squads" are being formed to kill Libyan dissidents abroad.

18 May

Donald H. Rumsfeld resigns his post of special envoy to the Middle East.

Tunisia strengthens its guards along the Libyan border.

Greece affirms that it has expelled an American diplomat, claiming he was an agent of the CIA.

Iraqi aircraft attack a cargo ship in the Persian Gulf.

19 May

The Lebanese cabinet reaches an agreement on a policy statement that will provide for a new national accord.

Iraq claims to have cut Iran's oil exports by 55 percent as a result of its blockade of Iranian oil terminals.

The Arab League secretary general, Chedli Klibi of Tunisia, calls for the most influential states to end the war between Iran and Iraq.

Polisario spokesmen claim their forces destroyed the Western Sahara port terminal of Aiun.

In the aftermath of Hindu-Muslim riots in Bombay, police arrest 635 persons.

20 May

Israeli airplanes bomb two bases of pro-Iranian Shiite guerrillas in the Bekaa Valley of Lebanon.

The foreign ministers of the Arab League, meeting in Tunis, overrule objections from Syria and Libya and accuse Iran of aggression in connection with attacks on Arab shipping in the Persian Gulf.

21 May

Prime Minister Yitzhak Shamir of Israel denounces Jewish settlers in the West Bank who have plotted and carried out terrorist acts against Arabs.

Four Arabs convicted of the murder of Aharon Gross are given terms of life imprisonment by a military court.

President Reagan assures King Fahd of Saudi Arabia that the United States will support any Persian Gulf state in case of a confrontation with Iran; this statement was occasioned by recent Iranian attacks on Saudi tankers.

After four days of fighting between Muslims and Hindus, the death toll in Bombay reaches 107.

In Lahore, Pakistan, serious clashes occur between rival Muslim sects at a mosque; President Zia ul-Haq of Pakistan accuses India of massing its army on the border.

22 May The United States confers with its allies on the possibility of providing a military presence to protect shipping in the Persian Gulf.

In Turkey, thirteen persons are sentenced to death on charges of plotting to overthrow the government.

Turkish Cypriot leaders announce that a draft constitution has been prepared. Its provisions will allow general elections in order to establish a Turkish Republic of Northern Cyprus.

Diplomats in New Delhi assert that the U.S.S.R. is seeking a negotiated peace with insurgents in the Panjshir Valley.

23 May Twenty-five Jews are indicted by Israel's attorney general for belonging to a terrorist organization.

President Saddam Hussein of Iraq announces he will continue the blockade of Iran's oil terminal on Kharg Island.

High Syrian officials travel to Iran, reputedly to urge the Khomeini government to avoid any action in the Gulf that might cause American intervention.

President Reagan publicizes his administration's intention to provide 1,200 Stinger antiaircraft missiles to Saudi Arabia.

Pope Shenuda III, head of the Coptic church in Egypt, praises President Hosni Mubarak for resisting Islamic fundamentalists in Egypt.

Soviet forces are reported to be using "fuel-air explosive bombs" in Afghanistan.

Muslim-Hindu riots continue in the Bombay area of India; thirty-five are killed. Disturbances occur also in Hyderabad.

24 May Israeli aircraft attack a Palestinian guerrilla base at Bar Elias in the Bekaa Valley near the Syrian border.

Israeli officials indicate they will oppose the Reagan administration's proposal to sell Stinger antiaircraft missiles to Saudi Arabia.

Rabbi Eliezer Waldman, a candidate for parliament for the Tehiya party, is arrested in connection with Jewish terrorists' attacks on Arabs.

In Israel criminal charges are brought against two army officers for their part in the 1980 attacks on three Arab mayors.

Iran and Iraq attack Persian Gulf shipping: Iraq attacks two ships leaving Kharg Island, and Iran attacks a ship off the coast of Saudi Arabia.

The administration informs members of Congress that Iran may expand the Gulf war and attack targets in Saudi Arabia.

Hindus and Muslims continue clashes in Bombay; up to two hundred persons have perished in the eight days of fighting.

25 May   At the Security Council, talks commence on the Persian Gulf shipping situation; the chief delegate of Iran refuses to attend.

Iraq claims destruction of eight ships in a convoy north of Kharg Island.

War-risk insurance is doubled by Lloyd's of London for oil cargo in the Persian Gulf.

26 May   King Fahd of Saudi Arabia discusses ways to end attacks on Persian Gulf shipping with Syrian officials.

Japan announces a new tanker policy for the Gulf: henceforth Japanese ships will not go into the northern Gulf and vessels of other nations will be chartered for oil deliveries to Japan.

Continued clashes in Bombay between Muslims and Hindus raise the death toll to 215 persons.

27 May   The Reagan administration decides to sell four hundred Stinger missiles and two hundred launchers to Saudi Arabia, with delivery within four days. In addition U.S. Army specialists will be sent to train Saudis in the use of these antiaircraft weapons.

Israeli prime minister Yitzhak Shamir says his government will oppose the sale of Stinger missiles to Saudi Arabia; presidential candidate Walter F. Mondale also voices opposition to the delivery of missiles to Saudi Arabia.

Egypt holds elections for a new parliament.

Indian police authorities say they control the state of Maharashtra where 223 persons perished in recent Hindu-Muslim riots.

28 May   Israel's defense ministry announces that two Arab gunmen who were captured alive last month while hijacking an Israeli bus were later killed by security officers; Defense Secretary Moshe Arens strongly condemns this action by Israeli security personnel.

U.S. officials reveal that four hundred Stinger antiaircraft missiles are being shipped to Saudi Arabia, which plans a protected zone along its Persian Gulf coastline.

29 May   The president of Iran, 'Ali Khamenei, says Iran will resist American intervention in the Persian Gulf.

President Reagan takes formal steps to provide Saudi Arabia with four hundred Stinger antiaircraft missiles; in addition, an air force KC-10 aerial tanker is being sent for possible refueling of Saudi Arabia's F-15s.

In Egypt, the National Democratic party of President Mubarak wins 391 of 448 seats up for election; the major opposition party, the New Wafd, receives 12.7 percent of the vote.

30 May   Defense Minister Moshe Arens of Israel confers in Washington with Secretary of Defense Weinberger on the sale of seventy-five American F-16s to Israel; in the course of the meeting, Arens reiterates his opposition to the sale of advanced American weapons to Arab countries.

Iran offers a $1.50 discount per barrel on oil loaded at Kharg Island.

1 June   The Security Council adopts a resolution that condemns Iran for attacking commercial shipping in the Persian Gulf.

2 June   The secretary general of the United Nations starts a ten-day tour of Lebanon, Syria, Jordan, Egypt, and Israel, intending to learn about the Arab-Israel dispute.

Iran formally rejects a Security Council resolution that condemned Iranian air attacks on Gulf shipping.

3 June   Iraqi aircraft attack and damage a Turkish oil tanker near Kharg Island.

Muhammad Sadr, Iran's political director for Europe and America, starts a five-day visit to the Soviet Union.

4 June   The Department of Defense says an AWACS aircraft was sent to Saudi Arabia to provide air and naval intelligence in the Persian Gulf.

The Department of State criticizes the settling of Turkish Cypriots in an area near Famagusta.

5 June   In an aerial engagement, two Saudi F-15s shoot down two Iranian F-4 aircraft near the Saudi island al-'Arabiyah.

The Defense Department says three additional AWACS are being sent to Saudi Arabia; the department also says that U.S. warships in the Persian Gulf will defend American oil tankers.

The Turkish government halts all oil pickups by Turkish ships at Iran's Kharg Island.

An Israeli diplomatic corp member is wounded in an assassination attempt in Ma'adi, Egypt.

A British relief organization called Afghan Aid reports that about 500,000 people in Afghanistan are in danger of starving.

6 June	Iran makes an official protest to Saudi Arabia for shooting down one of its aircraft over international waters.
8 June	The director general of Iran's foreign ministry visits Moscow and meets Foreign Minister Gromyko.
9 June	The president and prime minister of Lebanon ask help from the UN secretary general in getting Israeli forces out of southern Lebanon.
10 June	A Kuwaiti oil tanker is attacked by an unidentified airplane in the Persian Gulf.
11 June	A twelve-hour artillery battle between Muslim and Christian forces in Beirut leaves sixty-five persons dead.
	Richard Murphy, assistant secretary of state for Near East and South Asian affairs, states that victory by either Iran or Iraq is not desirable because it would destabilize the area.
12 June	The Lebanese cabinet gains a vote of confidence from parliament 53 to 15; parliament also votes to give special powers to the cabinet for a nine-month period. These powers include the right to revise or rescind earlier decrees.
	Sixty-five thousand teachers in Israel strike for higher wages.
	Iran and Iraq agree not to attack each other's cities; Iran reiterates its refusal to negotiate with Saddam Hussein of Iraq.
	Rauf Denktash, Turkish Cypriot leader, starts a two-day state visit in Turkey.
	Reports in Pakistan indicate the U.S.S.R. is launching a major assault on resistance forces near Herat, Afghanistan.
13 June	Israeli defense minister Moshe Arens tells visiting UN Secretary General de Cuéllar that the UN must recognize the Israeli-backed militia of Gen. Antoine Lahud in southern Lebanon.
	Foreign ministers of the Gulf Cooperation Council meet in Taif, Saudi Arabia, to agree on measures to take for the security of their oil shipments.
	The Sudanese army repels two attacks by rebels in southern Sudan.
14 June	The United States threatens to withdraw its delegates and stop its financial support to the Universal Postal Union if Israel is expelled from the organization.
15 June	The Iranian government announces it will not attack oil tankers in the Persian Gulf if Iraq stops its raids.
	Algerian and Moroccan troops clash near Bechar, Algeria.

16 June	In Israel, the Election Committee bars the Kach party of Rabbi Meir Kahane from participating in the 23 July elections.
	Iraq accuses Iran of shelling a town, thus violating a mutual agreement not to attack civilian cities.
19 June	The Election Committee in Israel bars the Progressive List for Peace, a new party of Palestinian Arabs and Jews, from participating in the 23 July elections.
	The Department of State informs Kuwait that because of congressional opposition the United States is unable to supply it with Stinger antiaircraft missiles.
	Hosni Mubarak, president of Egypt, appoints ten new deputies to the Egyptian parliament, including five Copts.
20 June	The United States and Israel carry out military exercises to practice medical airlifts; this is the first joint military exercise by the two countries.
	The Armenian Revolutionary Army claims responsibility for an explosion at the Turkish embassy in Vienna.
21 June	In Israel, Gilad Peli is sentenced to ten years in prison for attempting to blow up the Dome of the Rock in Jerusalem; he is also sentenced five additional years for transporting explosives.
22 June	Shimon Peres, Israel's Labor party leader, pledges to withdraw his country's troops from Lebanon three to six months after he becomes prime minister, if elected.
	A Libyan exile living in Greece is assassinated in Athens.
23 June	The Lebanese cabinet agrees to reorganize the army. Designed to achieve parity between Muslim and Christian elements, the agreement provides for a new commander, a six-man military council, and a National Security Department.
24 June	The newly elected parliament in Egypt opens; 85 percent of the seats belong to President Hosni Mubarak's National Democratic party.
	Iraq resumes attacks on tankers that carry Iranian oil in the Persian Gulf, damaging a Greek ship.
26 June	Talks are held in Bahrain on the Persian Gulf war: King Hussein of Jordan, President Zia ul-Haq of Pakistan, King Fahd of Saudi Arabia, and Egyptian chief of staff Muhammad Hilmi participate.
27 June	An agreement is reached between Israel and Syria on the exchange of war prisoners.
	Israeli aircraft attack Nakhil Island, near Tripoli, Lebanon.

Iraq damages a Swiss oil tanker near Kharg Island in the Persian Gulf.

The Reagan administration informs Congress that it intends to sell $82 million worth of antiaircraft equipment to Kuwait.

28 June   The Supreme Court of Israel overrules a ban on two political parties; both the Progressive List for Peace (Jews and Palestinian Arabs) and the Kach movement, led by American-born Meir Kahane, are now allowed to participate in the country's parliamentary elections.

Syria and Israel exchange prisoners.

29 June   Israeli naval units stop a ferry carrying Lebanese from Cyprus to West Beirut and remove nine passengers for interrogation.

In Tunis five groups within the PLO (including Arafat's al-Fatah) issue a communiqué announcing agreement on unity.

30 June   The Druze militia—the armed forces of the Progressive Socialist party—withdraws from Beirut to take up positions in the Shuf Mountains. This move is taken in cooperation with the Lebanese Military Council, which is putting into effect the security plan that will lead to the control of Beirut by the Lebanese government.

1 July   Iraq alleges it has damaged one Iranian airplane and sunk five ships today.

2 July   The Secret Army for the Liberation of Armenia warns that it will "strike all those who give help to the [Turkish] Olympic team in Los Angeles."

3 July   The Lebanese Forces, the militia of the Phalange party, withdraws its heavy armor from East Beirut in accord with the government's plan to reestablish authority in Beirut.

4 July   The Lebanese army moves nine thousand soldiers into Beirut to secure positions vacated by various militia groups, as the government asserts its sovereignty. The government also takes control of the airport.

5 July   The Lebanese army clears away barricades that were erected along the Green Line dividing Muslim and Christian sectors of Beirut.

Iranian aircraft attack and damage a Japanese oil tanker: this is the sixth attack credited to Iran.

6 July   Egypt and the Soviet Union reach an agreement on the exchange of ambassadors.

Rauf Denktash, leader of the Turkish Cypriots, accuses Greece of secretly building up Greek military forces on Cyprus.

7 July	Demonstrators in Beirut impede the Lebanese army's attempt to open crossings between East and West Beirut. The demonstrators are protesting the inability of the government to locate thousands of persons who were abducted by rival militias during the past several years.
	Military experts of the Gulf Cooperation Council meet in Kuwait to plan strategy against Iran's attacks on Gulf shipping.
	Iran claims its agents killed dozens of Iraqi agents by setting off a truck bomb in Baghdad. The attackers are said to be members of the Islamic Jihad organization.
8 July	Demonstrators in Beirut continue to impede government plans to open more crossings between East and West Beirut.
	The Reagan administration and the Pentagon consider denying surplus equipment to Greece because of that country's recent anti-American positions and its release of a terrorist.
	The U.S. embassy in Kabul, Afghanistan, is hit by a rocket in a series of shellings that are due to governmental infighting.
9 July	Protestors in Beirut shut down all crossing points between East and West Beirut in a general strike action.
	President Mitterrand of France and King Hussein of Jordan confer in Amman on the Iran-Iraq war and the Arab-Israeli conflict.
	The defense minister of Kuwait travels to Moscow, seeking to purchase military equipment to protect Kuwaiti oil shipments from Iranian attack. Earlier efforts by Kuwait to purchase antiaircraft missiles from the United States were not successful.
10 July	Protestors in Beirut call off their demonstrations: all crossings between East and West Beirut are opened, and the airport and seaport are functioning. The U.S. State Department welcomes the restoration of normalcy to Beirut and credits Syria with working toward a stable Beirut.
	Israeli Labor party leader Shimon Peres rejects an offer by Yitzhak Shamir, leader of the Likud bloc, that the two parties form a government of national unity after the 23 July elections.
	Tunisia raises the price of grain products 10 to 12 percent; last January extensive riots occurred, with the death toll over one hundred, when the government increased grain prices.
	Great Britain officially charges three Israelis and a Nigerian in the foiled kidnapping attempt of a wealthy Nigerian exile, which occurred at Stansted airport 5 July.
11 July	The Lebanese cabinet appoints a committee to obtain the release of hostages held by various militias; a second committee is named to investigate ways to open highways leading to southern Lebanon.

Heavy fighting breaks out in northern Lebanon in the Koura district between two pro-Syrian factions.

The American ambassador to Greece holds a meeting with Prime Minister Papandreou to discuss ways to reduce tensions between Greece and the United States.

The secretary general of the United Nations arrives in Moscow for discussions on Afghanistan.

12 July   Fighting continues in northern Lebanon between the Maronite Marada militia and forces of the National Syrian Social party.

13 July   Kuwait agrees to purchase $327 million in military equipment from the Soviet Union.

King Hassan II of Morocco meets envoys from Libya.

14 July   President Assad of Syria intervenes in the fighting between two pro-Syrian factions in northern Lebanon. Robert Franjieh, commander of the Maronite Marada militia, and In'am Ra'id, head of the National Syrian Social party, are called to Damascus for peace talks.

The Turkish parliament approves a five-year economic plan.

18 July   The Lebanese cabinet decides to restore diplomatic relations with Iran. Relations were severed last year when Iran refused to recall an Iranian military force stationed in Baalbak.

Israeli gunboats seize a small freighter leased to the PLO, claiming it was engaged in terrorist activities.

The Israeli liaison office in Beirut is ordered closed by the Lebanese minister of defense, Adel Osseiran.

19 July   Iraq claims its aircraft attacked and damaged a large ship near Kharg Island.

20 July   The Soviet embassy in Beirut is hit by a rocket.

21 July   Israeli occupation officials close the only presently traveled road between northern and southern Lebanon.

The foreign minister of West Germany, Hans-Dietrich Genscher, on a two-day visit to Tehran, calls for increased trade between his country and Iran.

22 July   The government of Sudan announces its troops have pushed rebel forces back into Ethiopia.

24 July   Israeli occupation forces in Lebanon reopen the only road running between Beirut and southern Lebanon.

Israel shuts its office for diplomatic liaison in Dbayeh, a suburb of Beirut.

The results of the Israeli national elections are indecisive.

Reports reaching Pakistan and India indicate the U.S.S.R. has undertaken major offensives against Afghan insurgents in the Logar Valley south of Kabul, in the Shomali Valley north of Kabul, and in Herat Province in the northwestern part of the country.

26 July   Rashid Karami, prime minister of Lebanon, says his coalition government "respects" the guerrillas in southern Lebanon because they represent the will of the Lebanese people.

A Department of State official says that the election of Meir Kahane to the Israeli parliament may result in the loss of his American citizenship.

28 July   The Lebanese government begins to remove barricades remaining along the Green Line separating East and West Beirut.

29 July   Druze forces of the Progressive Socialist party and the Murabitun, who are mostly Sunni Muslims, clash in heavy fighting in Beirut.

Iran reports it has been fighting Kurdish rebels for several days near Sardasht.

30 July   Guarded by Druze militiamen, the last Marine combat troops who were part of the multinational force leave Beirut.

In the West Bank town of Nablus, al-Najah University is closed down for four months after students demonstrate over the forced removal of an exhibit celebrating Palestine Week.

The Pakistan government takes measures to force all Afghan mujahedin (freedom fighters) out of Peshawar.

31 July   Greek workers end a twenty-seven-day strike at American naval bases in Greece.

1 August   Israel launches a sea and air attack on guerrilla bases near Tripoli, Lebanon. These bases house members of the Abu Musa faction of the PLO and the Popular Struggle Front.

Yitzhak Shamir and Shimon Peres announce their readiness to consider forming a coalition government in Israel.

2 August   Five or six ships are damaged by mines in the Red Sea.

American experts arrive in Cairo to investigate mine explosions in the Gulf of Suez.

3 August   Israeli forces in Lebanon shut down fifty shops in Nabatiyah after guerrillas attack an Israeli patrol.

4 August   Five thousand Israeli Arabs and Jews demonstrate at Umm al-Faham against Rabbi Meir Kahane's plans to set up an emigration office for Palestinian Arabs.

5 August	The president of Israel, Chaim Herzog, asks the leader of the Labor party, Shimon Peres, to form a new government.

An oil tanker is damaged by an underwater explosion in the Red Sea; this is the fifteenth ship to be damaged by such explosions during the past two weeks.

6 August

The Lebanese cabinet cancels an emergency meeting. Nabih Berri, leader of the Shiites, and Walid Jumblat, leader of the Druze, differ on the question of what part of Lebanon should be brought under the control of the Lebanese army. The question of political refugees, who are mostly Christians, occupies other cabinet members.

The prime minister of Lebanon, Rashid Karami, meets with the U.S.S.R.'s chief Middle East expert, Vladimir P. Polyakov, who wants Lebanese support for an international Middle East conference. Karami instead wants to expand the UN peace-keeping force in southern Lebanon, which the Soviets oppose.

Egypt requests assistance from the United States and Great Britain in clearing mines from the Red Sea. The United States will send four special helicopters, and Britain will provide minesweepers. So far, more than fifteen ships have been damaged by underwater explosions in the Gulf of Suez and the Red Sea.

7 August

The U.S. Navy dispatches about two hundred servicemen and some minesweeping helicopters to the Gulf of Suez.

Yasir Arafat, speaking at an Arab-African solidarity conference in Tunis, advises Arabs to adopt rigorous anti–United States positions.

The government of Iran praises recent attacks on shipping in the Red Sea, responsibility for which is claimed by the Islamic Jihad, but says it is not involved in the attacks.

Iraq renews its attacks on Iranian oil shipments in the Persian Gulf by damaging a Greek-owned tanker near Kharg Island.

8 August

The Lebanese cabinet agrees on a plan to restore army control in the mountains south of Beirut, where Walid Jumblat's Druze troops are firmly entrenched.

The Iranian foreign ministry accuses the United States and Israel of placing mines in the Red Sea.

Iranian hijackers of a jet airliner surrender in Rome.

9 August

The Ayatollah Khomeini denounces the mining of the Red Sea.

11 August

Iraq claims destruction of five ships and three Iranian F-14 airplanes in the Persian Gulf.

12 August	Chadian rebels, meeting in Ouagadougou, Bourkina Fasso (Upper Volta) resolve to form a group opposed to both the government of Hissen Habré and the main opposition group.
13 August	The United States sends three helicopter minesweepers to the Red Sea.
	The International Conference on Population, meeting in Mexico City, condemns the settlement policy of Israel.
	Afghan aircraft bomb a Pakistani village.
	Various Jewish groups in the United States protest a suggested change in Israel's law of return that would bar all converts from the Reform and Conservative movements from entering Israel as Jews.
14 August	Morocco and Libya announce plans for a union; Colonel Qaddafi and King Hassan II meet in Oujda and issue a statement outlining the plan for mutual defense and nonaggression.
15 August	Saudi Arabia confirms it has concluded a barter deal, exchanging 30 million barrels of oil for ten Boeing 747 airplanes.
	Kuwait signs an accord with the Soviet Union for the improvement of Kuwait's air defenses.
	The Iranian parliament dismisses five members of the cabinet; the move is seen as an effort by Prime Minister Musavi to increase diplomatic contacts with the Western world.
16 August	Israeli jets attack a Palestinian base at Bar Elias, twenty-five miles east of Beirut.
18 August	A tanker is hit by a missile fired from an unidentified airplane in the Persian Gulf.
19 August	Iran warns Iraq it is preparing a new offensive.
	The Afghan army shells Pakistani territory, killing eighteen persons. This raises the death toll of the present series of four similar attacks to thirty Pakistanis.
20 August	Israeli forces in Lebanon again close the north-south highway at Batar.
	Prime Minister Papandreou of Greece cancels plans for joint military exercises with the United States.
	Pakistan is again shelled by Afghan army units near the border town of Parachinar.
21 August	Unusually heavy fighting breaks out in Tripoli, Lebanon, between Sunni Muslim forces and a Syrian-backed militia known locally as the Pink Panthers. Up to 450 persons have been killed this year in Tripoli.

The chief of staff of Egypt's armed forces asserts that Libya is responsible for placing mines in the Gulf of Suez and the Red Sea.

The United States criticizes Greece for abruptly canceling a planned joint military exercise. Greece justifies its action in canceling the maneuvers, which have been held annually twenty times, on the grounds that NATO does not acknowledge Turkish provocations.

22 August   Factional warfare continues in Tripoli, Lebanon; fifteen persons are killed today.

Two Soviet minesweepers join naval units of Italy, France, Great Britain, and the United States in searching for mines in the Red Sea.

23 August   The chief of staff of the Lebanese army dies in a helicopter crash. Gen. Nadim al-Hakim, a Druze, was involved with the Gemayel government's plan to extend its authority to the Druze-held Shuf Mountains.

Iraq claims a successful attack on a ship near Kharg Island.

A bomb explosion kills seventeen and injures three hundred in Tehran. Opponents of the Khomeini government are implicated.

24 August   In Beirut the Saudi Arabian consulate is burned and the British embassy is struck by rocket-propelled grenades. The Islamic Jihad claims responsibility.

25 August   Lebanese Druze leader Walid Jumblat refers to the recent death of General Nadim al-Hakim, a Druze, in a helicopter accident as an assassination and says the Lebanese army is not to be trusted.

26 August   A cease-fire is arranged in Tripoli, Lebanon, where recent fighting between local Sunni Muslims and a Syrian-backed militia has killed about one hundred people.

President Chaim Herzog of Israel gives Shimon Peres an additional twenty-one days to put together a new government coalition.

Foreign ministers of seven Arab countries meet in Baghdad to seek ways to end the Iran-Iraq war.

27 August   Syrian president Hafiz al-Assad visits Libya for the second time within a week for more talks with Colonel Qaddafi on issues that have strained their relationship.

A Senate Foreign Relations Committee special staff report reveals that Iraq, because of recent acquisitions of weaponry from France and Russia, holds an advantage over Iran.

The leaders of two rival Afghan rebel groups, Gulbuddin

Hekmatyar and Burhanuddin Rabbani, pledge cooperation against the U.S.S.R.

28 August   The Israeli air force attacks the Palestinian guerrilla base at Majd al-Anjar in the Bekaa Valley of Lebanon; casualties may reach one hundred.

Moroccan minister of state Ahmad 'Alawi says that Libya has formally recognized Morocco's sovereignty over Western Sahara.

29 August   Pierre Gemayel, prominent Maronite leader in Lebanon and the founder of the Phalangist party in 1936, dies of natural causes at age seventy-eight.

When Rabbi Meir Kahane and three busloads of his armed supporters attempt to enter the Arab town of Umm al-Faham, he is detained by police and removed from the scene. Many local Jews join Arabs to protest Kahane's announced intention of entering the town.

30 August   Two Iranians fly an F-4 Phantom jet to Iraq and request asylum.

Afghan rebel groups begin to move out of Peshawar in accordance with an order of the government of Pakistan.

31 August   The Iranian foreign ministry criticizes various international agencies for their failure to end the hijacking of an Iranian jetliner to Iraq.

Libyan diplomats at the United Nations are placed under special travel restrictions by the United States.

A bomb explodes at the Kabul airport and kills about thirty persons.

1 September   Israel puts into effect new antismuggling regulations governing traffic between Lebanon and Israeli-held Lebanese territory: no cars, taxis, or trucks are allowed to pass from one zone to another. Instead, goods must be unloaded from vehicles on one side and carried across the border to be loaded onto different vehicles.

According to reports in Bahrain, Iran is closing its major oil export terminal on Kharg Island for repairs.

Colonel Qaddafi of Libya announces he has sent troops and military equipment to Nicaragua to back the Sandinista government against the United States.

Greek and Turkish Cypriots approve the peace initiative proposed by the United Nations.

Four men are indicted in the U.S. District Court in New Haven, Conn., for attempting to export 400,000 chemical warfare suits to Iran.

3 September	President Gemayel of Lebanon confers in Damascus with Syrian president al-Assad on means of resolving the deadlock within the Lebanese cabinet. This deadlock stems from the refusal of the Muslim members of the Government of National Unity to permit the Lebanese army (which is largely Christian) to be deployed outside of Beirut until the Muslims of Lebanon achieve a greater degree of political power.
4 September	Afghan rebel or exile groups in Pakistan claim to have recently bombed three hotels and a movie theater in Kabul.
5 September	A car bomb in Beirut, apparently intended to kill high-level civil and religious officials, kills four persons and injures twenty-seven.
	Political leaders in Israel say they have reached a basic accord on a multipartisan government; certain parties in the Likud bloc threaten to leave the coalition if the West Bank settlement program is not continued.
	Sen. Patrick Moynihan (Dem., N.Y.) calls the recently concluded treaty between Morocco and Libya a diplomatic defeat for the United States.
6 September	The United States vetoes a Security Council resolution calling on Israel to lift its restrictions on civilian traffic in southern Lebanon.
7 September	The presidents of Iran and Syria meet in Damascus to discuss the Gulf war.
	The Iranian exile group Mujahedin-i Khalq makes public a list of the names of more than ten thousand persons said to have been executed by the Khomeini government.
8 September	A hijacked Iranian airplane is seized in Cairo.
	'Ali Khamenei, president of Iran, ends a three-day visit to Syria.
9 September	Nabih Berri, who is leader of Lebanon's Shiites, justice minister, and minister of state for southern Lebanon, warns Israel that he is prepared to launch suicide car-bomb attacks on Israeli installations in Lebanon.
	Iranian nationals hijack an Iran Air flight and are granted asylum in Iraq.
	The Office of Technology Transfer reports that most Islamic Middle Eastern countries will be unable to develop nuclear weapons on their own by the year 2000.
10 September	Nabih Berri, cabinet member and Shiite leader, and Walid Jumblat, cabinet member and Druze leader, accuse the Lebanese army intelligence of complicity in the 5 September assassination attempt against Education Minister Salim al-Hoss and high-level Shiite dignitaries.

Israeli warplanes attack targets at Bhamdun, Lebanon.

The Israeli Labor party votes to approve a proposal calling for a coalition government.

Iraq reports it attacked an oil tanker near Kharg Island.

In Ethiopia, a Communist party is officially formed, with Lt. Col. Mengistu Haile Mariam, the country's leader, becoming secretary general.

11 September The defense minister of Syria, Mustafa Tlas, is quoted as saying that Rif'at al-Assad, brother of Syrian president Hafiz al-Assad, has been declared "persona non grata forever" in Syria. A report in Lebanon says that six army officers were arrested in Syria on charges of supporting Rif'at.

At a Malta meeting of nonaligned nations, Egypt declines to accept a communiqué that criticizes the Camp David accords.

Reports in New Delhi allege that Muslim insurgents have recently recaptured the upper part of the Panjshir Valley.

12 September Nabih Berri and Walid Jumblat boycott the weekly meeting of the Lebanese cabinet; President Gemayel agrees to a three-day special conclave next week on political changes.

Iraqi aircraft attack a convoy of oil tankers headed for Bandar Khomeini.

Iranian agents on a domestic flight foil a hijacking attempt.

An aide to Rif'at al-Assad, brother of the president of Syria, dismisses a recent *Der Spiegel* article that spoke of Rif'at's exile.

Rioting occurs in northern Jakarta, Indonesia, by "Muslim activists"; twenty persons are killed.

14 September The Israeli parliament votes approval of a government of national unity including both the Labor party and the Likud bloc, with a rotating prime ministership.

The Palestinian mayor of Rafa, 'Abd al-Karim Kishta, is assassinated by unknown persons; Kishta had been appointed mayor by the Israeli government.

The prime minister of Turkey, Turgut Özal, warns the United States that relations between the two countries can be harmed by the recently passed House of Representatives resolution calling for a day of remembrance for Armenian massacre victims; that resolution and the effort made by the Senate Foreign Relations Committee to have American foreign policy take account of the "genocide of the Armenian people" are seen by Özal as lending support to international terrorism by Armenian fanatics.

The president of Iran, 'Ali Khamenei, announces a committee has been formed in Iran to safeguard the rights of black Americans.

15 September	Calvin H. Plimpton, M.D., is named president of the American University of Beirut, succeeding the assassinated Dr. Malcolm Kerr.
16 September	Israel devalues the shekel by 9 percent. Budget Minister Yitzhak Modai aims to reduce the standard of living to 1982 levels and to cut $1 billion from the state's $20 billion budget.
	Trial begins in Israel for twenty Jews indicted for three major terrorist attacks on Arabs.
	Two oil tankers are damaged in the Persian Gulf by unidentified airplanes.
17 September	The Lebanese cabinet begins a series of special meetings to seek ways to redistribute political power.
	Following a secret trip to Libya by Claude Cheysson, foreign minister of France, Libya and France agree to a "total and simultaneous" withdrawal of their troops from Chad to begin on 25 September.
18 September	Members of the Lebanese cabinet agree to ask their respective militias to release all prisoners. Up to three thousand Lebanese have been reported missing during the past few years. The cabinet also agrees that a forty-member committee be formed to discuss constitutional changes.
	Fighting breaks out again in Tripoli, where the Sunni fundamentalist group Tawhid has been fighting with a Syrian-backed Alawite militia called the Pink Panthers.
19 September	The Reagan administration asks the new Israeli government to provide a comprehensive plan to cut the budget before asking for a big increase in aid from America.
	A tribunal of judges that was formed to hear U.S. claims against Iran is indefinitely suspended by tribunal president Gunnar Lagergren because the two Iranian judges punched one of their fellows.
20 September	The U.S. embassy in Beirut is seriously damaged by a car-bomb explosion; twenty-three persons die in the explosion at the embassy annex in East Beirut, to which all embassy operations had moved recently from West Beirut for greater safety. The Islamic Jihad claims credit for the attack.
	Troops of the South Lebanon Army, an Israeli-backed force, massacre thirteen Shiites from Sukmur in retaliation for the deaths of four of their fellow militiamen.
	Iraq claims it has raided Iran's major oil outlet at Kharg Island.
	An underwater explosion damages a Saudi ship in the Gulf of Suez. This is the nineteenth vessel to be damaged, presumably by mines, since 9 July.

21 September	The South Lebanon Army has detained for court-martial fifteen of its Druze militiamen who participated in a revenge-style attack on the Lebanese village of Sukmur on 20 September.
22 September	The Lebanese information officer, Joseph Skaf, accuses Israel of direct responsibility in the recent slaying of thirteen civilian Shiite villagers by members of the South Lebanon Army; according to Israeli army sources, Druze militiamen of the South Lebanon Army killed the villagers in retaliation for the deaths of their Druze comrades.
	Yitzhak Shamir, foreign minister of Israel, says his government intends to ask the United States to negotiate with Syria for a withdrawal of Israeli forces from Lebanon.
	Iraqi aircraft raid an Iranian petrochemical site at Bandar Khomeini. This is Iraq's eighth air strike at the complex, which is being constructed by a Japanese consortium.
23 September	The U.S. Navy positions three warships off the coast of Lebanon.
	Israel announces the imposition of new measures to reduce its high rate of inflation (400 percent); certain food prices will be raised, certain taxes levied, and various subsidies will be rolled back.
24 September	Richard W. Murphy, assistant secretary of state for Middle Eastern affairs, confers with President Hafiz al-Assad on the subject of Israeli troop withdrawal from southern Lebanon.
25 September	Jordan decides to restore diplomatic recognition of Egypt, becoming the first of the seventeen Arab states that broke relations with Egypt in 1979 to move to restore them.
	French troops begin withdrawing from Chad in accordance with an agreement with Libya, whose forces are expected to withdraw from northern Chad.
	Greece and Libya sign an economic cooperation agreement; Greece is to supply technological assistance in return for a guaranteed supply of oil.
26 September	Libya and Syria denounce Jordan's decision to resume diplomatic relations with Egypt.
	Libya reports it has begun withdrawing troops from Chad.
	An Italian magistrate issues an arrest warrant for Yasir Arafat on allegations that he supplied Italian terrorists with weapons; the PLO denies the charge.
27 September	Richard W. Murphy, assistant secretary of state for Middle Eastern affairs, returns to Damascus for talks with Syrian officials.
	The Department of State imposes additional restrictions on

the export of American products to Iran; these restrictions are a response to Iran's support of terrorist activity.

28 September The government of Chad reports that Libya has not begun to withdraw its troops from Chad.

Pakistan reports that an Afghan airplane bombed the town of Teri Mangel, killing thirty-two persons.

29 September Iraq attacks petrochemical works under construction by a Japanese firm at Bandar Khomeini; an earlier attack took place on 22 September.

The president of Sudan, Ja'far al-Numayri, lifts a five-month state of national emergency.

The Chadian rebel group called the Transitional Government of National Unity declares it will attack Ndjamena as soon as the French complete their withdrawal from Chad.

30 September Syria rejects the call by King Hussein of Jordan for an Arab summit meeting at which the problem of diplomatic recognition of Egypt would be discussed. King Hussein accuses Syria and Libya of repeatedly violating past Arab summit resolutions, of giving support to Iran over Iraq, and of undermining Yasir Arafat.

Shimon Peres, prime minister of Israel, expresses the hope that Jordan's recognition of Egypt will renew the peace process.

Israeli military authorities adopt a new policy to keep Beirut-based Western correspondents out of the Israeli-occupied areas of southern Lebanon.

One hundred and seven Egyptians are sentenced to life imprisonment at hard labor for inciting riots in Asyut shortly after the assassination of Anwar Sadat. (Note: On 5 November, the *New York Times* says that only sixteen defendants were sentenced to life imprisonment.)

1 October Following riots in Kafr al-Dawar, the Egyptian government orders a rollback on prices of certain foods.

King Hussein of Jordan attacks an Israeli proposal that Jordan and other Arab states join in peace negotiations.

2 October Hosni Mubarak, in a newspaper interview, states that Libya has plotted to destroy the Aswan Dam; the Egyptian president also predicts that Iraq will soon resume diplomatic relations with his country.

Ahmed Zaki Yamani, the oil minister of Saudi Arabia and spokesman for OPEC, visits Egypt to discuss the oil market; this is the first visit to Egypt by a high-ranking Saudi official since the 1979 break in diplomatic relations.

Israeli police disperse a large crowd of Arabs demonstrating at the U.S. consulate to protest prison conditions in Israel.

Ariel Sharon, Israel's minister of industry and trade, announces a six-month ban on imports of luxury products to help preserve foreign currency reserves.

Two subcommittees of the House Foreign Affairs Committee approve nonbinding resolutions that the U.S. embassy in Israel be moved from Tel Aviv to Jerusalem; the Department of State strongly opposes the move.

Chad hands over 121 Sudanese prisoners of war to Sudan; these prisoners had been in the Libyan Islamic Legion.

'Ali Nasir Muhammad, leader of Southern Yemen, is in Moscow to discuss common issues with Soviet leader Chernenko.

The foreign minister of Pakistan, Sahabzada Ya'qub Khan, states in the UN General Assembly that the Russian presence in Afghanistan poses a "direct and tangible" danger to his country.

3 October

Israeli officials say that Prime Minister Peres will not ask for stopgap economic aid when he visits Washington next week; instead, the intention is to present a five-year plan in which the United States will assist in restructuring the Israeli economy, according to cabinet secretary Yossi Beilin.

Yitzhak Shamir. Israel's foreign minister, in an address at the United Nations calls for a concerted effort against terrorism and pledges that Israel will pull its forces out of Lebanon when appropriate security arrangements are made.

The Department of State concludes that there is "persuasive circumstantial evidence" that Libya mined the Red Sea waterway. Mines so far have damaged at least nineteen ships.

The prime minister of Greece, Andreas Papandreou, alleges that the Korean Air Lines jet that was shot down by a Russian warplane was on a CIA spy mission.

News sources in Pakistan report that Afghanistan is concentrating troops in its Baluchistan Province on the Pakistan border.

4 October

Prime Minster Karami of Lebanon says his government will not engage in direct talks with Israel about troop withdrawal; he suggests the United States undertake indirect negotiations between Israel and Lebanon.

A hunger strike by eight hundred Palestinian inmates of a West Bank prison ends with an agreement for improved conditions.

U.S. intelligence agencies indicate they have evidence linking the Hizb Allah (Party of God) to the 1983 and 1984 bombings of the American embassy in Beirut, the Marine barracks, and the embassy in Kuwait. The Hizb Allah is based in Baalbak, Lebanon, and receives munitions from Iran.

Libya denies it planned to destroy the Aswan High Dam and accuses Egyptian president Mubarak of acting in the interests of Israel and the United States.

Vahit Halefoglu, foreign minister of Turkey, calls for direct negotiations between Turkish and Greek Cypriots and gives support to the current United Nations–sponsored talks on the Cyprus problem.

Nine Afghan insurgents are sentenced to death for the 31 August bomb attack at the Kabul airport.

5 October
Rashid Karami, prime minister of Lebanon, in a speech at the General Assembly appeals to the United Nations and the United States for help in arranging a withdrawal of Israeli forces from Lebanon.

6 October
Israel's prime minister, Shimon Peres, begins a week-long visit to the United States with the objective of securing increased financial aid to meet his country's serious economic crisis.

In Karachi, Pakistan, Sunni and Shiite Muslims engage in numerous clashes that leave several persons dead and about three hundred injured.

Hindu-Muslim confrontations occur in Nagda, India.

7 October
Israeli officials indicate a willingness to consider withdrawing troops from Lebanon in return for a verbal commitment from Syria to keep its forces in their present locations in Lebanon.

Some Libyan military units begin to withdraw from Chad. This is the first evidence that Libya will observe the 25 September accord with France for mutual withdrawals.

8 October
Iraqi warplanes damage a supertanker in the Persian Gulf.

President Zia ul-Haq of Pakistan says there will be no opposition parties after the March 1985 elections for an "Islamic democracy."

9 October
President Hosni Mubarak of Egypt begins an official visit to Jordan.

President Reagan informs visiting prime minister Peres of Israel that the United States will assist Israel, but only after a joint economic development group looks into questions of aid, investment, and related financial issues.

10 October
Israeli officials say they expect an increase in American grants from $2.6 billion to more than $4 billion in 1985.

12 October
President Saddam Hussein of Iraq reveals in a newspaper interview that he is ready to restore diplomatic relations with the United States.

An Iranian airplane bombs an Indian-owned tanker in the Persian Gulf.

13 October   Great Britain terminates its search for mines in the Red Sea.

14 October   Defense Secretary Weinberger confers in Cairo with President Hosni Mubarak; Egyptian officials are optimistic about a breakthrough in Lebanese-Israeli-Syrian talks on the withdrawal of Israeli forces from Lebanon.

Prime Minister Peres of Israel says the defense ministry is drawing up plans for a pullout of troops from Lebanon.

15 October   President Hafiz al-Assad of Syria arrives in Moscow for talks; this is his first visit since 1980. It comes at a time in which the U.S.S.R. is making overtures to moderate Arab states and after a period of Syrian disappointment over the lack of Soviet support during the 1982 Israel invasion of Lebanon.

Israeli finance minister Yitzhak Modai states that the Reagan administration has agreed to defer payments for ninety days on Israel's debt; U.S. officials say that no offer to do this was made.

Iraq announces its air force has attacked a naval target in the Persian Gulf.

Chad's warring factions agree to meet in Brazzaville, Congo, on 20 October.

16 October   The Lebanese parliament elects a new speaker: Hussein Husseini replaces Kamal al-Assad. Although both are Shiites, al-Assad supported the Lebanese-Israeli peace agreement, and Husseini is a militant former Amal leader who is backed by Syria.

In Moscow, Hafiz al-Assad and Soviet leader Chernenko condemn the United States for blocking peace in the Middle East.

17 October   Secretary of Defense Weinberger announces in Israel that the United States will give Israel access to advanced technology so it can manufacture its own up-to-date jet fighter, the Lavi.

The General Assembly votes down an attempt by Iran to expel Israel.

Iran begins a ground drive against Iraqi positions on the northern front.

Great Britain cuts the price of its North Sea oil by $1.35 a barrel to $28.65; OPEC officials consider holding an emergency meeting in Geneva.

18 October   The president of Syria, Hafiz al-Assad, ends a three-day Moscow visit. Western observers point out various areas of concern for Syria: (1) Moscow's desire to improve relations with so-called moderate Arab states, (2) Moscow's continued and increasing military aid to Iraq, and (3) Moscow's continuing support for Yasir Arafat, head of the PLO.

The Iraqi foreign minister, Tariq 'Aziz, arrives in Moscow.

Iran launches a ground assault in the Sayf-Sa'd area, breaking an eight-month lull in major ground fighting in the war with Iraq.

Nigeria lowers its oil price by $2.00, becoming the first OPEC member to break with the current official price structure.

19 October An Iranian fighter-bomber attacks a ship in the Persian Gulf; the U.S. Navy airlifts injured crewmen to medical facilities.

20 October The Department of State announces it will significantly reduce the Beirut embassy staff to about thirty persons.

Delegates from the various factions that are contending for supremacy in Chad meet in Brazzaville, Congo; the United States supports the present government headed by Hissen Habré.

21 October Both Tehran and Baghdad report severe fighting about seventy miles east of Baghdad.

About one hundred delegates from rival factions in Chad's civil war gather in Brazzaville, Congo, to attend talks on peace; the National Unity group of Goukouni Oueddei refuses to attend the opening sessions.

22 October President Amin Gemayel of Lebanon leaves Beirut to visit Colonel Qaddafi in Libya. Gemayel's visit will come a week after Druze leader Walid Jumblat's visit.

Eight oil-producing states hold talks in Geneva in advance of the OPEC meeting scheduled for 29 October; Nigeria declines to attend the meeting, thus reducing the likelihood of reaching a firm position on prices. Egypt participates in today's meeting.

23 October President Gemayel of Lebanon confers with Pope John Paul II and with high officials of the Italian government.

Reports in New Delhi say that Soviet troops in Afghanistan pillaged the town of Kandahar twice during this month.

25 October Iraqi ships attack an Iranian convoy near Bandar Khomeini.

26 October The vice-consul of the United Arab Emirates is wounded by a Jordanian gunman in Rome.

27 October The Lebanese government resolves to seize a number of seaports presently operated by private militias.

28 October In Jerusalem an Arab bus is struck by an antitank rocket. Jewish terrorists are suspected, and Rabbi Moshe Levinger, who leads hard-line Jewish settlers on the West Bank, attributes the attack to the government's lenient attitude toward Israeli Arabs.

The peace negotiations being held in Brazzaville, Congo, to settle the dispute in Chad are terminated without success.

29 October Palestinian students at Bethlehem University demonstrate to protest a rocket attack on an Arab bus by a Jewish extremist group.

The government of Sudan reports it has foiled a coup by Libyan-backed conspirators.

OPEC, holding an emergency meeting in Geneva, agrees to decrease its oil production by 1.5 million barrels a day to 16 million barrels a day. However, no agreement is reached on how to apportion these cuts.

30 October A provisional peace treaty is reached between the government of Sudan and the Sudan People's Liberation army, a principal element of those in the south of Sudan who oppose the central government's imposition of Islamic law in non-Muslim areas.

OPEC, meeting in a secret emergency session in Geneva, agrees on a formula to distribute production reductions among its members. Discussion and action on the problem of pricing are postponed until OPEC's December meeting.

31 October Israeli military authorities shut down Bethlehem University because of rioting occasioned by an attack on an Arab bus by Jewish terrorists.

The United Nations announces that Lebanese and Israeli delegates will start talks on Israeli troop withdrawal from southern Lebanon.

1 November Syrian first vice-president 'Abd al-Halim Khaddam says his country welcomes the planned talks between Israel and Lebanon but will not guarantee the security of Israel's northern border or guarantee that the thirty thousand Syrian troops now in eastern Lebanon will not move into areas vacated by the Israelis.

Special U.S. envoy Richard W. Murphy informs Israel that the United States will not act as mediator between Israel and Syria.

3 November The Lebanese government sends its troops into the Beirut harbor area to seize a pier held by a private Christian militia.

4 November The Israeli cabinet approves measures designed to fight inflation by holding down wages and freezing prices.

Afghan insurgents fire rockets into the city of Kabul.

5 November	Egypt and the United States hold joint naval and air exercises in the Mediterranean Sea.
	Roelof F. Botha, foreign minister of South Africa, makes an unofficial visit to Israel.
8 November	Heavy fighting breaks out in Beirut along the Green Line between Muslim and Christian militias. The causes of the intense fighting are seen to lie in efforts by the government to extend its authority and in the opposition of Muslim fundamentalists to the Lebanese-Israeli talks in Naqura.
	Talks begin at Naqura, Lebanon, between Israeli and Lebanese military officials on conditions for an Israeli withdrawal from southern Lebanon. Two major differences seem to be the question of maintaining security in southern Lebanon and the future role, if any, of the United Nations in these talks.
	Foreign Minister Claude Cheysson informs parliament that French and Libyan forces will complete their withdrawal from Chad in a matter of hours.
9 November	Extremely heavy fighting continues in Beirut.
10 November	The government of Lebanon suspends troop-withdrawal negotiations with Israel. The reason advanced by Lebanon is that the Israelis arrested Mahmud Faqih and twelve other men of the Shiite Amal militia. Also contributing to the break-off is the increasing opposition of radical Shiite religious leaders to cabinet member and principal Shiite politician Nabih Berri.
	Yasir Arafat says the PLO will convene the Palestine National Council in Amman, Jordan, later in November; Syrian-backed factions within the PLO oppose holding the long-delayed meeting in Amman.
	In a joint communiqué France and Libya announce the withdrawal of their forces from Chad.
	Foreign Minister Cheysson says France will give over $33 million in development aid to Chad next year.
	Syria warns the PLO not to convene the Palestine National Council in Amman, Jordan. Although several hard-line factions in the PLO oppose the upcoming meeting, Naif Hawatmeh, leader of the Democratic Front for the Liberation of Palestine, says he will attend.
11 November	Israel offers to begin a cease-fire vis-à-vis the Shiite militia in southern Lebanon to facilitate the resumption of talks at Naqura.
	In Addis Ababa, as delegates to the meeting of the Organization of African Unity arrive, the Nigerian foreign minister announces his country will recognize the Polisario of Western Sahara.

Israeli authorities continue a recent effort to destroy Arab houses in the Jiftlik area of the West Bank; about eighty houses, supposedly illegal or a threat to security, have been destroyed recently.

12 November   In southern Lebanon a general strike begins to protest the arrests of Shiite militia leaders by the Israelis.

Morocco withdraws from the Organization of African Unity which is presently holding its twentieth summit meeting at Addis Ababa, because the OAU decided to seat a delegation from Western Sahara.

In Athens an anti-American demonstration is held outside the U.S. embassy.

13 November   American officials maintain that Libya has not withdrawn its forces from Chad despite announcements to that effect by Claude Cheysson, foreign minister of France.

14 November   The Lebanese cabinet decides to resume talks with Israel after Israel released eleven Shiite militants whom it captured recently.

Maj. Gen. Mahmud Abu Dargham, a Druze, is appointed chief of staff of Lebanon's army.

15 November   Colonel Qaddafi, leader of Libya, and President Mitterrand of France meet in Crete to discuss the situation in Chad; whereas France has withdrawn its forces, Libyan troops still remain in violation of the mutual agreement of 17 September.

The Organization of African Unity ends its four-day meeting in Addis Ababa.

In the discussions between Israel and Lebanon that resume today at Naqura, the Lebanese propose that their army take control of all of southern Lebanon and that Israel pay $8 billion in war reparations.

16 November   President Mitterrand acknowledges that Libyan troops remain in Chad.

The official Libyan press agency states that Colonel Qaddafi's "suicide squads" have murdered former Libyan prime minister 'Abd al-Hamid Bakkush in Cairo.

17 November   Egyptian officials release evidence showing how they tricked the Libyan government into believing that Qaddafi's "suicide squads" had assassinated former prime minister Bakkush.

18 November   President Hosni Mubarak of Egypt says Colonel Qaddafi of Libya is an international terrorist and is financing plots to execute various world leaders.

Vice-President Khaddam of Syria visits Tehran; Arab diplomats report that he is seeking to persuade the Iranian government to moderate its policies.

19 November	The third round of talks at Naqura between Israel and Lebanon produces discussion of concrete political matters.
	Foreign Minister Claude Cheysson of France informs Secretary of State Shultz that France is prepared to send forces to Chad if Libya does not carry out its promised troop withdrawal.
	Armenian terrorists assassinate a Turkish UN official in Vienna.
20 November	George Habash, leader of the Popular Front for the Liberation of Palestine, arrives in Moscow for discussions of ways to avoid the breakup of the PLO.
	In a news conference, French foreign minister Cheysson says the United States and France differ profoundly on policy toward Colonel Qaddafi.
21 November	Israeli troops break up student demonstrations in favor of Yasir Arafat at Bir Zeit University; one Arab student is killed.
22 November	The Palestine National Council convenes in Amman, Jordan; King Hussein delivers the opening address, calling for an international peace conference under UN auspices to settle the Palestine issue.
	Demonstrations continue in the West Bank; one Arab is killed by Israeli troops in Ramallah.
	'Ali 'Abd al-Salam Turyaki, foreign minister of Libya, assures France that his country will pull its troops out of Chad.
	The deputy foreign minister of Greece arrives in Libya to assist in implementing the French-Libyan accord over troop withdrawal from Chad.
23 November	Yasir Arafat gains increased strength within the PLO when a new pro-Arafat speaker of parliament is elected over the pro-Syrian incumbent.
24 November	The vice president of Syria, 'Abd al-Halim Khaddam, confers with President Gemayel of Lebanon on plans for the deployment of the Lebanese army along the coastal road south of Beirut.
	Prime Minister Musavi of Iran accuses the Red Cross of conducting espionage.
26 November	Iraq and the United States restore full diplomatic relations, and the United States asserts it will retain its attitude of neutrality in the Iran-Iraq war.
	Troop withdrawal talks resume between Israel and Lebanon at Naqura. This is the fifth session since 8 November.
	The Lebanese army takes up new positions in an effort to consolidate its control over Beirut.

Rif'at al-Assad, brother of the president of Syria, returns to Damascus from five months of exile in Paris.

President Mitterrand of France arrives in Damascus for a three-day official visit.

27 November   Israeli jets attack PLO bases in Qab Ilyas, twenty miles east of Beirut.

The Gulf Cooperation Council opens its fifth annual meeting.

The Reagan administration says that Italian and American agents have discovered and foiled a plot by a Lebanese group to bomb the U.S. embassy in Rome.

The British deputy high commissioner for western India is assassinated in Bombay by a member of the Revolutionary Organization of Socialist Muslims.

American officials indicate that military aid to Afghan insurgents will double in 1985.

29 November   The Gulf Cooperation Council announces it will create a rapid deployment force with a unified command to be used in case of emergencies that threaten any Persian Gulf state.

1 December   Shafiq al-Hut, the PLO representative in Beirut, says he doubts the PLO will ever be able to reestablish itself in southern Lebanon in the event of an Israeli withdrawal; al-Hut also indicates he fears for the safety of Palestinian refugees living in southern Lebanon if Israel withdraws without securing an agreement with the Lebanese government over control of Phalangist operations in the South.

King Hussein of Jordan begins a three-day state visit to Egypt.

3 December   Egypt endorses King Hussein's formula for a resolution of the Arab-Israeli conflict; included in the king's proposals is an international conference. Shimon Peres, speaking in the Israeli parliament, opposes the idea of an international conference and suggests direct talks between Israel and Jordan.

In Nablus, al-Najah University reopens after being closed for four months by Israeli authorities who objected to the theme of an exhibit at the school during Palestine Week.

Iraqi warplanes attack a Cypriot oil tanker in the Persian Gulf.

The defense minister of Afghanistan, General 'Abd al-Qadir, who is second in rank in Afghanistan and who led the 1978 coup, has been removed from his post and reassigned.

Guerrillas ambush a Nile River steamship carrying government forces near Bor, Sudan.

4 December   A Kuwaiti airliner is hijacked by Arabic-speaking gunmen and forced to fly to Tehran.

5 December	According to the hijackers of a Kuwaiti airliner, an American hostage and two Kuwaitis have been killed.
	'Azmi al-Mufti, Jordan's chargé d'affaires in Bucharest, is assassinated, probably by the Black September faction of the PLO.
6 December	'Ismat 'Abd al-Majid, foreign minister of Egypt, urges the United States to intervene in the Arab-Israeli dispute and to negotiate with the PLO.
8 December	Lebanese army detachments and Druze militia forces engage in battle near Suq al-Gharb.
10 December	In Tehran, security men seize the hijacked Kuwaiti airliner and free the remaining hostages, ending a six-day ordeal at the Tehran airport.
	Assistant Secretary of State Richard W. Murphy meets Lebanese officials to discuss the Lebanese-Israeli talks at Naqura and then goes to Damascus for talks with Syrian officials.
	Various sources in Israel reveal that an airlift operation has transported thousands of Ethiopian Jews to Israel.
11 December	The administration asserts that Iran encouraged the hijackers of the Kuwaiti airliner.
	Prime Minster Papandreou says Greece no longer follows NATO policies as a matter of course.
	Amnesty International reports that stiff sentences are levied on those who practice their religion in Albania, where the population is 70 percent Muslim.
12 December	Iran's prime minister, Hussein Musavi, indicates he will not permit the extradition of four Arab hijackers.
	A car bomb is detonated at the Druze religious center in Beirut.
	A bloodless coup in the Islamic Republic of Mauritania deposes Muhammad Khouna Ould Haidalla and places Colonel Sidi Ahmed Taya in power.
13 December	Israeli troops in southern Lebanon raid eight Shiite villages and arrest fourteen suspects.
14 December	Gunmen assassinate a high-ranking Druze officer of the Lebanese army in Beirut.
	The Security Council extends the mandate for the UN peacekeeping forces in Cyprus for six months.
15 December	Isma'il Darwish, a pro-Arafat PLO official, is assassinated in Rome by unknown gunmen.

16 December	Rabbi Yitzhak Peretz resigns from the Israeli cabinet. A member of the Orthodox Shas party, his resignation weakens the Likud bloc.
18 December	Egypt is reinstated in the forty-five-member Islamic Conference (plus the PLO) and takes its seat in the conference now underway in Yemen. Hard-line Arab states make no apparent objection.
	Iranian officials decide to try the four hijackers of a Kuwaiti airliner. The trial will be in accord with Iran's shari'ah-based penal code.
	The Shas party, led by Rabbi Yitzhak Peretz, leaves the National Unity cabinet of the Israeli government.
19 December	The government of Israel submits its annual request for American aid. The request for 1986 is $4.85 billion and an additional $800 million over the $2.6 billion allocated for 1985.
	Pakistan holds a nationwide referendum on the continued presidency of Zia ul-Haq and his program of Islamicization.
20 December	Israel asks the Lebanese government to expand the role of UN troops in southern Lebanon or risk the withdrawal of Israeli troops from that area.
	The Lebanese army takes control of Tripoli.
21 December	A car bomb is detonated outside a Druze school in Ra's al-Matn. The Yazbaki Revolutionary Organization claims responsibility, the Yazbakis being a right-wing Druze sect in opposition to Walid Jumblat's Druze group.
	The Department of State says it will not meet Israel's request for an emergency grant of $800 million until Israel imposes additional austerity measures.
22 December	The foreign ministers of Islamic states end a five-day meeting in Sana, Yemen. During the meeting, Iran resisted all efforts to pass a resolution that the Islamic Conference Organization mediate the Iran-Iraq war; Foreign Minister Velayeti maintained that Saddam Hussein must resign the presidency of Iraq before Iran would consider any move to terminate the war.
25 December	Prime Minster Peres of Israel reveals that Secretary of State Shultz has advised that Israel take strong measures for economic recovery and reduce consumption; the Israeli minister for economic planning, Gad Yaakobi, responds: "Israel does not need moral preaching."
	A car bomb is detonated in Tehran; several persons are killed and wounded and more than forty buildings are damaged.
	The prime minister of the U.S.S.R., N.A. Tikhonov, starts a two-day visit in Ankara, Turkey. The two countries are ex-

pected to discuss regional and international problems and to enter into a $6 billion trade agreement.

26 December   Iranian aircraft attack a Spanish supertanker approaching the Saudi terminal at Ras Tamura.

Israeli police prevent Rabbi Meir Kahane from entering the Arab village of Taibe, on suspicion of making a provocative visit.

27 December   Amin Gemayel and Hafiz al-Assad confer in Damascus on security problems and the Lebanese-Israeli negotiations.

At the end of the visit by Russian prime minister Tikhonov to Ankara, no communiqué is issued because of differences of opinion; nevertheless, Turkey and the Soviet Union agree to a ten-year program of economic and scientific cooperation.

28 December   The government of Jordan is reported to have approved death sentences for fifteen Jordanians who sold their properties in the occupied West Bank to Israelis.

29 December   Fahd Kawasmeh, a member of the PLO executive committee and former mayor of Hebron, is assassinated in Amman, Jordan. The Black September group claims responsibility.

The Egyptian government lifts the exile of Coptic leader Pope Shenuda, who had been banished by former president Sadat.

Iraq claims its airplanes shot down two Iranian F-4s.

OPEC, meeting in Geneva, concludes an agreement on oil pricing, but Algeria and Nigeria refuse to endorse it.

30 December   Yasir Arafat, PLO chairman, accuses Syria of responsibility for the assassination of Fahad Kawasmeh.

Saudi Arabia at the Threshold

J.E. Peterson

In the aftermath of the Iranian revolution, it was fashionable among Western pundits to predict the imminent downfall of the Saudi Arabian regime. A presidential declaration was deemed necessary to emphasize Saudi Arabia's vital importance to the United States and to put on the record Washington's refusal to accept any change there. Five years after the establishment of the Islamic Republic of Iran, however, the mutterings of coming collapse in Riyadh have faded to an almost inaudible whisper. The reason for the nonappearance of the "Saudi Arabian revolution" seems to have far less to do with events in the kingdom between the seas than with glaring defects in the crystal balls of the instant experts.

In the fifty-two years since the official establishment of the Kingdom of Saudi Arabia, this deeply traditional society has undergone socioeconomic transformation to a degree unmatched perhaps anywhere else in the world. These changes necessarily have been accompanied by rapid growth and evolution within the political system. Herein lies the apparent paradox of Saudi Arabia: a deeply conservative monarchy, based on what has been termed "the world's largest family-owned business," has presided over a truly radical process of modernization. Yet, rather than being a hotbed of widespread repression and simmering instability, the Saudi Arabia of today—and probably for the foreseeable future—projects an image of continued prosperity and political stability. One benefit of this prognosis is a continuation of close ties between this important Arab kingdom and the United States.

SAUDI ARABIA AND THE UNITED STATES

Saudi Arabia has been one of the United States' oldest friends in the Middle East. The description of a "special relationship" seems fully justified by the extent of the friendship and steady cooperation between the two countries throughout an often cataclysmic half-century. The relationship easily weathered such benchmarks as the emergence of oil and oil power in the region, the independence of most of the Arab states and Israel, five Arab-Israeli wars, the intrusion of several Soviet toeholds in the area, the waxing and waning of the "Arab cold war," the appearance of two revolutions in the Persian Gulf, and, most recently, the specter of anti-American and perhaps anti-Saudi Islamic radicalism. At the midpoint of the 1980s, U.S.-Saudi relations seemed stronger than ever, despite the continued presence of several thorns.

Saudi Arabia's Importance to the United States

At the beginning of the 1970s, only a few Americans who were connected with the oil industry or who specialized in Middle Eastern affairs were likely to have heard of Saudi Arabia. Over the following decade, however, discussion of the kingdom, its oil, its connection to the United States, and its foreign policy has become commonplace in U.S. government pronouncements, newspaper headlines, television news reports, and even scholarly publications. By late 1982, in a poll conducted by the Chicago Council on Foreign Relations, 77 percent of the American public felt that the United States had a vital interest in Saudi Arabia—a percentage exceeded by only Japan, Canada, and Great Britain.

There are many impressive reasons why Saudi Arabia is important to the United States as the following checklist demonstrates:

1. Oil, not surprisingly, stands at the head of the list. As a source of crude oil, Saudi Arabia has no equals, with approximately one-quarter of the world's total oil reserves to be found in the kingdom. Between 1976 and 1981, Saudi Arabia was the largest source of oil imported into the United States (although by 1984 it had slipped to sixth place) (*Washington Post*, 10 Feb. 1985). Saudi oil has been an even more important source of energy for American allies and friends around the world.

The Saudi oilfields also constitute a strategic asset. A 1975 Congressional Research Service study pointed out that the "Saudi core" would be the most likely target if the United States ever found it necessary to intervene militarily to control international oil deposits. This conclusion was based on its great size, compactness, proximity to seaports, and relative isolation from population centers, among other factors (U.S. Congress 1975).

2. Saudi Arabia long has served as a moderating influence within OPEC. Because of the capital-surplus nature of its economy and its great excess capacity, Riyadh possessed both the willingness and the ability to enforce its views of what should be a reasonable price for oil (essentially, price increases should keep pace with world inflation). The emergence of the world oil glut in the 1980s has severely diminished this capacity, and it was left to Saudi Arabia to try to maintain order in increasingly contentious OPEC ranks by absorbing the lion's share of production cutbacks.

3. Saudi Arabia's oil income gives it considerable importance and influence in a variety of arenas. The kingdom received well over $100 billion in oil income in 1981, more than the earned income of all of Africa or all of South America.

The kingdom has become a major consumer. U.S. exports to Saudi Arabia reached a high of $8 billion in 1982. By 1984, it had become the sixth largest market for U.S. goods, services, and technology, *excluding* arms sales. Not only do more than a thousand U.S. firms operate in Saudi Arabia but a number of U.S. government agencies are heavily involved as well, including the Interior, Treasury, Agriculture, Commerce, Energy, and Labor departments. The amount of military construction for which the U.S. Corps of Engineers has been responsible exceeds $19 billion (*Washington Post*, 25 Nov. 1984). In addition, U.S.-Saudi arms sales agreements through 1980 totaled nearly $35 billion and arms deliveries were over $11 billion (U.S. Congress 1981, 48). This figure does not include the $8.5 billion price tag for 5 AWACS and other equipment sold to the kingdom in 1982.

The mass of oil revenues also enabled Riyadh to provide vast subsidies to a wide variety of states and parties in the Arab world, Africa, and Islamic community. As a result, Saudi Arabia has been one of the world's principal sources of development assistance. In 1981, its official disbursements of $5.798 billion (4.77 percent of GNP) even topped the U.S. total of $5.783 billion (0.20 percent of GNP) (OECD 1982). (The oil glut has taken its toll on Saudi development efforts, with 1982 and 1983 totals dropping below $4 billion [OECD 1984].) In adition to development aid, Saudi financial assistance has been used to advance Islam (for example, the construction of mosques and distribution of Korans in a number of countries) and such political goals as building a "moderate" Arab consensus and shoring up anti-Communist alliances.

4. Saudi Arabia is the United States' principal partner in the Gulf, the last remaining pillar among the Gulf's Big Three states. Thus, its cooperation is especially important to Washington for several reasons. First, it occupies a strategic location astride both the Gulf and the Red Sea, fronting Israel and Jordan, Iraq, Iran, the Yemens, and the Horn of Africa, and it is much larger than all its immediate neighbors. Second, it provides a potential platform from which to counter a possible Soviet advance on the Gulf. Third, it provides a buffer against the potential of larger but less congenial Iraq and Iran for troublemaking in the region. Fourth, the kingdom embraces many of the same political goals as the United States, both in the region and in general; consequently, the implementation of Saudi policy generally advances U.S. policy interests. And fifth, Saudi Arabia cooperates militarily with the United States to a far greater degree than any other Arab state, and the United States has a massive arms transfer and training investment in the kingdom. According to many potential contingencies, the Saudi military establishment conceivably would act as an extension of U.S. capabilities. The overstocking of U.S. supplies and equipment there raises the possibility of use by American forces in an emergency. Furthermore, the two countries share intelligence to a considerable degree, whether through human sources or by electronic equipment as in the AWACS.

5. Saudi Arabia is a key actor in the region because of its predominance in the Arabian Peninsula and its leadership within the Gulf Cooperation Council (GCC). Riyadh can strongly influence, if not dictate, the policies of the smaller states. This is particularly important for the United States, since the other states (apart from Oman) tend to be relatively more inclined toward neutrality or nonalignment.

6. Saudi Arabia also has an important role to play in the Eastern Mediterranean. In the last seventeen years, Riyadh has developed a "moderating" influence within Arab politics, and has used its moral capital and financial means in efforts to persuade Jordan, the PLO, Syria, and especially Egypt

(prior to the Sadat initiative) to remain within the pale of Arab consensus. Given the closeness of American and Saudi goals on most issues, Saudi diplomacy in the Arab world often serves American interests. Nevertheless, there are severe limits to Saudi ability to pressure its sister Arab states, and Saudi objectives do not automatically parallel American policy goals. The United States and Saudi Arabia fundamentally share the same goal of constructive movement toward a comprehensive Arab-Israeli peace, although the two countries differ on the means to the end and the final status of the Palestinians.

7.   The capital-surplus years have provided Saudi Arabia with considerable financial clout. Saudi investment in the United States is substantial, even though the precise amount is open to widely varying interpretations, and the movement of Saudi (and other Gulf states') liquid assets potentially could wreak havoc with the U.S. dollar. It should be realized, of course, that the growth of Saudi importance on the international financial scene, as exemplified by its seat on the International Monetary Fund's Board of Governors, has been matched by a commensurate exercise of responsibility: the Saudi stake in the international economic order proportionally is just as great as any industrialized country.

8.   The United States has a considerable stake in Saudi development efforts. One indication of the degree of American involvement is the formation of the U.S.-Saudi Joint Commission for Economic Cooperation, formed in 1974; another is the presence of over sixty thousand U.S. citizens in the kingdom.

9.   More intangibly but perhaps even more important than the above reasons, Saudi stability carries great importance for U.S. prestige and credibility abroad. Simply put, the United States has a big stake in Saudi Arabia's future. Much of the development and evolution of the modern Saudi state, economy, and society has been influenced or shaped by an American input. The blueprints of Saudi Arabia's three development plans unmistakably reflect American thinking and operating methods. The thousands of Saudis educated in the United States have returned home to positions as prominent government officials, technocrats, businessmen, and intellectuals.

At a broader level, the United States faces the perennial problem of friendship and a favorable reception in the Third World. The fall of the shah's regime in Iran was one more blot on the ledger of Third World perceptions of the United States, following on the heels of Vietnam, Chile, and Central America. Washington's belief that it cannot afford to "lose" Saudi Arabia, and Reagan's codicil to the Carter Doctrine ("Saudi Arabia we will not permit to be an Iran") not only gives the world warning but puts the United States on the line.

Background to the U.S.-Saudi Relationship

Aramco

The nascent Saudi state faced extreme poverty in the 1920s and 1930s. Between 1915 and 1924, the government's principal income came from a British subsidy; with the conquest of the Hijaz, the *hajj* (pilgrimage) tax provided income—but the contribution from this source diminished as a result of the Great Depression. Consequently, receipt of a bonus for signing an oil concession represented a major source of income, even without considering the actual discovery of oil.

The prospects for a strike in Saudi Arabia were good enough to interest several companies, among them SOCAL (Standard of California), which had discovered oil in nearby Bahrain in 1932. SOCAL's success in gaining the Saudi concession over its British rivals was due principally to its willingness to pay $250,000 in gold upon King 'Abd al-'Aziz ibn Sa'ud's signature, as well as royalties of four gold shillings per ton in the event oil was found. Discovery came in 1938 at Dammam in the Hasa region of the Eastern Province, and California Arabian Oil (which comprised SOCAL and its new partner TEXACO) began exporting some oil to its Bahrain refinery soon after. The outbreak of World War II put a halt to production, however, and Saudi income was reduced again to British and American subsidies.

Saudi production began in earnest after the war ended, as Standard of New Jersey (now Exxon) and Standard Vacuum Oil (now Mobil) joined the earlier partners in the newly named Arabian American Oil Company (AR-AMCO). In 1949, the Saudi fields were producing ½ million barrels per day (mbd). Production doubled by 1955 and jumped to 3.5 mbd by 1960. The growing scarcity of worldwide oil resources in the 1960s and 1970s meant that Saudi production continued to grow annually, reaching an average in excess of 10 mbd until the early 1980s.

But ARAMCO served as more than simply a source of income for Saudi Arabia in those early days. The company provided the government with advice and expertise on a wide variety of subjects. It instituted the first formal educational system for its Saudi employees, both at its headquarters in Dhahran and abroad, and its local purchases paved the way for the emergence of present-day indigenous commercial concerns in the Eastern Province.

Foundations of Official Ties

Diplomatic ties began with the establishment of a U.S. legation in Jidda in 1943. In February 1945, King 'Abd al-'Aziz met with President Franklin Roosevelt on a yacht in the Great Bitter Lake of the Suez Canal; one month later, Saudi Arabia abandoned its neutrality and declared war on Germany. A full embassy was subsequently established in Jidda in 1948.

Military ties between the two countries date from the same period. By 1943, the Pentagon deemed it desirable to establish its own air facilities in the Gulf (rather than rely on British ones) to link the Middle Eastern–North African theater to South Asia and the Pacific. Negotiations over a base at Dhahran were started and the facility was completed shortly after the end of the war. The Dhahran airfield was used by the United States until the agreement was terminated by mutual choice in 1962.

U.S. teams were sent to survey Saudi military needs in 1944 and 1949, and the U.S. Military Training Mission was established in 1953, replacing earlier British teams. The first arms transfers from the United States to Saudi Arabia took place at this time as well, including M-41 light tanks and B-26 bombers. At first, the level of military assistance was extremely modest. Between 1950 and 1964, the grand total of sales agreements was only $87 million and deliveries totaled $75 million. But the level of sales agreements jumped to $342 million in 1965 and zoomed to over $2 billion in 1974. By 1980, nearly $35 billon in arms agreements had been negotiated, with over $11 billion of deliveries made (U.S. Congress 1981, 48).

The expansion of U.S.-Saudi ties in the 1950s and 1960s, especially in military matters, was prompted by a number of factors. A principal one involved the growing importance of Saudi oil fields (and increasing levels of production) at a time when the world's oil supplies were growing short. Just as important was the emergence of the Arab cold war between the new, radical Arab republics and the older, traditional regimes, mostly monarchies.

Saudi interest in an American partnership stemmed from its being subject to active aggression by such "progressive" Arab leaders as Egypt's Nasir and Iraq's Qasim. For its part, Washington sought allies against Soviet encroachment in the Middle East. The complexities of the situation were clearly illustrated by the civil war in neighboring Yemen (1962–67). Saudi Arabia provided as much aid as possible to the royalists fighting the Egyptian-backed republicans, and the United States briefly posted a squadron of F-100 aircraft and paratroops in southwestern Saudi Arabia in case Egypt should use its troops in Yemen to attack Saudi Arabia directly.

Relations between 1973 and 1978

Emphasis within the bilateral relationship during the mid-1970s appeared to be placed on Saudi development efforts and the Saudi role in the Eastern Mediterranean. Increased American involvement in the kingdom's development was encouraged by the U.S. government because of its favorable impact on recycling petrodollars.

At the same time, the October 1973 Arab-Israeli war and resultant oil boycott marked a troubling undercurrent in the two countries' ties. (As the fighting continued, Saudi Arabia and most other Arab oil producers reluctantly instituted production cutbacks and a boycott of the United States and the Netherlands for their pro-Israeli attitudes; the boycott was later extended to include Portugal and South Africa, for their antiblack policies in Africa.) Indeed, it has persisted as the only major thorn in an otherwise increasingly intimate relationship.

Washington looks at Riyadh as the key to Arab moderation regarding Israel—as a tool to bring other Arab actors into the moderate camp. Riyadh sees itself more as a force behind Arab consensus on many matters, including Israel. Its insistence on consensus derives from the experience of the Arab cold war and reluctance to return to the extreme polarization of Arab politics during those years. The Khartum Conference of 1967, which put an end to the cold war, also created pan-Arab obligations for Riyadh, particularly in regard to Arab-Israeli matters. Saudi Arabia is also bound by the decision of the Arab summit at Rabat in 1974 to recognize the PLO as the sole representative of the Palestinians.

Saudi encouragement and midwifery produced the rise of the short-lived U.S.-Saudi-Egyptian triangle of the 1970s. Saudi Arabia encouraged Sadat to turn from the Soviet Union to the United States. But Sadat's surprise decision to go to Jerusalem mocked Saudi concerns for a consensus approach and led to suspicions that Sadat's goal was a separate peace in which the other Arab states and the Palestinians would be sold out.

Relations between 1979 and the Present

The special relationship prospered during the subsequent half-decade and even grew more intimate, despite the frustrations of the Arab-Israeli impasse. The

Sadat initiative and resultant Camp David process alienated Egypt from most of the Arab world, including Saudi Arabia, and gave birth to only the Egyptian-Israeli treaty instead of a comprehensive peace. Saudi irritation at Sadat's tactlessness in pursuing a separate path with American encouragement was present in the U.S.-Saudi relationship, but it did not seriously jeopardize bilateral relations.

Once Alexander Haig's stillborn conception of a "strategic consensus" (based on close cooperation of all American friends in the Middle East, including Israel, in an anti-Soviet alliance) was dropped, and after Anwar Sadat was assassinated, the prospect of a rupture of U.S.-Saudi closeness because of Egypt began to dim. The Israeli invasion of Lebanon in 1982 and Hosni Mubarak's cautiousness gradually served to reorient Egypt back toward a centrist position in Arab politics. Egyptian support was forthcoming for Iraq in its war with Iran, Egyptian-Jordanian diplomatic relations were restored in late 1984, and it seemed only a matter of time before Cairo and Riyadh resumed official ties.

In large part, the limited impact of Sadat's policies on the U.S.-Saudi relationship was due to increasingly volatile developments in the Gulf, alarming both Riyadh and Washington. The security threat posed by the militantly anti-U.S. and anti-Saudi revolution in Iran in 1979 seemed to tie in with a resurgence of populist Islam. Saudi fears seemed justified, at least briefly, by the November 1979 takeover of the Great Mosque at Mecca by Islamic extremists. Suspicions of Soviet designs on the Gulf were intensified by the brief border war between Saudi-backed North Yemen and Moscow-influenced South Yemen in early 1979 and then by the Soviet takeover of Afghanistan at the end of that year.

One consequence of this highly charged atmosphere was an emerging U.S. emphasis on direct and indirect military options in the Gulf. The Carter Doctrine was promulgated in January 1980 to provide a warning to Moscow that any move to the Gulf would be met by U.S. force if necessary. Efforts were made to give teeth to that declaration through the Rapid Deployment Force, officially made the U.S. Central Command in 1983. Pressure was put on Riyadh to permit access to Saudi military facilities by the Central Command on an emergency basis and to allow the stockpiling of equipment there. Riyadh has continued to resist this kind of overt cooperation, as have the other GCC states with the exception of Oman.

The priority given to a possible Soviet attack in American planning for Gulf contingencies was forced to undergo reevaluation with the outbreak of the Iran-Iraq war in September 1980. It finally became apparent in official Washington circles that threats to Gulf security from regional sources were as great as, if not greater than, Soviet incursions. With the fall of Pahlavi Iran, Saudi Arabia had become the only remaining pillar of U.S. interests in the Gulf. Washington was determined to protect its influence in Saudi Arabia, even to the point of intervention if necessary (as expressed in the Reagan codicil). In addition, efforts were intensified to build up the Saudi military to the point of self-defense, if not some regional defense, capability.

U.S. apprehensions over the apparent deterioration of stability in the Gulf forced the acrimonious debate over the sale of five Airborne Warning and Control System (AWACS) radar aircraft to the kingdom in 1982, over the objections of Israel and its supporters in the United States, and those congressmen who feared that the Al Sa'ud state would collapse just as the Pahlavi regime had. The Saudi government, while anxious to maintain its close relations with Washington, including in the military realm, was notably and understandably reluctant to give carte blanche to a direct U.S. military presence in the kingdom. The tug-of-war between the Pentagon's desire for facilities in Saudi Arabia and the Saudis' wish to keep out American military units (as opposed to American military advisers to the Saudi armed forces) continued through the tanker war of 1984.

DOMESTIC DETERMINANTS IN SAUDI POLICYMAKING

Saudi Arabia is neither a traditional state nor an absolute monarchy. In fact, it is a very new creation. A process of unification early in the twentieth century joined the areas of Najd (the central Arabian homeland of the royal family), Shammar in the north, al-Hasa along the Gulf coast, the cosmopolitan region of Hijaz in the northeast, and fertile 'Asir along the Red Sea coast south of the Hijaz. The country assumed its present territory and structure only in the 1930s. Although ultimate political authority rests with the king, considerable restraints exist on his decisions and actions, as outlined below. The last two decades have been particularly important in developing an entirely new governmental apparatus and complex set of domestic and external concerns in Saudi policymaking.

The Structure of the Saudi Political System

Saudi Arabia is a new state built on traditional foundations. In the last several decades, the country has experienced a rapidly expanding state structure and the rooting of many of the solid, capable institutions necessary for the operation of a modern nation-state. In short, the skeleton of basic foundations has been put into place; it now remains to flesh it out.

Traditional Elements of Saudi Politics

A number of traditional elements still remain strongly entrenched in Saudi politics, however, and are likely to retain at least part of their importance for some time to come.

    Tribalism.   Despite all the changes in recent years, Saudi Arabian society retains many aspects of its tribal roots. The Al Sa'ud were originally tribal shaykhs and their traditional ability to wield power was based on tribal forces. The National Guard continues to serve as a reminder of this traditional relationship between the ruling family and the tribes. Beyond their tribal base in the Najd, the position of the Al Sa'ud over the kingdom was consolidated in this century through the forging of new tribal alliances, principally by intermarriage among the Al Sa'ud and other shaykhly clans. To some extent, the position of the ruling family today is maintained through continued reference to the myth of the legitimacy of the Al Sa'ud as preeminent tribal shaykhs.

    Personal Leadership.   Personal leadership is another traditional element that has carried over into the modern state. A leader, whether of the tribe or of the state, is expected to be *shadid* (capable, forceful, and strong); and respect is earned or lost according to an individual's performance as much as his rank. At the same time, according to traditional expectations, a leader must be accessible to his people and accommodate their desires and grievances. This right has been preserved in the *majlis* (an open audience where any citizen can come and speak directly to the king, the crown prince, provincial governors, and other figures of authority). As a consequence, the traditional precept of *shura* (consultation) has been retained. Similarly, the principle of *ijma'* (consensus) has evolved from a means of tribal democracy into an emphasis on acquiring the unanimous assent of the Al Sa'ud family on important decisions.

Islam.   The central role of Islam is more pronounced in Saudi politics than in many Islamic countries. In part, this derives from the traditional origins and emphasis of the kingdom. The *shari'ah* (corpus of Islamic law) is proclaimed to be the constitution of the country, and Saudi Arabia claims a special role within the Islamic community because of its guardianship of the holy cities of Mecca and Medina. On a more historical level, the roots of the Saudi state derive from the eighteenth-century alliance between the secular and tribal power of the Al Sa'ud and the austere fundamentalist teachings of a Najdi religious figure, Muhammad ibn 'Abd al-Wahhab. As a consequence, the majority of Saudis are today Wahhabis (or as they prefer to be known, Muwahhidun, or "unitarians"), a movement following a strict interpretation of the Hanbali school of law within the Sunni sect of Islam.

Another element in the legitimacy of the present regime rests upon its claim to be defenders of the faith, based on the Saudi role in advancing the reformist tenets of Wahhabism throughout the Arabian Peninsula. The *'ulama'* (religious scholars) play a prominent role in Saudi Arabia, upholding the shari'ah, opposing the disintegration of traditional society, and even issuing *fatwas* (legal opinions) regarding government policy. The descendants of Muhammad ibn 'Abd al-Wahhab, known as the Al al-Shaykh, hold influential positions within the 'ulama' and goverment.

Even the late king 'Abd al-'Aziz, who was responsible for unifying the country, had difficulty in reconciling the traditional, religious nature of his subjects with the requirements of a modern state. The swords of the *Ikhwan*, sedentarized bedouin organized into settlements and fighting units in order to advance the Wahhabi version of Islam, turned against 'Abd al-'Aziz in the late 1920s when he prevented them from raiding British-controlled Iraq and Transjordan. Although the schisms between traditionalism and modernization are no longer as sharp as they were, they still present a problem for Saudi rulers.

The Role of the Al Sa'ud
It is unquestionable that the ruling family constitutes the unchallenged source of authority in Saudi Arabia. At the same time, however, it bears emphasizing that Saudi Arabia is not an absolute monarchy, dependent on the unrestricted actions of a single individual or even a single family.

The King.   The king is at the apex of this unchallengeable authority, but he must rule in accordance with the shari'ah and a family consensus, and on the basis of an uncertain balance between traditional precepts and modern expectations of a ruler. As John Shaw and David Long have written, "Saudi decision making in general is based on two traditional concepts: *shura*, or consultation, and *ijma'*, or consensus. The role of the king, in this context, is to guide the consultation to a favorable consensus on which to base decisions" (Shaw and Long 1982, 60).

The successful evolution of the institution of Al Sa'ud shaykh, or *imam* (the quasi-religious title by which Saudi leaders were traditionally known), into monarch undoubtedly has benefited from the role played by two strong and capable kings. 'Abd al-'Aziz (r. 1932–53) unified Saudi Arabia and laid the foundations of the modern state. He presided over the integration of the heterogeneous Najd, Eastern Province, Shammar, Hijaz, and 'Asir into a single state, over the discovery and production of oil, over the opening to the outside world, and over the beginning of the relationship with the United States.

His son Faysal (r. 1964–75) provided the authoritative presence behind the throne during his brother Sa'ud's troubled reign (r. 1953–64) and then succeeded to the throne when Sa'ud was deposed by the family. Faysal was responsible for bringing Saudi Arabia into the mainstream of Arab politics following the end of the Arab cold war and providing leadership on Arab-Israeli matters; for fully implementing the choice to forego traditional isolation and interact fully with the outside world; for laying the groundwork for a thorough development process; for seeking to create a community of interests among the Islamic countries; for deepening the U.S.-Saudi relationship, particularly in military matters; and for transforming the traditional enmity with the smaller Arab Gulf states to a close working relationship.

These two kings were basically men of the desert, deeply pious and respected by the 'ulama' for their piety and religious learning. They were also well skilled in traditional tribal politics, yet they were men of vision beyond tribal limits. The state apparatus they presided over was small and uncomplicated. They depended on a few trusted advisers, often of non-Saudi origin, and rarely delegated authority on even the most unimportant details.

The last two kings lived most of their lives in the oil era, during a period embracing rapid socioeconomic change, the impact of modernization, and the emergence of a complex foreign policy environment. Leadership has become more collegial and less conservative or traditional. King Khalid (r. 1975–83) was in frail health upon his succession and generally left routine matters to be handled by his brother Fahd. Fahd (r. 1983–present) has a playboy reputation to live down and exerts less charisma than Faysal, which may mean some less respect or control within the family and among the citizenry in general. Nevertheless, he has proved to be a competent, decisive ruler.

The outlooks and requirements of Saudi Arabia's kings are undergoing evolution, just as the state and society are. It is likely that future monarchs will be less attuned to a traditional/religious/conservative constituency (with perhaps the exception of the current crown prince) and will be required to demonstrate sensitivity to changing and increasingly complex circumstances.

It is possible that future strains will appear in the process of determining succession to the throne. There is no formal rule of primogeniture, and succession has not strictly followed family lines of seniority. Through 1984, succession has proceeded through sons of 'Abd al-'Aziz. Among these are the so-called Sudayri Seven—sons of King 'Abd al-'Aziz by the same mother (their ranks include King Fahd; Sultan, the minister of national defense and aviation; and Nayif, the minister of the interior). Another son, 'Abd Allah, serves as crown prince and heir apparent (as well as deputy prime minister and commander of the National Guard). 'Abd Allah, a rival of the Sudayri Seven, is regarded as the spokesman for conservatives in the country and appears somewhat more skeptical of the value of the U.S.-Saudi special relationship.

Upon Khalid's death, a modus vivendi was reached between the Al Sa'ud conservatives and the Sudayris. In return for recognition of 'Abd Allah as crown prince, Sultan received the title of second deputy prime minister and the understanding that he would follow 'Abd Allah as crown prince. Sultan is considered more "modernist" and relatively more congenial to the continuation of close ties to the United States. The balance among different factions among the sons of 'Abd al-'Aziz thereby was preserved. Nevertheless, it does not formally resolve the succession problem, especially in terms of the transition of power from the sons of 'Abd al-'Aziz to the next generation of grandsons.

Other Members of the Al Sa'ud. Although consideration of the kings of the present and the future may figure most importantly in the overall political picture, the role of the Al Sa'ud in the system is not limited to them. With more than five thousand male members, the family constitutes a key interest group and sociopolitical elite by itself. As a family unit, it presently exercises more say in the decision-making process than at any time since the reign and deposition of King Sa'ud. Consequently, the decision-making process in Riyadh appears to have become more impenetrable, increasingly protracted, and fuzzier in its overall direction.

Rivalries and differences of opinion exist, although tightly shielded against exposure outside the family. A significant number of princes (allegedly including 'Abdullah) question the strengthening of ties to the United States, and their views received some weight by the embarrassing and insulting American domestic debate over the AWACS sale. Some senior princes in family protocol, such as 'Abd al-'Aziz's oldest living son Muhammad, do not hold government positions but nevertheless are influential in family councils. In addition, there are various collateral branches of the family, some of which hold seniority to the descendants of 'Abd al-'Aziz.

Generational differences are another potential source of strain within the Al Sa'ud. An emerging generation of younger princes—modernized, often college educated, ambitious, and frequently serving as dedicated public servants—can be found among the descendants of 'Abd al-'Aziz (as well as in the collateral branches). Their ranks include Sa'ud al-Faysal (son of the late king Faysal, with a B.A. from Princeton and presently holding the position of foreign minister), Turki al-Faysal (Sa'ud's brother, holder of an M.A. from the University of London, and now head of Saudi intelligence), and Bandar ibn Sultan (son of the minister of defense, with an M.A. from Johns Hopkins School of Advanced International Studies and now the Saudi ambassador to the United States). Despite their obvious qualifications and dedication, so far they stand outside the inner circle of real power and their turns at the throne are many years down the road, if ever.

Other Elites

There is no other group, or combination of groups, that can seriously challenge the role of the Al Sa'ud within the political system. Nevertheless, there are a number of elites that do wield significant power and whose views and opinions must be taken into account by the government. Broadly speaking, these can be categorized as traditional and newly emerging elites.

Traditional Elites. The 'ulama' form perhaps the most obvious traditional elite, their position being most obvious in Saudi Arabia owing to the kingdom's reliance on the shari'ah and the continuing strong social and ideological, as well as religious, impact of Islam on this country. Prominent among this group is the Al al-Shaykh family, members of which have intermarried with the Al Sa'ud and hold key positions within the government. In some ways, the influence of the 'ulama' may be weakening through the effects of modernization. On the other hand, they may be the recipients of increased attention because of the less overtly pious background of recent kings and the growing challenge of Islamic political activism. In this connection, it is worth noting that the government took care to receive a favorable fatwa before sending in the troops to recapture the Mecca mosque in 1979.

The old merchant families, as in other Gulf states, traditionally played an important role, partly because they tended to hold the government's purse-strings in an era of scarcity and also because of their education and widespread connections. In Saudi Arabia, this applied particularly aptly to the merchants of the Hijaz. The established families were well placed to take advantage of the oil boom to expand their operations and increase their dominance of local commerce. But the ranks of Saudi businessmen have been swelled by nontraditional entrepreneurs (of which 'Adnan Khashoggi and Ghaith Pharaon have received the most attention abroad) and by "part-time" government officials who run their own businesses on the side. There are many among the Al Sa'ud, as well as nonmembers of the royal family, who have become wealthy through collecting distribution rights for imported goods or in joint ventures with foreign contractors.

But the almost unlimited opportunities of oil wealth terminated the traditional leverage of merchants over ruling families. In fact, the wheel has turned and the merchants have become dependent on the regime: Saudi businessmen have fared exceedingly well under the Al Sa'ud government and their proclivity to plow their investments back into Saudi Arabia, especially in real estate, has kept their assets captive to the fortunes of the regime.

A third traditional elite that definitely has seen its relative position in the political system decline is the tribal establishment. Once a central factor in the building of a supratribal state through tribal alliances and the armed might of thousands of loyal tribesmen, the shaykhs and their followers have very little of a political role left to play. This trend is inevitable as the kingdom becomes less and less of a tribal state, despite its recent origins and nostalgically conservative intentions. Even the National Guard, built on the principle of loyal tribal backing for the royal family (not necessarily "the state"), is modernizing and gradually shedding its old aura of part-time tribal levies.

New Elites. Among the new elites, two deserve special consideration: military officers and technocrats. The armed forces have grown impressively since the first major military modernization programs in the 1960s and now boast a strength of about fifty-five thousand men (excluding the National Guard). To ensure the loyalty of the armed forces and because of national manpower shortages, the government has treated both officers and ranks extremely well, providing numerous material advantages and acquiring advanced arms systems and other equipment for their use. Because of the prominent U.S. role in Saudi Arabia's military modernization, many of the officers have been trained by Americans, often in the United States, and tend to get along well with their U.S. counterparts.

But it bears noting that the military remains undertrained and basically untested. Although loyalty to the regime seems secure at present, external factors (such as perceived government inaction in another prolonged Arab-Israeli war) may change that. The regime has been careful to put members of the Al Sa'ud and other "trustworthy" individuals in key positions, but middle-grade officers conceivably may become frustrated over obstacles to career advancement and the government's concern with radical ideologies (which have contributed to military coups in various Arab states in the past) rather than with traditional values and goals.

An even more potent influence on the Saudi scene has been the burgeoning of technocrats and perhaps the creation of a Saudi "middle class." Saudi Arabia, again like other Gulf states, possessed no traditional bureaucracy, and so one had to be created entirely from scratch. As a consequence, a founding generation of modestly educated, often non-Saudi, officials appeared in the 1940s and 1950s. But this generation has long since been replaced, initially by a first generation of modern, formally educated Saudis who moved into position in the 1960s. Prominent among these men are Ahmed Zaki Yamani (minister of petroleum and natural resources; M.A., Harvard) and Hisham Nazir (minister of planning; M.A., University of California).

Just behind them came another generation (or perhaps more accurately, only a half-generation later) who took charge in the early 1970s. These included Muhammad Abu al-Khayl (minister of finance; B.A., Cairo University); 'Abd al-'Aziz al-Qurayshi (governor of the Saudi Arabian Monetary Agency; M.B.A., University of Southern California); Ghazi al-Gosaybi (former minister of both industry and health; Ph.D., University of London).

Shortly after, in the mid-1970s, as technocrats occupied many of the cabinet positions and the country's administration was strengthened, the roles of deputy ministers became increasingly important and an even younger generation of qualified individuals emerged: Faysal al-Bashir (deputy minister of planning; Ph.D., University of Arizona); Fu'ad al-Farsi (deputy minister of industry; Ph.D., Duke University); and Faruk Akhdar (director general of the Royal Commission for Jubayl and Yanbu'; Ph.D., University of California). All those mentioned above are commoners—demonstrating the willingness and need of the royal family to bring as many Saudis into responsible positions as possible—but many among the Al Sa'ud fit into these categories as well, including Sa'ud and Turki al-Faysal and Bandar ibn Sultan.

One result of this advancement of modernists into high positions, when combined with the extremely rapid expansion of government institutions and administrative functions, has been the emergence of an exceptionally capable high-level cadre of officials. As early as the Carter administration, it could be observed that there were more American-trained Ph.D.s in the Saudi council of ministers than there were in the U.S. cabinet.

It is possible that the filling up of top-level positions, and the consequent inability of younger technocrats to provide a direct input into policymaking, may result in frustration and restlessness. At present, however, two factors work in the other direction. The rapid expansion in the government and public sector of the economy and the increased complexity of business to be done require greater delegation of authority and heavier responsibility at lower levels than in the past. In addition, for the present, the emergence of discontent of even a semipolitical nature still seems to be deflected by the multitudinous opportunities to amass personal fortunes.

The Saudi political structure seems solidly situated for the near future. There is very little indication at present that real discontent with the Al Sa'ud–dominated regime exists among Saudi elites, whether civilian or military. Certainly, tensions continue within the royal family, but the continued emphasis on policymaking by consensus defuses potential splits (as in the compromise in determining the present and next crown princes). Dissatisfaction among commoners is not strong enough to challenge the system, even where it does exist. In some ways, the absence of a real threat mirrors the situation throughout the Arab world; the strengthening of political institutions has made nearly every Arab regime secure in tenure to a degree unthinkable only a decade ago.

Even where grievances exist, they are resolved within the system. When Ghazi al-Gosaybi, as minister of health in early 1984, clashed with powerful vested interests in his drive against corruption within the Health Ministry, he pleaded his case to the king through a poem in a Riyadh newspaper. It did not appear to be enough, as Gosaybi was removed from his cabinet position and sent off to Bahrain as ambassador (*Washington Post*, 27 Nov. 1984).

The Impact of Modernization and Development

Development Obstacles
The kingdom's development goals have been among the most ambitious in the world. Yet the attainment of "developed" status is made difficult by a number of inherent constraints. The lack of adequate manpower, in terms of both size and quality, constitutes one severe problem. The indigenous population of Saudi Arabia is only 4–5 million. The severe restrictions on the participation of women in the work force leaves a total Saudi work force of about 1.1 million. At the same time, the expansion of manpower requirements over the past decade has resulted in a non-Saudi work force of 2.1 million, whose long-term presence in the kingdom promises serious social and economic problems (Shaw and Long 1982, 46–47). Beyond sheer numbers, the country also faces a shortage of adequately trained Saudis in technical and other demanding positions.

The lack of water and agricultural resources also poses a severe constraint on development efforts. Despite being a quarter of the size of the United States, Saudi Arabia contains no permanent bodies of water; instead, it boasts the world's largest sand desert in the Rub' al-Khali, or Empty Quarter. Only 1 percent of its land is used for agricultural purposes (compared to the 19 percent of U.S. total land in cultivation, with another 27 percent used for grazing and 32 percent forested). The kingdom has begun the world's largest desalinization program, but it still may not be able to achieve self-sufficiency in food.

There are few natural resources, apart from oil and gas, to be exploited, making any prospect of industrialization outside the petroleum sector virtually impossible. It is touch and go whether Saudi Arabia can achieve economic self-sufficiency after the oil runs out. Not surprisingly, oil remains the key to the country's development. Even with recent economic expansion, oil continues to rank overwhelmingly first in export earnings (approximately 98 percent of the total) and total government revenue (90 percent), while the oil industry alone accounts for 65 percent of total Gross Domestic Product (McHale 1980, 630).

Before the oil glut, Saudi Arabia produced over 10 mbd, and production at that level could be sustained for well over fifty years. (The full extent of Saudi reserves has never been determined precisely, but even conservative estimates put them at one-quarter of the world's total reserves.) Furthermore, unlike most other producers (before the oil glut forced production levels down), the kingdom possessed considerable spare production capacity—making it theoretically possible to produce at a maximum level of at least 15 mbd (about double the present U.S. capacity). Given the severity of these constraints and the abundance of oil and gas reserves, it is clear that the best hope for Saudi Arabia's "life after oil" and economic diversification away from crude oil production seems to lie in the ambitious plans for the petrochemical industry.

Development Planning

Economic development in the kingdom began in earnest in the 1960s and accelerated dramatically with the rise in oil income in 1974. The principal value of the First Development Plan (1970–75) was as a learning process: it provided the government with a central direction for development purposes and involved decisions lasting beyond a single year. Necessarily, heavy emphasis was placed on infrastructural development and economic growth in all areas of the economy. The Second Plan (1975–80) continued the emphasis on physical infrastructure but also embraced the goal of diversification to reduce near-total dependence on a single exhaustible resource. For the first time, development planning was not constrained by lack of finance, although it did face the major problem of finding adequate domestic avenues for absorbing surplus funds.

The Third Plan (1980–85) was far more ambitious, originally entailing the expenditure of $239 billion (not including defense and foreign aid), compared to its predecessor's $149 billion. At the same time, it was also more selective in approach than the Second Plan, emphasizing economic diversification into capital-intensive hydrocarbon industries where the country seemed to possess a long-term comparative advantage. Although the Third Plan began under more favorable conditions (since considerable infrastructure was already in place and inflation had been reduced drastically), it still faced serious obstacles. One of these was the dilemma between the continuing need for manpower growth to meet the expectations of the plan and the difficulty of "Saudization," or incorporating Saudis into all sectors of the labor force (El Mallakh 1982). Another problem was, of course, the shortfall in income as a result of the halving of Saudi Arabia's oil production.

Of special interest in these plans is the Jubayl/Yanbu' project, one of the most ambitious development schemes ever conceived. It involves the creation of two major cities, with over 100,000 inhabitants each, out of villages on the Gulf (Jubayl) and the Red Sea (Yanbu'). The industrial complexes served by these cities are to include a full range of refining, petrochemical, and steel-manufacturing industries, linked by the trans–Saudi Arabian pipeline and fueled by the kingdom's extensive gas reserves.

By the end of 1984, basic socioeconomic infrastructural prerequisites had been or were close to being put in place across the country. These included massive investments in health care, transport, sewage, housing, education, and communications. Potentially at least, the Saudi government was able to provide the physical necessities and amenities of life for its citizens to a degree equal to the most developed countries in the world.

Traditionalism and Modernization

Despite the extent of change, it is undeniable that serious problems remain. Any economic development necessarily involves social change, no matter how carefully considered or opposed. In Saudi Arabia, development has produced, among other things, near-total sedentarization of the formerly large proportion of bedouin; changes in the occupations and life-styles of the majority of the people; a rising dominance of Western or Western-style education; and significant alterations to family structure (as demonstrated in the change from housing based on the extended family to homes designed for use by only the nuclear family).

As in most developing countries, socioeconomic development involves a tug-of-war between the resisting forces of traditionalism and the impatient proponents of modernization. Saudi Arabia's traditionalists—as strongly entrenched in the kingdom as anywhere in the Middle East—have fought social change in the past and will continue to do so in the future. They can call on widespread support by charging that many of these changes are antithetical to Islam.

From another point of view, even though Saudi Arabia's development effort has been comprehensive in both its scope and its neutral orientation toward "who gets what," some groups have benefited more than others. Those who have done particularly well over the past decade include the royal family, both old and new merchants, and the urban population in general. On the other hand, relatively less prosperity has come to the bedouin (who have been less well placed to take advantage of progress) and especially the Shi'a of the Eastern Province. The Shi'i population of 300,000–400,000 constitutes the largest indigenous minority in the country and accounts for approximately one-third of ARAMCO's work force. One effect of the Iranian revolution has been to reduce the reluctance of some Shi'a to complain openly about discrimination.

An additional problem with which the regime must grapple is the necessity of coming to grips with a changing role for women. There has been a breakdown of the traditional family structure in which women ruled an active and busy household. Many Saudi wives find themselves restricted to homes where servants and governesses do the work and take care of the children, leaving them with little to do or occupy their time. Just as there has been an explosion in education for male Saudis, there is a burgeoning pool of well-educated, sophisticated, and ambitious female Saudis, who largely have been denied the rights and opportunities accorded the other sex. Government policy generally has been to take the middle path, supporting the basic rights of women but avoiding offense to the traditionalists. Thus, the education of women, although of high priority, has been confined to segregated institutions.

The Impact of the Oil Glut

From a production high of over 10 mbd before the oil glut took hold, Saudi production has dropped to 4 or 4.5 mbd. Naturally, a drop of 50 percent in government revenues in a country where nearly all economic activity derives from oil income is cause for grave concern. One analyst concluded at the beginning of 1984 that continued production below 6.5 mbd would force basic reductions in the pace of development and that continued production below 4.7 mbd would not generate enough gas to provide for local industry needs (Knauerhase 1984). A year later, it had become clear that production was not going to rise substantially at any time in the near future.

At the end of 1984, an average production level of 4.5 mbd was reportedly forcing the government to make up a budget deficit in excess of $1 billion per month out of the estimated $100 billion of realizable assets abroad—this in spite of the severe slashes in government spending over the course of the year (*Economist*, 15 Dec. 1984). Further reductions in production in order to prevent the collapse of OPEC stood to enlarge the budget shortfall an additional 20 percent, putting even more pressure on official savings. Only defense expenditures have been considered sacrosanct in the belt-tightening process. Contractors have been hardest hit, as government agencies routinely delay payments: several liquidations were recorded during the year and some foreign firms have pulled out (*Middle East Economic Digest*, 14 Dec. 1984).

The adverse affects resulting from this decline in economic fortunes have been kept to a minimum for several reasons. Most of the massive construction projects and contracts of the 1970s are well on their way to completion now. As a consequence, the spending slowdown and budget cutbacks are relatively manageable—and even desirable—at present. Second, if necessary, the scope and size of projected industrialization schemes can be scaled back and the expatriate labor force reduced. Third, the kingdom has healthy reserves of liquid investments abroad that can be drawn down for some time to come. Fourth, many Saudis have done well by the years of plenty, and although the tremendous personal financial opportunities of the last decade may no longer exist, the average citizen is not likely to find his or her life-style terribly crimped. Fifth, the petrochemical complexes under construction in the last few years are just beginning to come onstream and will be able to provide income independent of crude oil production (provided the Saudis are able to crack trade barriers in industrialized countries).

Political Opposition

Given the amount of ferment and political upheaval in the Third World over the past quarter-century, to which the Arab world contributed a sizable share, it is astounding that Saudi Arabia has experienced only the merest hint of dissident political activity while undergoing such a plethora of changes. In the last twenty-five years, the only clear threats to the internal security of the regime have been clashes along the southwestern border with Egypt (1962–67), an incident within the air force that collapsed far before it achieved attempted coup status (1969), the assassination of King Faysal by a relative (1975), and the capture of the Great Mosque at Mecca by Islamic extremists (1979). Few countries in the world can match the kingdom's record of stability.

The Secular Left. The heyday of opposition from the secular left would seem to be the 1960s, with the widespread appeal of pan-Arab socialist ideologies—Nasirism, Ba'thism and even Marxism—and the active support of such Arab regimes as Egypt and nearby Iraq in promoting them. Since then, there seems to be little significant Saudi support for opposition along these lines. Several small leftist groups do exist, including a Communist party, but they are based outside Saudi Arabia and do not appear to have any following inside the country.

The Islamic Right.   In November 1979, in the immediate aftermath of the Iranian revolution, a small group of extremists—mostly Saudis but also including Yemenis, Kuwaitis, and Egyptians—seized the Great Mosque of Mecca in the name of their *mahdi* (an Islamic messiah). It was not until several weeks later that Saudi security forces were able to regain control of the mosque in intense fighting. Those extremists who survived were captured and tried, and most were executed. The enduring lesson of this episode is not that Islamic extremists were able to carry out such acts but that they were unable to generate any sympathy, let alone support, from the general population. In fact, reaction was quite the opposite: revulsion at the invasion of the sacred precincts of the mosque and the shedding of blood there.

But the emerging strength of populist Islam, evident even before the Iranian revolution but given particular impetus by that cataclysmic event, has led the Saudi government to tighten up, to adopt a more conservative stance, and to enforce the shari'ah more closely—and to push its smaller neighboring states toward similar policies. (The term *populist Islam—al-Islam al-sha'bi—* is James A. Bill's, who defines it as "a general social and political movement generated from below rather than a movement sponsored by governments and their supporting bureaucratic apparatus," which he labels *establishment Islam—al-Islam al-rasmi* [Bill 1984, 109n1].) The kingdom's inherent conservatism and reliance on Islam constituted its defense against the earlier radical challenge. But the new surge of populism has raised the possibility of outflanking, especially as development and modernization (with its strong overtones of Westernization) proceeds and materialism, even ostentatiousness, becomes obvious.

Populist Islamic sentiments are especially strong among Saudi Arabia's Shi'i minority, and in particular among the Shi'i youth who regard themselves as less middle class and less beholden to ARAMCO than their elders. They were responsible for the demonstrations in al-Qatif and al-Hasa in 1979 and 1980, which caused the government considerable apprehension and resulted in highly visible efforts by senior officials to provide promises of better living and working conditions. Shi'i opponents of the regime have formed the Islamic Revolutionary Organization in the Arabian Peninsula, presumably with support from Tehran. There is no evidence that this group has been able to gain effective support among the general population, and Iran seemingly has had second thoughts about underwriting it.

The Consultative Assembly.   The events of recent years spurred tentative moves toward a consultative asembly (*majlis al-shura*). Such a step would serve to remold the traditional institution of shura into a formal political body. Mention of such an assembly was first made a number of years ago, and it was promised again in the aftermath of the Mecca mosque takeover. No concrete action was taken at that time, however. The idea was brought up again by

King Fahd in a December 1984 interview with the *Sunday Times* (London), who promised to set up the assembly within "three or four months" and also to provide the country with a written constitution.

The assembly would consist initially of appointed members—presumably drawn from among the 'ulama,' technocrats, and merchants—followed by indirect election of half the membership through provincial assemblies in several years and then, at a later date, direct elections. The regime's intention to follow through with the assembly was given weight by the late 1984 letting of a $1.2 billion contract for the construction of the King's Office, Council of Ministers, and Majlis al-Shura complex in Riyadh (*Middle East Economic Digest*, 14 Dec. 1984).

EXTERNAL DETERMINANTS IN SAUDI POLICYMAKING

The other half of Saudi decision making involves the constraints and pressures placed upon the kingdom by its increasing involvement in regional and international affairs. The foci of Saudi concern and interaction can be viewed as a series of concentric circles, comprising the Arabian Peninsula, the Gulf region, the Arab world, the Islamic community, OPEC and oil matters, and relations with the superpowers. As David Long has written:

> Isolation in the vast desert reaches of Najd . . . has over the
> centuries produced an insular attitude of encirclement by
> enemies. This "encirclement syndrome" historically focused
> on rival tribes, expanded during the 19th and 20th centuries
> to include outside powers and currently includes Zionist
> Israel, Marxist Ethiopia, South Yemen and Afghanistan,
> revolutionary Islamic Iran and also Libya. Radical Syria and
> Iraq cannot be ruled out as future threats. This sense of
> encirclement has helped to instill among the Saudi
> leadership a continuing search for security, which is
> reflected in every aspect of U.S.-Saudi relations.
> (Long 1983, 17)

The Saudi Role in the Arabian Peninsula

If it were not for the British, nearly all the Arabian Peninsula might now be part of Saudi Arabia. Consequently, it should not be surprising that the Saudis often tend to act as though they hold proprietary rights to the rest of the peninsula. They dominate the newly formed Gulf Cooperation Council (GCC) both in policy formulation and in military contributions. To the south, Riyadh has long pursued active interference in North Yemeni affairs. The Saudis have been suspicious of South Yemen ever since Aden gained its independence in 1967 and long supported the subversive efforts of South Yemeni exiles against that government. Only recently have they been willing, albeit cautiously, to participate in a Riyadh-Aden rapproachement. (An earlier, even more tentative, rapprochement in 1978 was scuttled when the South Yemeni president was tried and executed by his Adeni rivals.)

The formation of the GCC in 1981 formalized the already strong ties among its six members (Saudi Arabia, Kuwait, Bahrain, Qatar, the United Arab Emirates, and Oman) that developed in the 1970s and intensified with the emergence of the Iranian revolution. There is no question that Saudi Arabia provides the central direction to the GCC, whether politically, economically, or militarily. Saudi predominance will be strengthened by the intended creation of a joint air defense system, which will rely on Saudi Arabia's AWACS.

The Saudi Role in the Gulf

Although Saudi Arabia clearly is the preeminent power within the peninsula, it ranks third in capabilities among the Gulf littoral states. Both Iran and Iraq are far larger in population (42 million and 14 million, respectively, to Saudi Arabia's 7 million) and possess far bigger armed forces (nearly 2 million and 517,000 men to 55,000), as well as predominating in most other measurements of power.

Saudi Arabia and its smaller neighbors have faced active Iraqi attempts at subversion in the past (beginning shortly after the 1958 revolution in Baghdad) and conceivably could face renewed efforts after the Iran-Iraq war. GCC-ally Kuwait is especially vulnerable to Iraqi pressure and remains a target of Iraqi on claims to part of its territory, despite its wartime assistance to Baghdad.

From the other side of the Gulf, Iran always has appeared somewhat menacing to the Arab Gulf states. Long before the revolution, the ambitions and rapid militarization of the shah raised suspicions of his ultimate intentions, particularly in light of long memories of Iranian incursions across the Gulf. The fall of the Pahlavi regime only served to intensify these fears. The new revolutionary government was not reluctant in conveying its disapproval of existing regimes in the Islamic world, and Saudi Arabia was singled out as the second enemy after Iraq. Active efforts were evident in Tehran during the first few months of the new order to destabilize and overthrow Arab regimes, the best known example being the abortive coup attempt in Bahrain during December 1981.

The outbreak of the Iran-Iraq war in September 1980 seemed to remove temporarily the threats from these two states, but the question remains of future intentions once (if?) the war ends. In the meantime, Saudi Arabia and its GCC allies face the very real threat of an expansion of the war to involve them directly. The tanker war of 1984 appeared to come perilously close to engulfing the entire region. The crisis began in late 1983 when Iraq announced its purchase from France of Super-Etendard fighters—which Argentina employed so successfully in the Falklands war to launch Exocet missiles against British naval vessels. (Iraq already possessed Exocets, but affixing them to Super-Etendards instead of helicopters meant that the missiles could be fired from a considerably longer, and thus safer, distance.)

Baghdad's apparent intention was to pressure Tehran toward negotiations by threatening to attack the main Iranian oil terminal at Kharg Island. When this ploy failed to achieve desired results, Iraq began to attack oil tankers making their way to and from the Kharg terminal. (Given Iraq's reluctance to risk its planes and the unsuitability of the antiship Exocets for attacking a ground installation, Kharg was virtually untouched.) Iran escalated the crisis with attacks on shipping along the Arab shore, particularly vessels bound for

Kuwaiti and Saudi ports. Finally in June, after Riyadh had given Iran public warning, Saudi F-15s shot down an Iranian fighter that had intruded into Saudi territorial waters. Both countries chose to play down the incident, and although the tanker war continued at a less intense level into early 1985, the risk of direct Iranian-GCC confrontation abated.

But these threats in the Gulf have led to Saudi Arabia's continuing concern for self-defense and consequent emphasis on military modernization. Defense spending was increased by 6 percent in the 1984–85 budget, despite the financial crunch, and accounted for nearly one-third of total budgeted expenditures. The biggest elements in defense during 1984 were a $4 billion French contract for the Shahine ground-to-air missile system, and $3–4 billion for the Peace Shield project, an integrated command, control, and communications system based on the AWACS.

The Arab Stage and the Arab-Israeli Imbroglio

The reversal from Saudi Arabia's traditional isolation to its prominent role in various international arenas has been nothing short of dramatic. A major feature of regional politics in the last two decades has been the increased importance of the kingdom in Arab councils. But the Saudis have been given a difficult task to do and few tools with which to do it. Essentially, there are only two weapons in the Saudi arsenal: moral suasion, involving the Saudi emphasis—and patience—on achieving consensus around a moderate center, and a sweetener based on financial subsidies. But a strategy based on these tools is severely limiting, and Saudi Arabia's position in the Arab world seems far more tenuous than that of Egypt, Syria, and Iraq.

One aspect of Saudi Arabia's emergence as an Arab power has been assumption of its share of responsibility for Arab-Israeli concerns, formalized by the Khartum Conference of 1967, and support for the rights of the Palestinians and their representative, the PLO, as decided at the Rabat Conference of 1975. As one Saudi official has explained Saudi obligations to pan-Arab and Palestinian concerns, "Saudi Arabia is a state within a nation of states" (al-Awaji 1983–84, 58). Its Arab obligations—overriding purely Saudi self-interest—have forced Riyadh to take the reluctant step of imposing oil embargoes against Western friends during several Arab-Isaeli wars. To these obligations may be added the late King Faysal's concern over the status of Jerusalem because of its importance in Islam.

The Saudi view of a solution to the imbroglio was made public in the Fahd peace plan of August 1981, adopted with minor changes at the Arab summit in Fez, which affirmed the right of all states in the region to peaceful existence. The Saudi plan essentially differs from the subsequent Reagan plan (September 1982) in its conception of the future status of the Palestinians. The Saudis insist on the establishment of an independent Palestinian state in the West Bank and Gaza, recognition of East Jerusalem as its capital, and the removal of all Israeli settlements from the West Bank. The Reagan plan, however, called only for limited Palestinian autonomy in political association with Jordan, determination of the status of Jerusalem through negotiations, and a freeze on Israel's existing West Bank settlements.

Saudi Arabia's strategy in implementing its plan is twofold. First, Riyadh sees its proper role in the region as building Arab consensus around a peaceful solution to the conflict, based on the West Bank–Gaza state. Second, Riyadh wishes to convince Washington to use its influence with Israel to accept this solution. This appears to have been a key objective in King Fahd's official visit to Washington in February 1985, the first by a Saudi monarch in fourteen years. Failure to reach a settlement along these lines is, in the Saudi point of view, dangerous for all parties concerned. Saudi Arabia argues that Israel's intrasigence in providing justice for the Palestinians and its aggressive military actions against neighboring Arab states destroy the ground under moderates within the Arab world and encourages extremists among Palestinians, Lebanese, and other Arab groups, and also provides a basis for Soviet inroads in the region.

Serious limitations confront this approach, however. First, Saudi Arabia cannot force its views on all the Arab states but can only plead for their consideration. Egypt's defection from Arab ranks in the late 1970s and Syria's obstinacy in the early 1980s clearly illustrated the inherent weakness of the Saudi position: subsidies, once employed, are difficult to cut off, yet they do not guarantee compliance with the donor's wishes.

Second, the United States, which theoretically has the ability to force Israeli compliance with its policies, has been unwilling to expend the political capital necessary, both in terms of domestic American politics and in head-to-head confrontation with Israel. Given that U.S. reluctance has been evident in situations where the administration has clearly taken issue with Israeli actions, such as the 1981 attack on the Iraq nuclear reactor and the 1982 siege of Beirut, the chances of Riyadh's success in getting Washington to apply pressure on Israel to negotiate on an independent Palestinian state would appear very grim.

Third, all the maneuvering by Saudi Arabia and the United States on this question is for naught as long the two immediate parties continue their intransigence and/or vacillation. Rather than providing a clear mandate for either Likud or Labor, the 1984 Israeli elections gave birth to an unwieldy coalition government that is unlikely to take any bold steps on the matter of territory and status of the Palestinians. The PLO, as an organization and as personified in its leader Yasir Arafat, has been buffeted severely by the forced exile from Beirut and the Syrian-instigated mutiny. Consequently, it has found itself trapped in muddled indecision over the next step and fearful of alienating its more extreme constituent groups. Favorable circumstances for a positive step toward peace are dim.

Saudi Arabia and the Islamic Community

If the kingdom has real difficulties in pursuing its goals within just the Arab world, it stands to reason that its problems should be even greater in dealing with a much larger and contentious community of states whose common bond of Islam masks deep ethnic, cultural, historical, geographical, economic, and political heterogeneity.

In this arena, Saudi Arabia has tended to concentrate its attention on two concerns. One of these involves religious aspects of Islam and the building of mosques, distribution of Korans, subsidization of hajj pilgrims, and provision of foreign aid as a kind of international *zakat* (Islamic alms tax). At the same time, the kingdom has orchestrated politically achievable but pragmatically meaningless consensus on a few issues on which all or most Islamic states can agree, such as Third World economic grievances, the status of Jerusalem, and the Soviet invasion of Afghanistan.

Practical successes have tended to be on a bilateral level, where the primary motives have had little to do with Islam. One of these has been a tacit Saudi-Pakistani alliance, which has served to enhance regional perceptions of Gulf security and provided civilian and military manpower for Saudi Arabia in exchange for remittances and foreign aid for Pakistan. There are said to be two thousand to ten thousand Pakistani troops stationed along Saudi Arabia's southwestern frontier. (Some Pakistanis apparently were captured by Yemeni forces in a 1984 border incident [Washington Post, 25 Nov. 1984].) Saudi activity on the fighting in Eritrea and Afghanistan, and Riyadh's attempts to bring its neighbors and fellow Islamic countries in line behind it, derives from the kingdom's strong anticommunist stance and fears of a Soviet pincer move on the Gulf itself.

The Saudi Role in OPEC

There is a rough parallel between OPEC and the Islamic community. Both consist of highly heterogeneous states uncertainly clinging together because of a single common factor: oil and Islam, respectively. The varieties of countries within OPEC are perhaps even more pronounced. OPEC's inherent unwieldiness did not matter as long as there was a worldwide scarcity of oil and every member, with the important exception of Saudi Arabia, could produce at full capacity and easily sell all it produced.

As the swing producer, Saudi Arabia could counteract the pressure of some OPEC members to raise prices too quickly by adjusting its production accordingly. By the late 1970s, however, world demand for oil had grown so much that Saudi Arabia's production permanently was close to its current capacity, thus eliminating its traditional role and rendering it helpless to act as a brake on upward prices. As a result, the revolution in Iran acted as the catalyst for an explosion of prices in 1979–80 from around $13 a barrel to more than $28.

A continuing scarcity of supplies allowed the official OPEC marker price to rise to $34 a barrel in 1981. But shortly after this, the expansion of worldwide oil production, made profitable by the inflated prices for crude oil, combined with slackening demand to create the oil glut. Declining demand for its members' oil forced total OPEC production to drop from about 31 mbd to 14 mbd in the early 1980s (or from two-thirds of noncommunist world production down to less than half). As a consequence, OPEC has been absorbed in bitter disputes over how much reduced production each country should absorb.

As the largest producer, Saudi Arabia bore the brunt of the biggest cutback, more than halving its output. Nevertheless, this sacrifice, the March 1983 adoption of OPEC's first official price cut (from $34 to $29 a barrel for marker crude), and the establishment of an organization-wide production ceiling of 17.5 mbd, were not enough to balance supply and demand. Nearly all OPEC members have continued to discount their oil in order to keep their own production up. The problem of maintaining internal discipline within OPEC ranks has been made more difficult by the actions of non-OPEC producers, such as Britain, Norway, Mexico, and Egypt, who have no reason to be bound by OPEC agreements on market sharing.

The continuing strength of the glut was illustrated by the absence of any significant rise in prices—or concern—during the Gulf tanker war in mid-1984. Instead, a forecasted increase in demand failed to materialize, and the annual OPEC meeting in December 1984 revealed that the cracks in the organization had grown even deeper. A reduced production ceiling of 16 mbd, adopted in October, had proved meaningless, and plans were drawn up for OPEC inspectors to keep the members from cheating on their production quotas. As the year ended, the $29 marker price still remained in jeopardy and was saved for the moment only by a "realignment of differentials" between the various types of crude oil—effectively lowering the price of most OPEC crudes.

The once powerful Saudi role within OPEC had been reduced to Ahmed Zaki Yamani's skills at persuading other members not to recklessly destroy OPEC. Most projections for the remainder of the 1980s point to only a modest rise in demand for OPEC oil at best. As a consequence, the diminished power of Saudi Arabia in OPEC councils is likely to hold true for the foreseeable future.

Saudi Views of the Superpowers

Riyadh maintains diplomatic relations with only one of the two superpowers, clearly demonstrating the kingdom's heavy tilt toward the West and jaundiced view of the Soviet Union. The mostly positive feelings Saudis hold about the United States derive from a number of causes. These include the American role as a partner in Saudi Arabia's economic development, its role as a partner in the kingdom's military modernization, a common anticommunist view of the world, the perception that only Washington has leverage over Israel, and a heartfelt basic compatibility or camaraderie between the two peoples (the Saudis are sometimes referred to as the Texans of the Middle East).

On the other hand, the Soviet Union has never been able to capitalize on the early ties between the two countries (a commercial treaty was signed in 1926). Moscow's position suffers from a prevailing Saudi ideology that is the antithesis of communism and fears of Soviet expansion and designs on the Middle East and especially the Gulf.

But the picture is not entirely black and white. Saudis do have reservations regarding the United States over: (1) the U.S. role vis-à-vis Israeli policies and the Palestinians, (2) American conceptions of non-Soviet threats to Gulf security and the insistence on an official U.S. military presence in Saudi Arabia (the kingdom understandably is skittish about any foreign military presence on its soil, especially one of the superpowers), and (3) occasionally raised differences over oil matters (and a lingering suspicion that the United States might decide after all to invade the kingdom to secure its oil supplies).

At the same time, the Saudi government displays some vacillation over the value of diplomatic relations with Moscow. Such official ties might prove useful in reducing the chances of a direct Soviet threat to the kingdom. Riyadh could gain input into Soviet policy regarding its anti-Saudi clients in the region. There might be a possibility of some leverage over the United States in Arab-Israeli matters.

Expectations of closer ties were raised by Foreign Minister Saʻud al-Faysal's visit to Moscow in December 1982 as part of a pan-Arab delegation, the first prominent Saudi to travel to the Soviet Union since Saʻud's father Faysal went in 1932. (Rumors have been rife as well of impending relations between the UAE and the Soviet Union, for which the UAE would almost certainly need Riyadh's approval.) Despite the cautiously raised possibility of Saudi-Soviet ties, no further movement in this direction was in evidence by the end of 1984.

THE FUTURE OF U.S.-SAUDI RELATIONS

It seems extremely unlikely that the fundamental nature of the relationship between the two countries will be altered in the near future, although minor differences and even adjustments toward a lesser degree of intimacy may be forthcoming. There are several logical reasons for this optimistic conclusion.

The present regime and social/economic/political structure of Saudi Arabia most probably will remain intact—at least in the short run. Furthermore, the assumption that this situation will hold true for a longer term can be justified by pointing to a long succession of favorable, and accurate, short-run prognostications. Despite the massive changes that the country has undergone in the recent past and will continue to experience in the future, most indications point to a remarkable political stability. It is in the interests of both countries—the United States and Saudi Arabia—to work together closely.

Despite the possibility of increased friction in several arenas, notably regarding Israel, Saudi Arabia really has nowhere else to turn. While Riyadh will not burn its bridges to Washington, it is possible that it may make public its exasperation over aspects of U.S. policy in the region, such as the U.S. relationship with Israel or its skewed role in Lebanon. It may also grow more resentful of its perceived negative treatment in the United States, as occurred during the AWACS debate or in the sudden postponement ("pending a comprehensive review") of expected arms sales on the eve of King Fahd's February 1985 visit to the United States. This could lead to an ascendancy of those in Saudi Arabia who favor more distance from the United States and greater reliance on Western Europe.

But it should also be remembered that if Saudi Arabia is dependent on the United States so is this country on Saudi Arabia. No matter how long the oil glut lasts, the largest concentration of oil reserves will remain in Saudi Arabia; that country will continue to exercise the most prominent role in OPEC and perhaps exert considerable influence on non-OPEC producers as well.

Furthermore, Saudi Arabia is the most important U.S. ally in matters of Gulf security. Iran is definitely out, U.S.-Iraqi ties constitute a marriage of convenience, Pakistan is too far away and perhaps too unstable, and the smaller Gulf states are not as strategically advantageous and are less willing to cooperate (with perhaps the exception of Oman). But a Gulf security partnership must be just that—a real partnership. Saudi Arabia and the GCC must handle full responsibility for internal and regional issues of security importance, with the United States providing essentially backup in case of a Soviet thrust and serving as only a junior partner in extending assistance in other contingencies.

Finally, the United States needs Saudi Arabia to play a central role in Arab, Islamic, and perhaps even Third World (or anticommunist) circles. If it is true that Riyadh must depend on the United States to talk tough to Israel, it also can be said that Washington must rely on Saudi Arabia to do the same with Syria. There are not many Third World countries with which the United States enjoys such close cooperation, and although Saudi Arabia's power and influence may be limited, it is not necessarily ephemeral. The advantages in maintaining the special relationship far outweigh any potential disadvantages or temporary upsets.

REFERENCES

al-Awaji, Ibrahim Mohamed. 1983–84. U.S.-Saudi economic and political relations. *American-Arab Affairs*, no. 7 (Winter): 55–59.

Bill, James A. 1984. Resurgent Islam in the Persian Gulf. *Foreign Affairs* 63, no. 1 (Fall): 108–27.

El Mallakh, Ragaei. 1982. *Saudi Arabia: Rush to development*. London: Croom Helm.

Knauerhase, Ramon. 1984. Saudi Arabian oil policies. *Current History* 83, no. 489 (Jan.): 29–32, 36–37.

Long, David E. 1983. U.S.-Saudi relations: A foundation of mutual needs. *American-Arab Affairs*, no. 4 (Spring): 12–22.

McHale, T.R. 1980. A prospect of Saudi Arabia. *International Affairs* (London) 56, no. 4:622–47.

Organization for Economic Cooperation and Development. Development Assistance Committee. 1982. *Development cooperation, 1982 review*. Paris, OECD.

———, 1984. *Development cooperation, 1984 review*. Paris, OECD.

Shaw, John A., and David E. Long. 1982. *Saudi Arabian modernization: The impact of change on stability*. Washington Papers, no. 89. New York: Praeger, with the Georgetown University Center for Strategic and International Studies.

U.S. Congress. House. 1975. Committee on International Relations. *Oil Fields as military objectives: A feasibility study*. Prepared by the Congressional Research Service, Library of Congress. Washington: U.S. Government Printing Office. Updated in John M. Collins, Clyde R. Mark, and Elizabeth Ann Severns. 1980. Petroleum imports from the Persian Gulf: Use of U.S. armed force to ensure supplies. Issue Brief No. IB 79046. Washington: Library of Congress, Congressional Research Service.

U.S. Congress. House. 1981. Committee on Foreign Affairs. Subcommittee on Europe and the Middle East. *Saudi Arabia and the United States: The new context in an* evolving "special relationship." Report prepared by the Congressional Research Service, Library of Congress. Washington: U.S. Government Printing Office.

ADDITIONAL READINGS

Aburdene, Odeh. "U.S. Economic and Financial Relations with Saudi Arabia, Kuwait, and the United Arab Emirates." *American-Arab Affairs*, no. 7 (Winter 1983–84): 76–84.

Beling, Willard A., ed. *King Faisal and the Modernisation of Saudi Arabia*. London: Croom Helm; Boulder, Colo.: Westview Press, 1980.

Carre, Olivier. "Ideologie et pouvoir en Arabie Saoudite et dans son entourage." In Paul Bonnenfant, ed., *La Peninsule Arabique d'Aujourd'hui*, edited by Paul Bonnenfant, 219–45. Paris: Centre National de la Recherche Scientifique, 1982.

Champenois, Lucien, and Jean-Louis Soulie. "Le royaume d'Arabie Saoudite." In *La Peninsule Arabique d'aujourd'hui*, edited by Paul Bonnenfant, 565–97. Paris: Centre National de la Recherche Scientifique, 1982.

———. "Chronologie du royaume d'Arabie Saoudite." In *La Peninsule Arabique d'aujourd'hui*, edited by Paul Bonnenfont, 597-603. Paris: Centre National de la Recherche Scientifique, 1982.

Cordesman, Anthony W. *Saudi Arabia, AWACS, and America's Search for Strategic Stability in the Near East*. Woodrow Wilson Center for International Scholars. Washington: Smithsonian Institution, 1981.

———. *The Gulf and the Search for Strategic Stability: Saudi Arabia, the Military Balance in the Gulf, and Trends in the Arab-Israeli Military Balance*. Boulder, Colo.: Westview Press, 1984.

Dawisha, Adeed. "Internal Values and External Threats: The Making of Saudi Foreign Policy." *Orbis* 23, no. 1 (Spring 1979): 129–43.

———. *Saudi Arabia's Search for Security*. Adelphi Papers, no. 158. London: International Institute for Strategic Studies, 1979–80.

———. "Saudi Arabia and the Arab-Israeli Conflict: The Ups and Downs of Pragmatic Moderation." *International Journal* 38, no. 4 (Autumn 1983): 674–89.

El Azhary, M.S. "Aspects of North Yemen's Relations with Saudi Arabia." In *Contemporary Yemen: Politics and Historical Background*, edited by B.R. Pridham, 195–207. London: Croom Helm, for the University of Exeter Centre for Arab Gulf Studies, 1984.

Exxon Corporation. Public Affairs Department. *Middle East Oil and Gas*. Exxon Background Series. New York, December 1984.

al-Farsy, Fouad. *Saudi Arabia: A Case Study in Development*. London: Stacey International, 1978.

Haass, Richard. "Saudi Arabia and Iran: The Twin Pillars in Revolutionary Times." In *The Security of the Persian Gulf,* edited by Hossein Amirsadeghi, 151–69. London: Croom Helm; New York: St. Martin's Press, 1981.

Helms, Christine Moss. *The Cohesion of Saudi Arabia: Evolution of Political Identity.* London: Croom Helm; Baltimore: Johns Hopkins University Press, 1981.

Hill, Enid. "Saudi Labor and Industrialization Policy in Saudi Arabia." *International Review of Modern Sociology* 12, no. 1 (1982): 147–74.

Hoagland, Jim, and J.P. Smith. "Saudi Arabia and the United States: Security and Interdependence." *Survival* 20, no. 2 (Mar.-Apr. 1978): 80–83.

Holden, David, and Richard Johns, with James Buchan. *The House of Saud: The Rise and Rule of the Most Powerful Dynasty in the Arab World.* New York: Holt, Rinehart & Winston, 1982.

Howarth, David. *The Desert King: A Life of Ibn Saud.* London: Collins, 1964.

Islami, A. Reza S., and Rostam Mehraban Kavoussi. *The Political Economy of Saudi Arabia.* Near Eastern Studies, no. 1. Seattle: University of Washington, 1984.

Jabber, Paul. "Oil, Arms, and Regional Diplomacy: Strategic Dimensions of the Saudi-Egyptian Relationship." In *Rich and Poor States in the Middle East: Egypt and the New Arab Order,* edited by Malcolm H. Kerr and El Sayed Yassin, 415–47. Boulder, Colo.: Westview Press; Cairo: American University in Cairo Press, 1982.

Jordan, Amos A., Jr. "Saudi Arabia: The Next Iran?" *Parameters: Journal of the U.S. Army War College* 9, no. 1 (Mar. 1979): 2–8.

Kelidar, A.R. "The Problem of Succession in Saudi Arabia." *Asian Affairs* (London) 65, n.s. 9, pt. 1 (Feb. 1978): 23–30.

Knauerhase, Ramon. "Saudi Arabia: Fifty Years of Economic Change." *Current History* 82, no. 480 (Jan. 1983): 19–23, 35–36.

Koury, Enver M. *The Saudi Decision-Making Body.* Hyattsville, Md.: Institute of Middle Eastern and North African Affairs, 1978.

Kuniholm, Bruce R. "What the Saudis Really Want: A Primer for the Reagan Administration." *Orbis* 25, no. 1 (1981): 107–21.

Lacey, Robert. *The Kingdom: Arabia and the House of Saud.* New York: Harcourt Brace Jovanovich, 1982.

———. "Saudi Arabia: A More Visible Role in the Middle East." *World Today* 38, no. 1 (Jan. 1982): 4–12.

Lackner, Helen. *A House Built on Sand: A Political Economy of Saudi Arabia.* London: Ithaca Press, 1978.

Leatherdale, Clive. *Britain and Saudi Arabia, 1925–1939: The Imperial Oasis.* London: Frank Cass, 1983.

Lonchampt, Jacques. "La planification en Arabie Saoudite." In *La Peninsule Arabique d'aujourd'hui*, edited by Paul Bonnenfant, 603–23. Paris: Centre National de la Recherche Scientifique, 1982.

Long, David E. *Saudi Arabia*. Washington Papers, no. 39. Beverly Hills, Calif.: Sage Publications, for the Georgetown University Center for Strategic and International Studies, 1976.

———. *The United States and Saudi Arabia: Ambivalent Allies* (Boulder, Colo.: Westview Press, forthcoming).

Malone, Joseph J. "Involvement and Change: The Coming of the Oil Age to Saudi Arabia." In *Social and Economic Development in the Arab Gulf*, edited by Tim Niblock, 20–48. London: Croom Helm, for the University of Exeter Centre for Arab Gulf Studies, 1980.

Nevo, Joseph. "The Saudi Royal Family: The Third Generation." *Jerusalem Quarterly*, no. 31 (Spring 1984): 79–90.

Niblock, Tim, ed. *State, Society and Economy in Saudi Arabia*. London: Croom Helm, for the University of Exeter Centre for Arab Gulf Studies, 1982.

Ochsenwald, William. "Saudi Arabia and the Islamic Revival." *International Journal of Middle East Studies* 13, no. 3 (Aug. 1981): 271–86.

Paul, Jim. "Insurrection at Mecca." *MERIP Reports*, no. 91 (Oct. 1980): 3–4.

Piscatori, James P. "The Roles of Islam in Saudi Arabia's Political Development." In *Islam and Development: Religion and Sociopolitical Change*, edited by John L. Esposito, 123–38. Syracuse: Syracuse University Press, 1980.

———. "Islamic Values and National Interest: The Foreign Policy of Saudi Arabia." In *Islam in Foreign Policy*, edited by Adeed Dawisha, 33–53. Cambridge: Cambridge University Press, 1983; in association with the Royal Institute of International Affairs.

Piscatori, James P., ed. "Ideological Politics in Sa'udi Arabia." In *Islam in the Political Process*, 56–72. Cambridge: Cambridge University Press, 1983; in association with the Royal Institute of International Affairs.

Pounds, Bonnie. "The U.S.–Saudi Arabian Joint Commission: A Model for Bilateral Economic Cooperation." *American-Arab Affairs*, no. 7 (Winter 1983–84): 60–68.

Presley, John R. "Trade and Foreign Aid: The Saudi Arabian Experience." *Arab Gulf Journal* 3, no. 1 (Apr. 1983): 41–59.

———. *A Guide to the Saudi Arabian Economy*. London: Macmillan; New York: St. Martin's Press, 1984.

Quandt, William B. "Riyadh between the Superpowers." *Foreign Policy*, no. 44 (1981): 37–56.

———. *Saudi Arabia in the 1980s: Foreign Policy, Security, and Oil*. Washington: Brookings Institution, 1981.

———. *Saudi Arabia's Oil Policy*. Washington: Brookings Institution, 1982.

Rustow, Dankwart A. "U.S.-Saudi Relations and the Oil Crises of the 1980s."*Foreign Affairs* 55, no. 3 (Apr. 1977): 494–516.

Salameh, Ghassane. "Political Power and the Saudi State." Translated by Vivian Steir. *MERIP Reports*, no. 91 (Oct. 1980): 5–22.

Stookey, Robert W., ed. *The Arabian Peninsula: Zone of Ferment*. Stanford, Calif.: Hoover Institution Press, 1984.

Tahir-Kheli, Shirin, and William O. Staudenmaier. "The Saudi-Pakistani Military Relationship: Implications for U.S. Policy." *Orbis* 26, no. 1 (1982): 155–71.

Tahtinen, Dale R. *National Security Challenges to Saudi Arabia*. AEI Studies, no. 194. Washington: American Enterprise Institute for Public Policy Research, 1978.

Troeller, Gary. *The Birth of Saudi Arabia: Britain and the Rise of the House of Sa'ud*. London: Frank Cass, 1976.

Turner, Louis, and James Bedore. "Saudi Arabia: The Power of the Purse-Strings." *International Affairs* (London) 54, no. 3 (July 1978): 405–20.

U.S. Congress. Senate. Committee on Appropriations. Subcommittee on Foreign Assistance and Related Programs. *Sales of Stinger Missiles to Saudi Arabia*. Hearing. Washington: U.S. Government Printing Office, 1984.

U.S. Congress. Senate. Committee on Foreign Relations. *War in the Gulf*. Staff Report. Washington: U.S. Government Printing Office, 1984.

Winder, Bayly. "Saudi Arabia: Sociopolitical Developments." *AEI Foreign Policy and Defense Review* 2, nos. 3–4 (1980): 14–20.

Conflict and Cooperation in the Gulf: Problems and Prospects

R. Hrair Dekmejian

POLITICAL AND ECONOMIC SETTING

The Persian or Arabian Gulf, one of the most important waterways in the world, is almost an inland sea of ninety thousand square miles. At its northern tip is the mouth of the Shatt al-'Arab, formed by the confluence of the Tigris and Euphrates rivers. The distance from the Shatt al-'Arab to the southeastern entrance of the Gulf—the Strait of Hormuz—is over five hundred miles. The states of the Gulf littoral are Iran, Iraq, Kuwait, Saudi Arabia, Bahrain, Qatar, Oman, and the United Arab Emirates (UAE). Iran, Iraq, and Saudi Arabia are the three largest states of the region and its primary political actors; the remaining five states are smaller in size, population, and political influence. The Gulf states are Islamic in faith and civilization; all are dominated by Sunnis except Iran and Oman, where the Shiite and Ibadi sects are dominant, respectively. The states on the western and northern parts of the Gulf are Arab, whereas Iran is Persian in language, history, and culture.[1]

The eight states of the Gulf are ruled by three types of elites and authority structures, ranging from Ba'thi secularism in Iraq to Islamic tribal Arab monarchies and the clerically led Republic of Iran. The Ba'thi elite rules Iraq in the name of secular Arab nationalism. In Saudi Arabia, monarchical rule is based on Islamic legitimacy and tribal consensus—a formula adopted in varying degrees by the smaller Gulf states.

The main economic resources of the Gulf region are petroleum, natural gas, and oil derivatives. Despite the recent decline of oil production, the Gulf still provides over one fifth of the world's petroleum. All the Gulf states are major or medium-level oil producers except Bahrain. During the 1970s the Gulf also became an important world financial and commercial center because of massive increases in oil-derived income and accelerated economic development. The great oil boom of the period accompanied by quantum price increases triggered large-scale developmental schemes that changed the face of the Gulf region in just over a decade. Rapid modernization, often of a haphazard nature, has unleashed a plethora of disruptive sociopolitical forces, one consequence of which was the Iranian revolution.

Iran

Iran is the second largest, most populous, and potentially most powerful state of the Gulf. The overthrow of the Pahlavi Dynasty marked the establishment of a provisional government led by the Ayatollah Khomeini in February 1979. On 2–3 December of that year, a national referendum approved the Islamic Constitution of Iran in the midst of a struggle for power among the various revolutionary factions. During 1980–81, the clerical faction associated with the Islamic Republican party (IRP) gained ascendance by purging the Mujahedin-i Khalq and other opposition groups. The IRP stood for the principle of clerical supervision and control of the government under the supreme guardianship of the Ayatollah Khomeini (vilayet-e-faqih).

During 1982, the Islamic regime was able to entrench itself despite the ravages of the war with Iraq. In fact, Iraq's early victories provided an important cause for the Islamic regime, which rallied the Iranians against the invading forces. After mid-1982, Iran was able to turn the tide of war by taking the offensive against Iraq. Iran's isolation and her consequent inability to acquire modern weaponry, however, has brought the war to a standstill. The large-scale financial aid to Iraq from the Arab Gulf states, combined with mass deployment of modern weaponry, enabled Iraq to halt the Iranian advance. Meanwhile, Iran's Islamic revolutionary zeal has become a dangerous threat to its neighbors.

Iraq

Iraq is the third largest state of the Gulf littoral and the second most populous after Iran. Its population of about 15 million includes a majority of Arab Shiites (55 percent) and a Sunni minority consisting of Arabs and Kurds. Since Iraq's independence in 1932, Sunni Arabs have been ascendant in the government. Until the July 1958 revolution, the country was ruled by the pro-British Hashimite Dynasty. In February 1963, the government of Brig. Gen. 'Abd al-Karim Qasim was overthrown and a coalition of Nasirites and Ba'thists assumed power under Col. 'Abd al-Salam 'Arif. In November 1963, Colonel 'Arif purged the Ba'th, which then led an underground existence until its takeover of power in July 1968. The Ba'th returned to power under Maj. Gen. Ahmad Hasan al-Bakr who retained the presidency until his resignation in July 1979 when Saddam Hussein assumed the leadership of the Ba'th party and the government.

Internal factionalism within the Ba'th party was compounded by opposition from the Kurdish minority in the North and the Shiite majority in the South. The Kurdish revolt led by Gen. Mustafa al-Barzani raged from 1961 to 1975 with support from Iran, Israel, and the United States. The revolt collapsed in March 1975 as a result of the Algiers agreement between Iraq and Iran, whereby the shah agreed to end all aid to the Kurds in return for Iraqi concessions on the Shatt al-'Arab waterway. More consequential was the growing Shiite rebellion after the mid-1970s, which found a new source of support and inspiration in the Islamic Republic of Iran. In September 1980, Iraq attacked Iran, initiating the bloody conflict that has continued to this date.

Oil is Iraq's leading natural resource, which once accounted for over half of its GNP. Between 1979 and the end of 1981, however, oil output fell by 75 percent annually because of the war with Iran. Thus, Iraq has been forced to rely on large-scale financial aid from the Arab Gulf states to counter the Iranian military threat. Simultaneously, Iraq has repaired its strained relations with the United States and the Soviet Union, the latter being a primary source of arms. Meanwhile, relations with Syria have remained antagonistic owing to the old enmity between factions of the Ba'th party ruling the two countries.

Saudi Arabia

The Kingdom of Saudi Arabia occupies much of the land mass of the Arabian Peninsula. It is a vast, largely desert country with an indigenous population of over 9 million and an imported work force of over 1.5 million. The kingdom is the world's largest exporter of oil and possesses vast petroleum reserves. As a result of rapidly increasing oil revenues during the 1970s, Saudi Arabia launched its Third Five-Year Plan in 1980, budgeted at $250 billion for agricultural expansion, social infrastructure, and petrochemical export-oriented industries. Despite the modernization of the kingdom, the Saudi government has continued to rely on the Islamic puritanical doctrines of Shaykh Muhammad ibn 'Abd al-Wahhab, the great Hanbali reformer of the eighteenth century. Thus, Wahhabism constitutes the official ideology of the Saudi state.

The present kingdom was founded in 1932 by King 'Abd al-'Aziz who restored the power of his ancestors by uniting much of the peninsula. After his death in 1953, the king was succeeded by an ineffectual son, Sa'ud ibn 'Abd al-'Aziz, who was deposed by the royal family in November 1964. He was replaced by his brother Faysal who initiated wide-ranging reforms in the kingdom's administrative and socioeconomic domains. Faysal's assassination by a nephew on 25 March 1975 brought his brother Khalid to the throne. Because of Khalid's illness, however, Crown Prince Fahd assumed many of the king's administrative duties. Upon his brother's death, Fahd acceded to the throne and his half-brother 'Abd Allah was designated crown prince. Despite a number of coup attempts and the takeover of the Great Mosque in November 1979 by Islamic radicals, the royal family has managed to preserve stability in the midst of rapid socioeconomic development. While maintaining close defense ties with the United States, the Saudis have opposed the Camp David accords of 1979 and given financial support to the PLO and the Arab states confronting Israel. In addition, the kingdom has been at the forefront of the Pan-Islamic movement, supporting missionary activities and aiding the anticommunist fighters (Mujahedin) in Afghanistan.

Kuwait

Kuwait gained independence from Britain in June 1961 as a hereditary emirate under the Al Sabah family. It is unique in the Gulf region in the constitutional character of its government, which features a legislature and a degree of democratic participation. Since independence, Kuwait has become the most modernized state of the Gulf with oil revenues of $19.7 billion in 1980. Its affluence

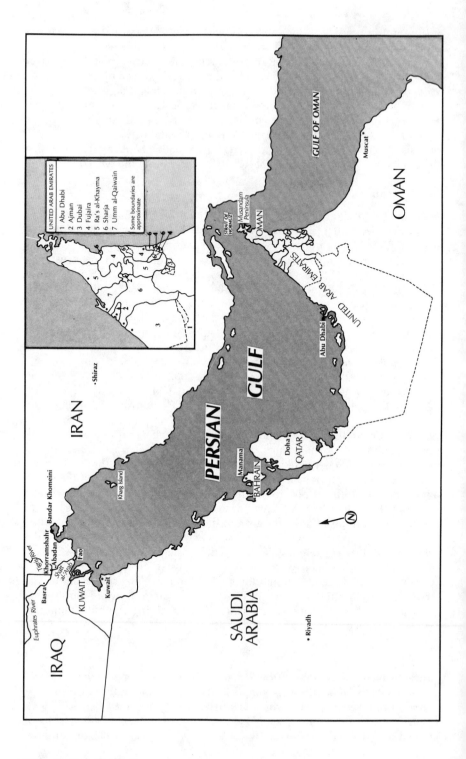

and relative liberalism, however, have been accompanied by serious internal and external security problems. In the early 1960s, Iraqi attempts to annex Kuwait were rebuffed with British and Egyptian support. In August 1976, Shaykh Sabah al-Salim dissolved the National Assembly, postponed new elections, and placed limitations on the press because of the impact of the Lebanese war on the large Palestinian community. These Palestinians, along with Iranian Shiites and other Arab immigrants, have been mostly excluded from political life. In February 1981, new elections were held for the fifty-member National Assembly when Kuwait returned to constitutional rule.

The decline in oil production has prompted considerable belt-tightening, although Kuwait has retained its economic strength and wealth since it possesses the world's third largest oil reserves. Its support of Iraq in the war, however, has made Kuwait a target of Iranian propaganda and subversion. In foreign policy, the country pursues a strongly Arab nationalist line by supporting the Palestinian cause. It is the only Arab Gulf monarchy that maintains diplomatic relations with the Soviet Union in keeping with the policy of positive neutralism.

Bahrain

The archipelago of Bahrain is the smallest of the Gulf states in terms of both area and population. A British protectorate after 1861, Bahrain became independent in August 1971. It is ruled by the Al Khalifah family, which is closely allied with Saudi Arabia. A brief experiment with constitutional government failed with the dissolution of the National Assembly in August 1975. In recent years, Bahrain has emerged as a major Gulf financial and banking center as its petroleum resources have declined. Historically, its main external threat has come from Iran, which has territorial claims to the island. Iran's Islamic regime has attempted to foment opposition to the Sunni Al Khalifah family by appealing to the Shiite community, which makes up over half of Bahrain's population. In December 1981, the government announced the discovery of a plot to overthrow the monarchy; ostensibly the conspiracy was the work of the Tehran-based Shiite group called the Islamic Front for the Liberation of Bahrain. This episode prompted the conclusion of a security agreement between Bahrain and Saudi Arabia.

Qatar

Qatar is an oil-producing shaykhdom ruled by the Al Thani family. The country occupies an arid peninsula that projects into the Persian Gulf from the Arabian mainland. Indigenous Qataris are mostly Wahhabis, and the country is closely tied to Saudi Arabia. Since gaining independence from Britain in 1971, Qatar has experienced significant modernization funded by oil revenues. Recent efforts at economic diversification have resulted in the construction of petrochemical, fertilizer, and steel plants and port facilities. Qatar is one of the more traditional shaykhdoms of the Gulf; the ruling family exercises control through the cabinet and the Advisory Council of thirty members. The major issues facing the shaykhdom include its territorial disputes with Bahrain and the UAE and the small size of the indigenous Arab population, which constitutes a minority. Faced with the depletion of petroleum reserves, Qatar is expected eventually to tap its substantial natural gas deposits to sustain its future economic well-being.

The United Arab Emirates

The British decision to withdraw from the Gulf prompted the Trucial States to form the Federation of the United Arab Emirates (UAE) in 1971. The UAE consists of Abu Dhabi, Dubai, Sharjah, Ra's al-Khayma, Ajman, Fujaira, and Umm al-Qaiwain. The combined population of over 1 million includes a majority of nonindigenous people. The discovery of major oil reserves in 1958 in Abu Dhabi and subsequently in Dubai and Sharjah radically altered the economy and society. By 1980, the UAE had attained the world's highest per capita GNP of $30,000; however, this wealth was unevenly distributed among the constituent emirates. In fact, inequalities in wealth, territory, and power have created considerable tension among the seven emirates, threatening the integrity of the federation. The two largest and richest emirates, Abu Dhabi and Dubai, have been rivals; the smaller emirates are dependent on federal aid, which mostly comes from Abu Dhabi.

The president of the federation is Shaykh Zayid Al Nahayyan, ruler of Abu Dhabi, who was elected by the other rulers in December 1971 and re-elected in November 1981. Similarly Shaykh Rashid Al Maktum of Dubai was elected vice president; in April 1979, he assumed the prime ministry of the federation by decision of the Supreme Council, which includes all seven rulers. As president, Shaykh Zayid has led the proponents of a tighter federal union, whereas Shaykh Rashid has advocated a loose federal structure. Clearly, Dubai sees a unified federal structure as a threat to its commercial and political independence, despite popular support for a tighter federation. The deadlock has cast doubts on the future viability of the UAE as a federal state.

Oman

The Sultanate of Oman, formerly known as Muscat and Oman, occupies the southeast portion of the Arabian Peninsula. A small noncontiguous area belonging to Oman at the tip of the Musandam Peninsula extends toward the Strait of Hormuz. Oman's population is predominantly Arab, although it also includes Baluchis, Indians, Iranians, East Africans, and Pakistanis. The political life of the sultanate is dominated by the Ibadi sect of Islam to which over half of the natives belong, as does the ruling Al Bu Sa'id family. The Ibadism of Oman sets it apart from the predominantly Sunni Arab world. The Ibadis trace their origins to the Khawarij of early Islamic history who assassinated the fourth caliph, 'Ali, and opposed the practice of choosing successors to the Prophet exclusively from his family or tribe.

The history of Oman has been strongly influenced by Britain's protective role after 1798 and by religious and tribal opposition to the Al Bu Sa'id Dynasty. Revolts against Sultan Sa'id ibn Taymur by the Ibadis of the interior were ended in 1959 with British help. Similarly, the Dhufar rebellion was crushed during the mid-1970s with British, Iranian, Jordanian, Saudi Arabian, and Pakistani assistance. Meanwhile, Sultan Qabus ibn Sa'id had taken power from his father in July 1970 through a British-supported coup d'état. The new sultan had opposed his father's conservative and isolationist policies and favored modernization and sociopolitical reforms. Substantial economic modernization has taken place since the discovery of oil in 1967. But the sultan has been reluctant to introduce political reforms beyond the establishment of a consultative assembly of forty-five appointed members. To sustain his conservative rule, the sultan has continued to maintain close ties with Britain while establishing strong defense and economic links with the United States. Oman's strongly pro-Western orientation has brought condemnation from both Arab nationalists and Islamic fundamentalists. Despite the importance of oil production, Oman has chosen to remain outside OPEC and OAPEC.

MAJOR ISSUES AND PROBLEMS

A number of major external and internal problems face the Gulf states in the mid-1980s. During 1984, these problems, which assumed new urgency as a consequence of unpropitious developments, centered on certain destabilizing factors:

1. The ongoing war between Iran and Iraq

2. The precipitous decline of oil prices and the resulting reduction of the national incomes of the Gulf countries

3. The persistence of security problems in the Gulf and the continuing inability of the Arab Gulf monarchies to assume the burdens of self-defense

4. The external and internal threat of Islamic fundamentalism, particularly of the Shiite variety, in the context of the continuing challenge posed by the Islamic regime in Iran

5. The exacerbation of ethnic, sectarian, and class conflicts and the quest for popular participation in monarchical settings

These clusters of destabilizing factors could produce a mutually reinforcing dynamic that may have serious repercussions on world finance, energy, and the strategic balance.

Iran-Iraq War

In its fifth year, the Iran-Iraq war constitutes perhaps the greatest threat to the Gulf's stability. Despite the deadlock on the warfront, the conflict during the last two years has spread to the Gulf region as a result of Iraqi and Iranian attacks on oil shipping. On the whole, most of the Arab monarchies have supported Iraq mainly through massive financial aid. This effort has become an ever-increasing burden for the monarchies at a time of decreasing oil revenues. Yet it has been impossible for most of the Gulf rulers to escape the burden of assisting Iraq, considering the potentially disastrous consequences of an Iranian victory. Indeed, an Iranian breakthrough would pose a clear strategic threat to the oil-producing monarchies, combined with an ideological threat in the form of Islamic fundamentalism.

In view of the continuing dangers of the war, the Gulf rulers have lost no opportunity to seek an end to the conflict. To this end, they have worked through the United Nations, the Islamic Conference, and the Arab League to encourage the two sides to negotiate a settlement. Moreover, several of the Gulf shaykhdoms led by Shaykh Zayid Al Nahayyan of the UAE have attempted to mediate between the warring sides without success.

Decline of Oil Income

The world economic recession, coupled with increasing levels of production in non-OPEC countries, have produced an oil glut and a consequent decline of oil prices. The impact of the oil glut on the Gulf producers can be seen in Tables 1 and 2.

Saudi Arabia experienced the most precipitous decrease of oil production and income; between 1980 and 1983, the kingdom's oil production was cut in half and its income dropped by over 50 percent. Kuwait's production declined by about 30 percent and its income by 50 percent. Similar reductions occurred in the production and income figures of the UAE and Qatar.

Aside from the oil glut, the Iraq-Iran war has had some impact on oil production. Despite the attacks on Gulf shipping, Iran, Saudi Arabia, Kuwait, and the producers of the lower Gulf have managed to transport their petroleum to foreign markets. The major loser has been Iraq whose access to the Gulf has been effectively blocked by the proximity of Iranian forces. Between 1980 and 1983, Iraq's oil production decreased by over 60 percent and its income by over 65 percent. The only exception to the Gulf countries' downward trend was Iran, which increased its oil production between 1980 and 1983 by about 45 percent and its income by almost 50 percent. Iraq's attempts to reduce Iranian oil exports by means of air attacks on ports and shipping have been only moderately successful.

The decrease of revenues from oil production is likely to have negative short- and long-range consequences for the Gulf states. For Iraq the decrease of oil income has produced a drop in the standard of living and a serious financial strain on its war economy. It has meant an ever-increasing Iraqi reliance on the largesse of the Arab Gulf rulers, who are themselves experiencing financial difficulties. In the last three years, Saudi Arabia, Kuwait, and the other shaykhdoms have responded to the income crunch with sharp reductions in their overall expenditures, including curtailment of large development projects, cuts in salary increases, and cutbacks in economic aid and philanthropic contributions to poorer countries. Simultaneously, these Gulf states have begun to shift attention to their developing petroleum-related industries, such as chemicals and plastics, which as exports are expected to produce new sources of income. Yet, these enterprises are unlikely to compensate for the large losses of income from oil production. As a result, the Gulf states will be forced to adjust to lower levels of revenues and affluence than they enjoyed at the height of the seventies' oil boom. This will require a fundamental readjustment of lifeways and consumption patterns, which could prove difficult to achieve.

Security Problems

The security of the Gulf area has continued to be a source of great concern both for the regional powers and for the West. The proximity of Soviet power to the

Table 1. Crude Oil Production
(million barrels per day)

	1980	1982	1983
Saudi Arabia	10.000	6.965	5.040
Kuwait	1.465	0.740	0.930
Neutral zone	0.540	0.300	0.370
Iran	1.485	1.975	2.505
Iraq	2.645	0.990	0.970
UAE-Abu Dhabi	1.375	0.970	0.900
UAE-Dubai	0.360	0.365	0.350
UAE-Sharjah	0.010	0.015	0.050
Qatar	0.480	0.350	0.315

Source: Europa Year Book 1984 (London: Europa Publications, 1984), p. 106.

Table 2. Government Oil Revenues
(million U.S. dollars)

	1978	1979	1980	1981	1982	1983
Iran	20,900	18,800	11,600	8,500	19,000	21,700
Saudi Arabia	36,700	59,200	104,200	113,300	76,000	46,000
Kuwait	9,500	16,300	18,300	14,800	10,000	9,900
Iraq	11,600	21,200	26,500	10,400	9,500	8,400
Abu Dhabi/UAE	8,700	13,000	19,200	18,700	16,000	12,800
Qatar	2,200	3,100	5,200	5,300	4,200	3,000

Source: Europa Year Book 1984 (London: Europa Publications, 1984), p. 108.

Gulf, coupled with West European and Japanese dependence on Gulf oil, have highlighted the strategic vulnerability of the region. Although the Soviet Union does not seem to constitute an immediate threat in the perception of the Gulf states, it is seen as a major long-range threat. The most immediate security concern for the Arab Gulf states is the Islamic regime of Iran. The rulers also feel threatened both by Israeli power and by subversion emanating from Arab and other countries.

American efforts to fill the power vacuum have been vehemently opposed by Iran; nor have the Arab monarchies, except Oman, shown eagerness to publicize their defense ties with the United States. They are convinced that the introduction of a large U.S. presence in the Gulf is likely to be countered by the expansion of the Soviet position in the People's Democratic Republic of Yemen. Moreover, because of the closeness of the U.S.-Israeli relationship, any overt cooperation with the United States invariably encounters opposition from Arab nationalists and Islamic fundamentalist elements. Consequently, the Gulf rulers have preferred to deemphasize their security ties with the United States, while seeking assurances of American readiness to assist militarily in situations of emergency. Meanwhile, the rulers have sought to develop their own joint defense capabilities within the Gulf Cooperation Council (GCC). Despite their recent efforts, however, security cooperation within the GCC has not reached the level of full integration of forces.[2]

Islamic Fundamentalism and the Iranian Threat

The rise of Islamic fundamentalism of both the Sunni and Shi'i varieties has become a pervasive feature in Gulf society. Islamic resurgence has taken on different manifestations ranging from the mystical quietism of the Sufi orders to the militancy of revolutionary groups.[3] In the Arab states of the Gulf's western periphery, Islamic fundamentalism has gained ascendance over Arab nationalist and leftist sentiments. In Iran, the revolution has entrenched a Shiite clerical oligarchy led by the Ayatollah Khomeini.

It is beyond doubt that the establishment of a theocratic state in Iran has given impetus to movements of Islamic resurgence throughout the Arab countries and the Muslim world. Iran's revolutionary impact has been most apparent among the large Shiite communities of Iraq, Saudi Arabia, and the Gulf shaykhdoms. However, the Sunni Muslims of the Arab world have also felt the politicospiritual wave of Islamic fervor emanating from Iran. Indeed, for both Sunni and Shi'i militant fundamentalists, the Iranian revolution constitutes an example to emulate in their efforts to assume power. The potency of the Iranian model is reinforced by the Islamic regime's unceasing efforts to propagate its revolutionary ideology, while supporting indigenous groups in their subversive activities. The propaganda apparatus of the Islamic Republic aims to promote popular resistance to the ruling authorities of the Arab states, particularly to Iraq's Ba'thi regime, the Saudi monarchy, and the Egyptian government. Other primary targets of Iranian propaganda include Kuwait and Bahrain, while the remaining shaykhdoms have generally been spared the full weight of Iranian attacks. Aside from the call to overthrow the "sinful" ruling elites, Khomeini and other leading clerics have challenged the Sunni 'ulama' to emulate their Shiite counterparts and form Islamist vanguards to revolutionize the faithful as a prelude to the seizure of power. The Iranian propaganda effort has had considerable success in the Shiite communities of Iraq, Saudi Arabia, Bahrain, and Kuwait, while those of Qatar and the UAE have remained generally passive.[4]

Of all the Arab Gulf states, Iraq has borne the brunt of the Iranian propaganda offensive and subversion. The internal Shiite opposition to the Ba'thi government, however, predated the Iranian revolution by almost a decade. A variety of socioeconomic and political reasons combined to inflame Iraq's Shiite majority against the Sunni-led Ba'th regime. The government's secularist policies and the lowly economic status of the recently urbanized Shiite peasant-tribesmen were critical factors in the establishment of al-Hizb al-Da'wah al-Islamiyah and other militant groups seeking the regime's overthrow. The Shiite political resurgence was reinforced by certain members of Iraq's clerical establishment led by the supreme Marji' (religious authority) Ayatollah Muhsin al-Hakim and his younger colleague al-Sayyid Muhammad Baqir al-Sadr.[5] These clerics were alarmed by the atrophy of faith among the Shiites under the impact of secular ideologies like communism and Ba'thi socialism. Baqir al-Sadr's emergence as the leading ideologue of the Shiite resurgent movement during the early 1970s marked the beginning of escalating confrontation between the Ba'th and the Shiite militant groups led by the Da'wah party. This resulted in a series of clashes and terrorism, which the government suppressed with vehemence. After the shah's overthrow, Baqir al-Sadr expressed his total support for the Ayatollah Khomeini and his regime and persisted in opposing the Iraqi government, which led to his execution in April 1980. The death of the Arab ayatollah removed one of the most prominent religious intellectuals of the Shiite world and weakened the opposition to the regime. The combination of repressive measures and financial contributions to nonpolitical Shiite clergy has enabled the Ba'th to neutralize the Da'wah party and its smaller offshoots to a substantial degree.[6] Also, many Iraqi Shiites have been reluctant to follow Iranian dictates because of their Arab identity.

Another focus of Shiite fundamentalism has been Bahrain, which had been claimed by Iran under the monarchy. Under Khomeini, Iranian propaganda was directed at Bahrain's Shiite community which constituted a majority in a state ruled by the Sunni Al Khalifah family. In December 1981, the government reported the discovery of an Iranian-inspired conspiracy, which brought arrests and a pledge by Saudi Arabian interior minister Prince Nayif to defend Bahrain. Equally consequential has been the renewed manifestations of militancy in the large Shiite community centered in Saudi Arabia's oil-producing Eastern Province. There have been repeated expressions of Shiite dissatisfaction with Saudi rule, which is based on strict Wahhabism. These have led to periodic clashes between the Saudi National Guard and the Shiites who have demanded equal rights and even an end to monarchical rule. In recent years, these sentiments have been encouraged by the Iranian clerical authorities who regard the Saudi family as a primary foe. In December 1979, nine months after the Iranian revolution, the Saudis were confronted with Shiite unrest in al-Qatif and Sayhat in the Eastern Province. Once again the National Guard was deployed to impose order.[7]

More recently, Kuwait has been the scene of terrorist attacks attributed to Shiite militants supported by Iran. On 12 December 1983, truck-bomb attacks were directed against the American and French embassies and other important targets in Kuwait. Iran denied responsibility for these attacks, and the Kuwaiti authorities arrested a number of Shiites belonging to the Iraq-based Hizb al-Da'wah, who were said to have perpetrated the bombings.[8] A lower level of activism is discernible among the Shiite minorities of Qatar and the UAE. Iran and the UAE have maintained a degree of amicable relations, and the large Iranian Shiite community of merchants in Dubai has played an important role in the substantial commercial relations between this emirate and Iran. On the whole, the Gulf rulers have adopted reformist policies to reduce the Shiites' dissatisfaction, which is often the result of local conditions. These reforms may not be enough, however, to stem the tide of Shiite militancy.

Shiite fundamentalism is not the only religious factor of potential instability in the Arab Gulf states. Equally significant is the resurgence of Sunni Islam, which can be seen in all aspects of daily life. This can be witnessed in the return of conservative life-styles and the appearance of many religious societies. The latter include Sufi brotherhoods promoting asceticism. reformist associations seeking to spread Islamic practices, and militant societies pressing for the establishment of Islamic polities. To cope with this resurgence, Gulf rulers have sought to reinforce their own bases of legitimacy by adopting stricter laws of Islamic conduct and limiting the infusion of Western influences into their societies.

The catalysts of Islamic resurgence in the larger Arab-Islamic setting have included crises in identity, culture, and political legitimacy; maldistribution of wealth; corruption and arbitrary rule; and a feeling of military impotence vis-à-vis the West, Israel, and the Soviet Union.[9] In the Gulf the massive presence of foreign workers and Western-style profligacy of ruling elites have constituted the two primary triggers of Islamist opposition. The most dramatic manifestation of militant fundamentalism occurred in Saudi Arabia when a group of radicals occupied for two weeks the Great Mosque of Mecca. A former national guardsman, Juhayman al-'Utaybi, led the insurgents who called themselves the Ikhwan (the Brothers), after the tribal warriors who fought to establish Saudi power in the early 1900s. Juhayman's brother-in-law declared himself the mahdi—whose manifestation as savior is associated with Islamic eschatological belief. The Ikhwan called for the overthrow of Saudi rule and the establishment of a strict Islamic order patterned after the community founded by the Prophet Muhammad.

After a period of hesitation, King Khalid convened a council of 'ulama' to secure a legal ruling (fatwa) to storm the mosque. The dissidents were eventually overpowered and executed. Although many Saudis did not share the Ikhwan's extremism and desecration of the Holy Sanctuary, they empathized with the rebels' call for Islamic puritanism and their challenge of the regime. In response, the government tightened security and declared its intention to institute major socioeconomic and political reforms. The adoption of these measures has had a strengthening effect on the monarchy.[10]

The Islamist current is also discernible in the smaller Gulf states. Violent expressions of Sunni fundamentalism, however, have been absent in these affluent societies, although the potential for conflict is present. Indications of friction became apparent in Kuwait during 1984 on the question of secular lifeways among university students. Armed with a fatwa from Shaykh 'Abd al-'Aziz ibn Baz of Saudi Arabia, Kuwaiti fundamentalists pressed for the imposition of strict Islamic rules on university and student life. They were vehemently opposed by the secularists who appeared to have government support. A showdown was averted by the intervention of the regime. Yet political Islam shall remain a medium of revolutionary protest and an alternative ideology of governance should the Gulf regimes lose legitimacy and their grip on power.

Communal Conflict and the Quest for Political Participation

The potential for communal conflict and the quest for political participation are two interrelated problems of consequence confronting the Gulf states. These twin problems are major challenges to the stability of the region. In Iran, muted rivalries are already apparent among clerical factions as a prelude to the struggle for succession in the post-Khomeini era. In this context, renewed opposition from the Mujahedin as well as from the Kurds, Azeris, and Baluchis may pose challenges to the stability of the Islamic regime. In Iraq, Shiite resistance is likely to persist amid renewed Kurdish attempts to seek political autonomy in the North.

More serious is the potential for ethnic conflict in the Gulf monarchies. Aside from its recalcitrant Shiite minority, Saudi Arabia has experienced regional and tribal conflicts. The most sociopolitically consequential issue for the Gulf monarchies, however, is the massive presence of imported laborers numbering in the millions. In their headlong quest for accelerated development, the Gulf states have created a long-term social, demographic, and political threat to their own stability. In Saudi Arabia, Yemenis constitute the largest expatriate group in addition to many Palestinians and other Arabs, Indians, Pakistanis, and South Asians. The same demographic pattern is discernible in the smaller Gulf states, which also contain large Iranian communities. The large foreign presence is a much greater sociopolitical threat to the Gulf shaykhdoms than to Saudi Arabia, which has a substantial indigenous population. In most of the Gulf shaykhdoms the native Arabs have become minorities in their own countries.

These expatriate communities were not meant to become permanent fixtures in the Gulf states. Yet many of them have acquired semipermanent status in view of the long-term technical and employment needs of the host countries. As foreigners, these expatriates are denied citizenship or participation in politics, although some hold important economic, educational, and even governmental positions. This is particularly true of expatriates from other Arab countries who have played a key role in the intellectual, religious, and economic life of Saudi Arabia and the other Arab Gulf states.

More centrally, the crisis of political participation has affected the native population.[11] Recent dramatic improvements in the socioeconomic and educational levels of the indigenous people have created strong pressures for popular participation in the political process. Only in Kuwait has there been a governmental attempt to open avenues and modalities of popular involvement in politics. Similarly, Bahrain, Saudi Arabia, Oman, and the UAE have taken tentative steps to permit some degree of popular participation in government, but it is too early to discern the success of these experiments.

IRAQ-IRAN WAR

Since its inception in September 1980, the Iraq-Iran war has become the Gulf's foremost security problem and a constant drain on the resources of all countries in the region. President Saddam Hussein's decision to attack Iran in 1980 was prompted by several factors: (1) the desire to recoup concessions given Iran on the Shatt al-'Arab under the 1975 Algiers agreement; (2) the apparent feasibility of achieving a quick victory over an internally divided revolutionary regime; (3) the wish to make Iraq the dominant power of the Gulf and the Arab world; and (4) the conviction that an Iranian defeat would destabilize the revolutionary regime and reduce its religious zeal and potential to foment unrest among Iraq's Shiites.

Less than two years after the attack, it became apparent that Iraq's initial assumptions and calculations were fallacious. In March 1982, Iran launched a major counteroffensive, forcing the Iraqis to give up their early territorial gains. While Saddam Hussein called for a cease-fire, Khomeini declared that Iran would continue the war until the "un-Islamic" Ba'thi regime was destroyed. Meanwhile, the fundamentalist clerical faction had consolidated its hold on Iran, subdued the Mujahedin and other internal opponents, and unleashed its Revolutionary Guards (*Pasdaran*) against the Iraqi forces. Imbued with Islamic fervor and readiness for martyrdom, the Pasdaran fought better than the regular Iranian army. Moreover, Iraq's irredentist ambitions toward Iranian territories such as Arabistan (Khuzistan) have been dampened; nor can Iraq claim a dominant position in Gulf and Arab affairs so long as the Iranian threat persists. Confronted with a determined enemy, Iraq has had to employ two strategies in dealing with the Iranian challenge.

The first strategy, thus far successful, is to block an Iranian breakthrough on land at any cost. This has been done by the deployment of the Iraqi forces in heavily fortified positions and the use of massive firepower and modern weaponry against the poorly equipped Iranian enemy. Iraq's second strategy is to employ its superior air power to block Iranian oil shipments from Kharg Island in an effort to reduce Tehran's oil revenues. This strategy has not been crowned with notable success until the present time for several reasons. Despite the proven effectiveness of the French-supplied Super-Etendard bombers and Exocet missiles, the Iraqis have not utilized the full potential of these weapons systems. Furthermore, Iraqi attacks on international shipping to and from Iran's Kharg Island have involved the ships of many nations including those of Iraq's Arab allies. Indeed, the Arab Gulf states have viewed the Iraqi escalation with great trepidation in view of Iran's counterattacks on Arab Gulf shipping. Consequently, Iran has succeeded in maintaining a high level of oil production and revenues without which its internal stability and war-making capabilities would be seriously jeopardized.

During 1983 and 1984 the Iraq-Iran armed confrontation had reached a deadlock. The great human losses on the Iranian side had created doubts among top leaders about the wisdom of further sacrifices. During 1984, there were repeated postponements of a major offensive, although a limited Iranian attack to dislodge the Iraqis from Manzali Heights proved successful. Significantly, Iran refrained from repeating its past threats to close the Strait of Hormuz; instead it stated its opposition to widening the war. In the meantime, there is no question that Iraq has succeeded in strengthening itself militarily and diplomatically by forging ties with Egypt, Jordan, France, Italy, and even the two superpowers—all of which fear the consequences of an Iranian victory. After a period of coolness in Iraqi-Soviet relations, the U.S.S.R. has resumed shipments of war matériel. Also, Iraq has reestablished diplomatic relations with the United States after a lapse of seventeen years. In contrast, Iran has generally remained isolated, except for the support given by Syria and Libya. In view of its enmity with Iraq, Syria has continued to prevent the transit of Iraqi oil to the Mediterranean. This has prompted Iraq to increase its shipments through the pipeline in Turkey; also Iraq has begun urgent consideration of plans to build a pipeline to the Red Sea through Jordan. Yet, manifestations of renewed Iraqi determination and strength have failed to induce the Iranians to end the war. Repeated attempts by the Islamic Conference, the Arab League, the United Nations, and Shaykh Zayid of Abu Dhabi to seek a negotiated settlement have been rejected by Iran. The Ayatollah Khomeini's primary condition to end the war remains the overthrow of President Saddam Hussein.[12]

THE GULF COOPERATION COUNCIL

During the late 1970s several major developments occurred to prompt the establishment in May 1981 of the Cooperation Council of the Gulf Arab States—*Majlis al-Ta'awun li-Duwal al-Khalij al-'Arabi*. These developments, which propelled the Gulf into a position of unprecedented economic, strategic, and political centrality, were (1) the world energy crisis, (2) the Islamic revolution, (3) the Soviet invasion of Afghanistan, and (4) the escalating risks of regional conflict, especially the Iraq-Iran war and the Arab-Israeli confrontation.[13] These factors combined with internal instability in the Gulf states provided the critical impetus for the creation of the Gulf Cooperation Council (GCC) consisting of Saudi Arabia, Kuwait, Bahrain, Qatar, Oman, and the United Arab Emirates (UAE).

Objectives

As an association of six sovereign dynastic states, the GCC began as a loose regional grouping. During its four-year existence, however, the council has made concerted efforts toward the establishment of a viable regional entity. There were four clusters of specific motivating factors among the member states for establishing the GCC: (1) external security, (2) internal security, (3) political unity, and (4) socioeconomic unity.[14] Unquestionably, the dual problems of external and internal security have been paramount in the perception of GCC members because of their weakness and vulnerability. Consequently, the GCC has committed itself to a policy of self-reliance and mutual cooperation in defense matters. But the GCC is concerned not only with self-defense but also with the maintenance of the free flow of oil. To this end its members have tried to achieve a strategic consensus with limited success. The lack of consensus flows from differences in foreign policy among the member states. While Kuwait advocates a nonaligned course, Oman has pressed for close cooperation with the West and has permitted a large U.S. military presence on its soil. Bahrain and Qatar usually support the Saudi position of maintaining security ties with the United States without permitting the stationing of American forces on their territories. The UAE has followed Kuwait's nonaligned course without following the latter's example of establishing diplomatic relations with the Soviet Union. During October 1983, the GCC held its first joint exercise in Abu Dhabi under the code name *Dir' al-jazirah* (Shield of the Peninsula).[15] A second joint maneuver was held during October 1984 in Saudi Arabia.

The problem of defense occupied center stage during the fifth summit conference of GCC rulers in Kuwait in November 1984. However, there has been no evidence that the GCC has been able to develop a rapid deployment force to counter threats from Iran, Israel, or the Soviet Union, which Gulf rulers consider their major potential foes. According to GCC statistics, the member states can marshal only 140,000 troops, which is considered insufficient to defend their territorial expanse. Yet the establishment of an integrated and well-trained Gulf force could prove useful in holding off a potential aggressor until the dispatch of foreign troops, possibly from Egypt and ultimately from the European countries and the United States.

Equally central is the issue of internal security. In recent years three

GCC member states—Saudi Arabia, Bahrain, and Kuwait—have experienced internal threats to their security. The Great Mosque episode and Shiite unrest plagued Saudi Arabia in late 1979, Bahrain faced Shiite recalcitrance and plots during December 1981, and Kuwait was hit by truck bombings in late 1983. In response, the GCC has prepared a draft security agreement that provides for substantial interstate cooperation in dealing with political opponents, subversive elements, and criminals.[16] However, Kuwait and the UAE, and possibly other members, have been reluctant to endorse all the clauses of the security agreement, particularly on the question of extradition. One major reason for GCC's failure to develop effective defense and internal security agreements is the apprehension of most members about the growth of Saudi influence on their domestic and foreign affairs.

More successful have been GCC's efforts to promote economic cooperation among its members. An economic agreement has been approved along with the establishment of the Gulf Investment Organization with capital of $2.1 billion to encourage industrialization.[17] Despite its low priority, the GCC has also registered considerable progress in social cooperation.

Structure and Leadership

The structural characteristics of the GCC are outlined in its charter, promulgated on 25 May 1981. The GCC possesses a three-tiered organizational structure consisting of (1) the Supreme Council, (2) the Ministerial Council, and (3) the General Secretariat (See Table 3).

The Supreme Council is GCC's highest authority, consisting of the heads of its member states. The council's presidency rotates among the six rulers in alphabetical order. Any member state has the right to call a council meeting as long as the call is seconded by at least one other member. In summary form, the functions of the Supreme Council are as follows:

1. To establish GCC's general policies and guidelines

2. To review recommendations, reports, and studies submitted by the Ministerial Council and the secretary-general

3. To establish policies to define GCC's relations with outside powers and international organizations

4. To approve GCC's internal rules and regulations and amendments to its charter

5. To approve GCC's budget and appoint its secretary-general[18]

Below the Supreme Council is the Ministerial Council, consisting of the foreign ministers of the member states. It meets once every two months, in addition to special meetings when requested by at least two member states. The functions of the Ministerial Council include:

1. Proposing policies to promote cooperation and coordination among member states

Table 3.

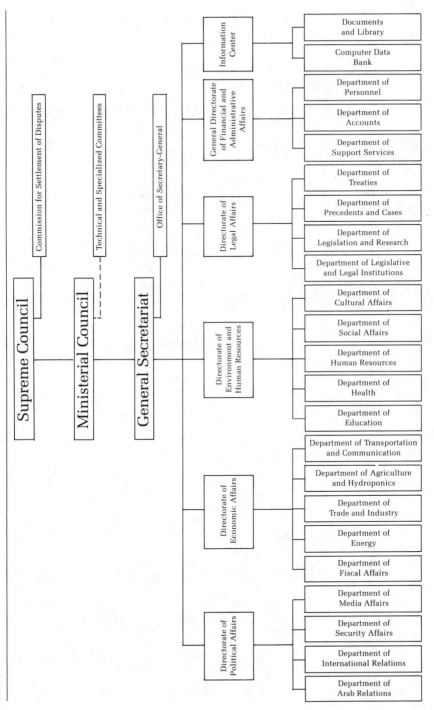

The organizational chart shows the following hierarchy:

Supreme Council
- Commission for Settlement of Disputes

Ministerial Council
- Technical and Specialized Committees

General Secretariat
- Office of Secretary-General

Directorates under General Secretariat:

Information Center
- Documents and Library
- Computer Data Bank

General Directorate of Financial and Administrative Affairs
- Department of Personnel
- Department of Accounts
- Department of Support Services

Directorate of Legal Affairs
- Department of Treaties
- Department of Precedents and Cases
- Department of Legislation and Research
- Department of Legislative and Legal Institutions

Directorate of Environment and Human Resources
- Department of Cultural Affairs
- Department of Social Affairs
- Department of Human Resources
- Department of Health
- Department of Education

Directorate of Economic Affairs
- Department of Transportation and Communication
- Department of Agriculture and Hydroponics
- Department of Trade and Industry
- Department of Energy
- Department of Fiscal Affairs

Directorate of Political Affairs
- Department of Media Affairs
- Department of Security Affairs
- Department of International Relations
- Department of Arab Relations

2. Encouraging and developing existing activities among member states

3. Stimulating cooperation among private sectors of the member states and the free flow of nationals across boundaries

4. Approving rules of procedures for the Ministerial Council and the General Secretariat

5. Arranging the meetings and agenda of the Supreme Council

6. Reviewing periodic reports on administrative and budgetary matters prepared by the secretary-general and submitting the appropriate recommendations to the Supreme Council[19]

The daily work of the GCC is conducted by the General Secretariat headed by a secretary-general. The latter oversees six directorates: Political Affairs, Economic Affairs, Environment and Human Resources, Legal Affairs, Financial and Adminstrative Affairs, and an Information Center. These directorates supervise twenty-three departments listed in Table 3. The General Secretariat's functions include:

1. Preparing studies on cooperation and coordination among member states and on their programs for integration

2. Preparing periodic reports on GCC's activities

3. Monitoring the implementation by member states of the resolutions and recommendations of the Supreme Council and Ministerial Council

4. Preparing reports and studies called for by the Supreme Council and Ministerial Council

5. Preparing budgets and accounts of the GCC and draft administrative and finance regulations[20]

The secretary-general is appointed by the Supreme Council for a three-year period. He must be a subject of one of the member states and is directly responsible for the General Secretariat's activities.

Rules of Procedure

The twenty-two-article charter is supplemented by rules of procedure designed to govern the operations of GCC's central organs. Under these rules, the Supreme Council must hold one summit meeting each year; at least two-thirds of the member states must attend to make the session valid. Thus, if four members are present, their decisions are considered binding on the others. The Supreme Council's resolutions on substantive matters must be carried by unanimous agreement of the member states present and voting; procedural resolutions require a majority vote.

At the present stage of its evolution, the GCC is still groping for an organizational and political identity. Its central organs are not fully operational, and the existing patterns of interstate relations are likely to keep the organization in flux. Indeed, GCC's present structure reflects the intentions of its founders rather than the optimistic pronouncements designed for popular consumption. With the possible exception of Saudi Arabia, the founding rulers did not wish to establish a federal or even a confederal union, but rather a loose framework for cooperation to strengthen their respective power and influence.

Consequently, in structural and operational terms, there is little to suggest a concerted move toward tighter forms of unity. The charter's stated aim of achieving a "confederal union" has not yet been realized despite recent progress toward the objective prompted by internal and external threats. The requirement of unanimity in the charter on all substantive matters brought to the Supreme Council and the Ministerial Council makes them subject to mutual veto, thereby producing *immobilisme* in the GCC's two top organs. This has been responsible for two modalities of GCC practice: consensus and incrementalism. The quest for unanimity by the six members prompts them to seek consensus through incremental adjustments in their positions.[21] This has resulted in slow progress through lengthy negotiations followed by expressions of optimism and solidarity.

GCC Elites: Composition and Decision Making

The GCC elite include three levels of officials: the six rulers of the Supreme Council, the six foreign ministers of the Ministerial Council and the Secretariat's top bureaucrats. The six rulers of the Supreme Council are GCC's supreme decisional body. These include King Fahd (Saudi Arabia), 'Isa Al Khalifah (Bahrain), Jabir Ahmad Al Sabah (Kuwait), Zayid Al Nahayyan (UAE), Sultan Qabus (Oman) and Khalifah Al Thani (Qatar). Collectively, they present a relatively homogeneous profile. All have had a modest education of the traditional Islamic type except Sultan Qabus, who briefly attended Sandhurst. In age the six rulers are mostly in their fifties and early sixties. All served in ministerial positions or were crown princes. In political orientation the group displays various degrees of conservatism and traditionalism; only in Kuwait and UAE do the rulers practice extensive *shura* (consultation), although Saudi Arabia and Bahrain have begun to institute procedures for greater popular participation. The rulers are not known to have significant familiarity with foreign languages except Qabus who knows English.[22]

The interpersonal relations of the six rulers are not always as harmonious as reflected in their statements after each summit conference. These relationships are determined by traditional rivalries, family and border disputes, personal conflicts, and divergent state interests and foreign policies. For example, there has been considerable coolness between the ruling families of Qatar and UAE and Qatar and Bahrain mainly because of territorial disputes. Yet both Qatar and Bahrain have forged close bilateral relationships with the Saudis.

The second level of GCC's elite structure consists of the six foreign ministers of the Ministerial Council. The collective profile of the foreign ministers reflects a degree of homogeneity. Most of these men are in their forties; they are better educated than the rulers, with several holding college degrees.

Except for the foreign ministers of the UAE and Oman, the rest are members of the ruling families. All have varying degrees of familiarity with English. Sa'ud al-Faysal of Saudi Arabia stands out as the most highly educated foreign minister with a graduate degree in political science. As a group, the Ministerial Council plays an important advisory role to the six rulers.

General Secretariat

Any future move by the member states toward a tighter confederal or federal union is likely to result in the strengthening of GCC's Secretariat and its leadership. Under the present arrangement, however, the Secretariat remains essentially an administrative organ that engages in planning, coordination, evaluation, and follow-up. Furthermore, the Secretariat is the hub of the complex and tortuous process of interstate negotiation, consensus building, and conflict management—a role in which it has demonstrated considerable effectiveness.

The Secretariat is headquartered in Riyadh in deference to Saudi Arabia's central role in the GCC. As secretary-general, 'Abd Allah Yusuf Bisharah heads a staff of three hundred, mostly consisting of technocratic and diplomatic personnel. In the recruitment of its staff, the Secretariat does not maintain a quota system, although it strives to achieve some degree of representativeness from all member states. Its present composition, however, does not appear to be fully representative. Omani officials are concentrated in the higher ranks because of the sultanate's practice of nominating many high-ranking officials to serve in the Secretariat. The middle and lower levels are mostly occupied by Bahraini and Saudi bureaucrats. Significantly, there is a low level of representation from Kuwait, Qatar, and the UAE. In view of the attractive business and other opportunities available in these countries for their nationals, it has been difficult to recruit civil servants from them to serve the GCC in Riyadh's harsh climate. This factor is likely to detract from the integrative and representational potential of the Secretariat.

Two additional factors have impeded the work of the Secretariat. The staff has been criticized as being too large; in fact, it appears to be "bottom heavy" as many top positions have gone unfilled. Secretary-General Bisharah is seconded by two assistant secretaries: Ibrahim al-Subhi of Oman, in charge of the Directorate of Political Affairs, and Dr. 'Abd Allah al-Quwayz of Saudi Arabia, in charge of the Directorate of Economic Affairs. The staffing process has not been completed; most appointees are college graduates.[23]

The moving force of the Secretariat is 'Abd Allah Bisharah, an activist secretary-general by any standard. A Kuwaiti national, Bisharah is placed at the confluence of opposing demands and pressures from the six member states. As a skillful diplomat of UN fame, Bisharah has manifested substantial skill as negotiator, administrator, and master of compromise. Moreover, Bisharah has moderated to some degree his outspoken UN style to make himself more compatible with GCC's conservative and slow-paced milieu. However, he has succeeded in providing dynamic leadership as initiator of programs despite periodic public and private criticism of his actions and statements.

Thus far, the member states have been reluctant to sacrifice enough of their individual interests and sovereignty to forge a tighter regional entity. The persistence of external challenges and internal threats, however, may push the GCC toward a more integrated confederal union.

U.S. POLICY TOWARD THE GULF

As a superpower, the United States has shown increasing concern for the Gulf area since World War II. The British decision to withdraw from east of Suez in 1968 and the growing economic importance of the area to the West during the 1970s were instrumental in heightening U.S. interest in the Gulf's security. In view of its wide-ranging security commitments extending from Vietnam to Europe, the United States during the 1960s was content to make Iran its surrogate policeman of the Gulf. This required strengthening the shah's regime both internally and externally, which enabled him to declare the Gulf an Iranian sphere of influence.[24]

The fall of the Iranian monarchy not only created a vacuum in the Gulf but also brought to power the Islamic Republic, which has dedicated itself to excluding U.S. interests from the region. In response, President Carter created the Rapid Deployment Force (RDF) to defend the Gulf countries and ensure the continued flow of oil to the West. The Soviet invasion of Afghanistan in December 1979 added another threat-dimension necessitating the establishment of the RDF.

The basic aims of U.S. security policy in the Gulf are (1) to sustain pro-American regimes against external and internal enemies, (2) to secure the production and export of oil, and (3) to prevent the expansion of Soviet influence and to checkmate any Soviet move into the region. In order to achieve these objectives, the Reagan administration has taken new initiatives in expanding U.S. security ties with key Gulf states and reconstituting the RDF as the Central Command to increase its military capabilities. In addition to the agreement with Bahrain to permit the U.S. Navy to use port facilities, the United States has concluded an accord with Oman to use Salalah and Masirah as staging bases. Simultaneously, the United States has sought to encourage GCC's efforts to develop its own rapid deployment force.

However, the concerted attempts of the Reagan administration to establish military bases on the territories of the GCC countries have been unsuccessful, except in Oman. Despite its manifest vulnerability vis-à-vis Iran, Kuwait has persisted in opposing a substantial U.S. presence in the Gulf. Similarly, Saudi Arabia has refused to permit the stationing of large U.S. forces in the kingdom; it appears to prefer to have American forces in Oman as a last resort in case of an emergency. The reluctance of most GCC states to allow a significant U.S. military presence is prompted by several reasons. In view of the special nature of the U.S.-Israeli relationship, many Gulf leaders remain suspicious of American intentions in the Gulf. More important, an American military presence is anathema to both Islamic fundamentalists and Arab nationalists. Thus, close military ties with the United States are bound to increase the domestic vulnerability of the Gulf Arab rulers.[25]

Finally, most GCC states fear that a large U.S. Gulf presence may provoke a Soviet response. This could come in the form of assistance to subversive groups and/or an expansion of the Soviet military presence in the Marxist People's Democratic Republic of Yemen. An expanded U.S. role in the Gulf could also trigger the intensification of Iranian-supported subversion and terrorism in GCC countries.

For the time being, the GCC countries have managed to contain Iran's subversive and propagandistic efforts to destabilize the ruling monarchies. In GCC's view, the first priority is to settle the Iran-Iraq war—a task that remains beyond the capabilities of the United States. Despite its tilt toward Iraq, the United States has shown some concern that a weakened Iran may turn to the Soviet Union for military support. Yet the United States and its West European allies remain the ultimate protectors of the GCC countries. This realization has produced a noticeable decline in anti-American statements in the Gulf media. In June 1984, the success of Saudi jet fighters guided by AWACS in downing an intruding Iranian F-4 jet may have strengthened U.S. credibility in the region. In all likelihood, U.S. military cooperation with the Gulf Arab states will intensify despite the preference of some GCC members for a nonaligned stance in foreign policy.

NOTES

1. For detailed information and data on the Gulf, see Arthur S. Banks, ed., *Political Handbook of the World* (New York: McGraw Hill, 1983); Lawrence Ziring, *The Middle East Political Dictionary* (Santa Barbara, Calif.: ABC-CLIO Information Services, 1984); Alvin J. Cottrell, ed., *The Persian Gulf States* (Baltimore: Johns Hopkins University Press, 1980).

2. R. Hrair Dekmejian, "Prospects for the Growth and Influence of the Gulf Cooperation Council" (Washington D.C.: Unpublished DOD Report, 1983), 60–68, 119, 121.

3. James A. Bill, "Islam, Politics and Shi'ism in the Gulf," *Middle East Insight* 3, no. 3 (Jan.-Feb. 1984): 7.

4. R. Hrair Dekmejian, *Islam in Revolution* (Syracuse, N.Y.: Syracuse University Press, 1985), 149–57.

5. Ibid., 129–36.

6. Ibid., 133–36.

7. Ibid., 144–45.

8. *Arabia*, April 1984.

9. Dekmejian, *Islam in Revolution*, 6–7, 25–31.

10. Ibid., 141–44.

11. Abdallah Fahd al-Nafisi, *Majlis al-Ta'awun al Khaliji* (The Gulf Cooperation Council) (London: Ta-Ha Publishers, 1982), 46–52.

12. On the war, see Stephen R. Grummon, *The Iran-Iraq War: Islam Embattled* (New York: Praeger, 1983).

13. Dekmejian, "Prospects," 1.

14. *Digest: Gulf Cooperation Council* (Kuwait News Agency) (Dec. 1982): 18–19.

15. *al-Dustur*, 10 Nov. 1983.

16. *FBIS*, 13 Oct. 1982; 17 Jan. 1983; 23 Feb. 1983.

17. *Arab Economist*, Mar. 1982, 36–37.

18. *Cooperation Council for the Arab States of the Gulf* (London: Gulf Information and Research Center, 1983).

19. Ibid.

20. Ibid.

21. Dekmejian, "Prospects," 41–42.

22. Ibid., 43.

23. Ibid., 45–46.

24. On the U.S. role, see Emile A. Nakhleh, *The Persian Gulf and American Policy* (New York: 1983).

25. For domestic criticism of the United States, see Muhammad Rumaihi, *The Gulf Cooperation Council: New Deal in the Gulf* (Lansing, Mich.: 1982), 11–15; *al-Mujtama'*, 12 Jan. 1982, 4; 21 Dec. 1982, 4–5; Nafisi, *Majlis*, pp. 32–58.

ADDITIONAL READINGS

Books

Amirsadeghi, Hossein, ed. *The Security of the Persian Gulf*. London: Croom Helm, 1981.

Bill, James A. "Islam, Politics and Shi'ism in the Gulf." *Middle East Insight* 3, no. 3 (Jan./Feb. 1984).

Chubin, Shahram. *Security in the Persian Gulf: The Role of Outside Powers*. London: International Institute for Strategic Studies, 1982.

Chubin, Shahram, ed. *Security in the Persian Gulf: Domestic Political Factors*. London: International Institute for Strategic Studies, 1982.

Farid, Abdel Majid, ed. *Oil and Security in the Arabian Gulf*. London: Croom Helm, 1981.

Helms, Christine Moss. *Iraq—Eastern Flank of the Arab World.* Washington, D.C.: Brookings Institution, 1984.

Litwak, Robert. *Security in the Persian Gulf: Sources of Inter-state Conflict.* London: International Institute for Strategic Studies, 1981.

Peterson, J.E. *The Politics of Middle Eastern Oil.* Washington, D.C.: Middle East Institute, 1983.

Piscatori, James P., ed. *Islam in the Political Process.* Cambridge: Cambridge University Press, 1984.

Plascov, Avi. *Security in the Persian Gulf: Modernization, Political Development and Stability.* London: International Institute for Strategic Studies, 1982.

Quandt, William B. *Saudi Arabia in the 1980s.* Washington, D.C.: Brookings Institution, 1981.

Tripp, Charles, ed. *Regional Security in the Middle East.* New York: St. Martin's Press, 1984.

Documents

Foreign Broadcast Information Service, 1981–84.
Digest: Gulf Cooperation Council. Kuwait News Agency, Dec. 1982.

The Military Balance 1984–85. London: International Institute for Strategic Studies, 1984.

Strategic Survey 1982–83, London: International Institute for Strategic Studies, 1983.

Strategic Survey 1983–84. London: International Institute for Strategic Studies, 1984.

Newspapers/Periodicals

al-Anba'

al-Dustur

al-Mujtama'

Arabia

Arab Economist

Israel After Its 1984 Elections

Don Peretz

Israel's eleventh Knesset (parliament) election in July 1984 brought to a head several of the critical problems facing the nation. It also underscored the deep divisions within Israeli society over the purposes and goals of Zionism, the national ideology, and over fundamental values. These rifts were manifest in approaches of the twenty-six political parties or factions that ran for the Knesset toward the economic crisis, the continuing occupation of Lebanon, and foreign policy, as well as in attitudes toward Arab-Jewish relations within Israel and relations between Oriental Jews[1] (from Asia and Africa) and Ashkenazis (from Europe and America).

BACKGROUND

Until the victory of Menachem Begin's Likud[2] bloc in 1977, national goals and the policies devised to attain them had been dominated by the Labor Zionists,[3] who planted the roots of the Jewish Yishuv (community) early in the century and who led the country to independence in 1948. Labor's ideology was a mixture of Jewish nationalism (Zionism) and socialism of the social democratic variety, with overtones emphasizing Jewish labor on Jewish land. Initially Labor Zionism was strongly land oriented—that is, it sought to establish Jewish agriculture as the economic and social base for national development. But as the Jewish population multiplied (by the 1980s, six times greater than 1948) and as world economic conditions changed, industry rapidly outpaced farming.

By 1977, the Labor Zionist establishment had become a vast multifaceted bureaucracy whose influence and activities reached into nearly all aspects of Israeli life from the army to banking, from publishing to food production. Often it seemed that bureaucracy for its own sake outweighed the ideas and ideals of Labor Zionism; in any case, many had become outmoded or lost as Israel sought to modernize by expanding the industrial and other nonagricultural components of the economy. Bureaucratization was accompanied by corruption and cronyism, and by increased public awareness that the Labor establishment was no longer the idealistic and idealized generation that had led the country to independence. Furthermore, Labor was held accountable for the severe losses sustained during the 1973 war, which, although a military victory, was a political and economic setback. Disenchantment by the electorate toppled the Labor establishment for the first time in 1977. However, the election was less a victory for Likud, the principal opposition bloc, than a defeat for Labor. Most voters who abandoned Labor cast their ballots for a new political faction, the Democratic Movement for Change (DMC)[4] rather than for Likud. Although Labor lost 19 of its 51 Knesset seats in 1977, Likud gained only 4. The DMC emerged as the third largest party with 15 of the Knesset's 120 seats representing voters who opposed the continued domination of Labor but were reluctant to vote for the right-of-center Likud.

As in all Israeli elections, no party or bloc won a majority; therefore it was necessary for Likud, with the largest number of seats (43) to form a coalition government with the National Religious party (NRP). After weeks of bargaining, the DMC also joined the coalition government, although many of its MKs felt uncomfortable in so close an association with Likud and the NRP. Within a few months, the DMC broke into factions, and by the tenth election in 1981 it had disappeared from the political scene.

Orthodox relations proved to be far more compatible with Likud than with Labor, especially after 1967. Israel's acquisition of the West Bank (called Judea and Samaria by Jewish nationalists) during the 1967 war sparked a nationalist revival among many Orthodox Jews who regarded the new territory as an integral part of Israel's holy patrimony, not to be surrendered under any circumstances. This attachment to territory gave the Orthodox parties, especially the NRP, largest in the religious bloc,[5] a close ideological tie with Likud.

Territorial Zionism, the aspiration to unify the historical land of Israel within the borders of the Jewish state, is the glue that has held Likud together. Likud was formed in 1973 from several factions that opposed territorial concessions for peace. Its components perceived the Labor government as overaccommodating in making compromises for a settlement with the Arab states.

The main component in the Likud bloc is the Herut party established by Menachem Begin in 1948. Begin was a close disciple of Vladimir Jabotinsky, founder of Revisionist Zionism early in the 1930s. Until 1977, Revisionism was the principal opposition ideology within the Zionist movement, regarded by Labor Zionism as reactionary, antiunion, and right wing.

The ideological rift between Begin and the Labor mainstream in the Yishuv was deep and bitter. Until the late 1960s when Herut joined the Liberal Zionists to form a common parliamentary bloc,[6] Begin and the Revisionists were regarded by the Labor establishment as political outcasts, even, according to some in the Labor movement, as fascists. Only after a wall-to-wall coalition government was formed on the eve of the 1967 war, which included Begin as a minister without portfolio, was Herut legitimized in the eyes of many staunch Laborites. (Begin left the coalition government in 1970 over disagreement with Prime Minister Golda Meir about possibilities of territorial concessions for peace).[7]

Likud also opposed Labor's economic and social orientation. It promised to diminish the power and influence of the Labor-dominated Histadrut

(Labor Federation), which was perceived as a behemoth that was stifling free enterprise and a market economy. In the campaign leading to his 1977 victory, Begin also promised to diminish the number of employees in the public sector, to cut inflation in half (to 15 percent) within a year, to reduce the adverse balance of trade, and to end government interference with the economic processes. An indication of Likud's economic and social orientation was Begin's invitation to the conservative economist Milton Friedman, of the University of Chicago, to become an Israeli government adviser.[8]

Few of these promises were realized by the tenth Knesset election in June 1981. Instead, inflation had increased to over 100 percent, the Histadrut was as powerful as ever, there were more public employees than in 1977, the national debt had grown, and the balance of payments was more unbalanced than before Begin's first victory. Public opinion polls before the election indicated that Labor would return to office and that economic issues were more important than others.

But this election too was a surprise. Begin's victory by one Knesset seat and less than 1 percent of the vote gave him another three years as prime minister (Likud received 37.11 percent of the vote and forty-eight seats; Labor, 36.57 percent and forty-seven seats).[9]

Two factors seemed to account for the unexpected Likud victory. One was Begin's charisma, the other, a continuing shift in Oriental Jewish voting patterns. During the 1981 campaign Begin emerged as the dominant political personality, with a fiery, aggressive, highly rhetorical style. None of the other political parties could compete with his oratory. In contrast, Shimon Peres, leader of the opposition Labor Alignment, was perceived as a colorless figure with no mass appeal. Begin's strong rhetoric on foreign policy appealed to a mood prevailing in Israel after the euphoria of the 1979 peace treaty with Egypt wore off. On one hand, Begin acquired a reputation as the man of peace, a Nobel Prize winner for his accord with Sadat. On the other hand, he demonstrated Israel's power and his own contempt for world opinion through acts that included the June 1981 bombing attack on and destruction of Iraq's nuclear reactor, annexation of Jerusalem and the Golan Heights, and personal insults to statesmen including West German chancellor Helmut Schmidt and French president Valéry Giscard d'Estaing. These demonstrations of Israeli vigor attracted many voters, especially in the Oriental Jewish community.

THE ORIENTAL FACTOR

Oriental Jews are not a single homogeneous community. Their diversity is as great as that in the world of Islam. In Israel, they have come from more than a score of North African and Asian countries, from Morocco to Afghanistan. Their first immigration into Israel was from Yemen before the state was established. After 1948, additional migrations came from Yemen, Iraq, Syria, Turkey, Egypt, Morocco, and other countries. The 1979 revolution in Iran caused thousands of Jews to emigrate from the new Islamic republic.[10]

The Oriental Jews are, rather than a community, a collection of communities with diverse languages and widely different cultures, attitudes toward life, and world perspectives. In fact, so great is their diversity that Orientals are probably more disparate than the Ashkenazis. Among the Orientals can be found rich and poor, highly educated and illiterate, some who were high government officials in their native lands and others who were outcasts. The majority who immigrated to Israel after 1948 reflected the cultural, social, and economic conditions prevailing in the societies of their origins.

What distinguished Orientals from Ashkenazis as a collective was the extent of their integration into the mainstream of Israeli society. By the time of mass Oriental immigration during the 1950s and 1960s, the great majority of pre- and postwar Ashkenazi immigrants was well on the way to integration. The earlier European immigrants were already housed; they held jobs, were members of the Histadrut, and had acquired a standing in Israeli society. Most Israeli leaders were Ashkenazi; they included cabinet and Knesset members, high army officers, Jewish Agency executives, and top figures in business, commercial, and cultural affairs. It was they who established the patterns of government bureaucracy and administration, the cultural and esthetic styles, and the values of the new state. As a result, Israelis perceived themselves, and were perceived by most of the rest of the world, as a "Western" nation rather than an integral part of the Middle East.[11]

Because of their late arrival and relative unfamiliarity with the Western values, techniques, and technology of the Yishuv, the Orientals often found only the least desirable occupations and were the poorest paid, the most deprived socially, and the least powerful politically. Until 1967, when Israel began to hire large numbers of Arab laborers from the West Bank and Gaza, the Orientals provided much of the work force at the bottom of the social scale: as hired hands in agriculture and construction, as menials in services such as restaurants and garages, as office, hospital, and household workers. Differences between Orientals and Ashkenazis were reflected by the gap in social and economic conditions. Orientals had considerably lower incomes with larger numbers living in poverty; their educational attainment was less. Moreover, some 90 percent of Jewish prison inmates still are Orientals.

Until the late 1960s most Oriental voters were coopted by the Labor bloc; the remainder of their ballots was divided between Likud and the NRP. Ben Gurion was the charismatic leader who aroused their enthusiasm. Attempts to organize the Orientals as a separate ethnic political bloc were largely unsuccessful until the 1981 elections. However, failure to organize significant Oriental political factions concealed the fact that growing numbers of Oriental Jews were becoming disenchanted with the Labor establishment. Furthermore, by the late 1970s, the Oriental Jewish population had increased from a minority of 25 percent when Israel was established to over 50 percent.

In the seventh Knesset election during 1969, Labor still captured the majority of Oriental votes, while Likud gained less than a third.[12] By 1973, Labor began to lag behind Likud with only 39 percent to Likud's 43 percent. The gap between Labor and Likud continued to grow until Labor was able to gain only a quarter of the Oriental vote, while Likud received 60 percent in 1981.[13]

Oriental Jews were now demanding more rapid economic improvement, better housing, and greater representation in and influence on national political decisions and policymaking. Although much of the Oriental population was upwardly mobile, with many more graduating from high school and university and becoming leaders of local political parties, mayors and municipal council members, and high-ranking police and army officers, the progress was not fast enough for them. Their growing impatience erupted into an almost violent hostility to the Labor establishment, especially during the 1981 election. Although Labor had been out of power since 1977, it was still perceived as the party of "status," representing the Jewish elite of Western European origin. Labor's attempts to improve economic and social conditions of those at the bottom of society and the increase of Orientals on the Labor electoral list were regarded, at best as paternalism, at worst as shrewd electioneering. With Ben Gurion, former father figure and fiery-tongued prophet, gone, Begin appeared as the new charismatic who would put the Laborites in their place and redeem Oriental honor.[14]

Much of the Israeli media labeled the 1981 election an "Oriental Revolt" because of the animosity to Ashkenazis that surfaced during the campaign. By 1981, Likud's constituency was heavily Oriental, young, religious, and blue collar. Ironically, the Labor Alignment, despite its socialist roots, represented the better educated white-collar workers of middle and upper income, most of them middle-aged and older Ashkenazis.[15]

These factors were fully exploited by Likud campaigners, especially Begin, who made political capital of the ethnic factor. There were frequent insinuations by Likud of Labor's discrimination against Orientals. One result was that the ethnic factor shook the whole political structure, bringing havoc to the third largest party, the NRP. Disagreements between its Oriental and Ashkenazi leaders over the electoral list finally split the NRP as Orientals departed to form a new religious faction called Tami, the Movement for Israel's Tradition. Tami greatly diminished the power of the NRP, which lost half of its twelve Knesset seats in 1981. The new religious party established itself as a political force, winning three seats of its own in the election.

Ethnicity remained a dominant theme in the election for Israel's eleventh Knesset during July 1984, but was less salient than in 1981. Although the economic and social gap between Orientals and Ashkenazis was closing and most parties now included a larger number of Orientals in "safe" positions on their electoral lists, ethnic voting patterns persisted. Likud captured a slightly larger number of Oriental votes than in 1981, and Labor remained the home of Westerns, with even fewer Oriental votes than in previous elections. Oriental voters still resented what appeared to them the superior or patronizing attitudes of the old Labor elites and their allies in the kibbutzim (collective settlements). It was Likud that was given credit for the increasing numbers of Orientals who were middle class and were entering the professions and technical occupations in large numbers.

Differences in income shrank from 35 percent during the 1960s to 19 percent by the early 1980s; possession of household goods among Orientals doubled during this period. Although the Oriental birthrate remained higher, 3.6 to 2.8 for the Ashkenazis, smaller families facilitated increasingly rapid upward economic mobility, greater educational opportunity and, consequently, social integration into the mainstream of Israeli life.[16] This was evident in the climb to political power of influential Orientals such as David Levi, an immigrant laborer from Morocco, who was Likud's second or third leading candidate for party leader and one of its inner cabinet members; in the appointment by Begin of Moshe Levi, son of Iraqi immigrants, as Israel's first Oriental chief of staff; and by the election to the Knesset of the largest number of Oriental MKs. They increased from twenty-two in the ninth Knesset to twenty-seven in the tenth and thirty-one in the eleventh. Of these, ten each were from the Labor Alignment and Likud; the others were scattered among six smaller factions.[17]

The 1981 "Oriental Revolt" spread in 1984 to the ultra-Orthodox camp, seen in the vote for the new Shas (Sephardi Torah Guardians) party. Whereas Tami was created by Oriental disaffection with the NRP, Shas was an expression of dissent within Aguda Israel, the ultra-Orthodox wing of the religious bloc. In 1984, many Orientals who voted for Tami during the previous election shifted to Shas or to other smaller parties because of disappointment with Tami. Its leader and founder Aharon Abuhatzeira, scion of Moroccan rabbinical notables, was convicted for misuse of public funds and forced to leave his cabinet post; and the party seemed to become transformed into a semisecular faction emphasizing social reforms for Orientals rather than Orthodox religious tradition. Shas members shunned Tami because, according to its leader, Rabbi Yitzhak Peretz, Tami lacked "rabbinical guidance." Even though Shas was an offshoot of Aguda Israel, it obtained spiritual guidance from a former Sephardi chief rabbi rather than from the Aguda Rabbinical Council of Torah Sages, a body distinct from Israel's officially recognized Chief Rabbinate.[18] Shas surpassed all expectations of its potential strength, winning four Knesset seats, as many as the once powerful NRP and twice as many as its Aguda Israel parent.

Although the Orthodox bloc as a whole maintained its collective strength with thirteen Knesset seats (NRP, four; Shas, four; Aguda Israel, two; Morasha, two; Tami, one), it was fragmented into five factions instead of the traditional two, NRP and Aguda Israel. The splits were both ideological and intrapersonal, as well as ethnic. Morasha, one of the new Orthodox factions, was formed from a splinter of the NRP and of Aguda Israel Workers demanding a more activist settlement policy in the occupied territories.

THE 1984 CAMPAIGN

A major difference between the 1981 and 1984 elections was Begin's absence from the hustings. After resigning from the prime ministry in September 1983, Begin withdrew from all political activity. He not only refused to continue as leader of Herut, but kept his name from the Likud electoral list and refused to endorse the party or any of its candidates. Begin's precipitous withdrawal was believed to be caused by political as well as personal disappointments. The 1982 invasion and war in Lebanon resulted in casualties far higher than anticipated and seemed to be a morass from which the Likud government found it hard to exit.[19] The war divided Israeli public opinion as it had never before been divided during a combat operation, and some held Begin accountable for the high casualties and unforeseen dire consequences. Many believed that Begin fell into depression over these events. The resulting infighting within Begin's own Herut movement added to his disillusionment with many of his followers. Additionally, Begin was depressed by the death of his wife several months before the election and by deterioration of his health following his wife's demise.

Even after Begin's retreat there were reports in the press of some not-so-well-informed voters who believed that they were casting their ballots for the prime minister when they voted Likud. But, by election time, they were few. Begin's disappearance from the campaign was perceived as a major factor in the characterization of the 1984 election as "the cleanest . . . . in the country's 36-year-old history" by Justice Gavriel Bach, chairman of the Central Election Committee, the official body designated to supervise the campaign.[20]

Begin's successor, Foreign Minister Yitzhak Shamir, was no more colorful or appealing to the electorate at large than his chief competitor, Labor's Shimon Peres. Neither could compete with Begin's former charisma; thus, the campaign was on a much lower key than in 1981. Only ex–defense minister Ariel (Arik) Sharon was deemed capable of replacing Begin's style, but his high-flown oratory and attempts to emulate Herut's founder failed to attract the following Begin commanded. Furthermore, Sharon had been in political limbo after Begin was censured by the official Kahan Commission for his activities in the Lebanon invasion.[21]

The 1984 campaign was such a contrast to 1981 that some observers called it Israel's dullest. There was almost no violence, much less bitter heckling of Labor candidates by Oriental Likud supporters, and few charges of disreputable activity by one side against the other. Both major parties, Likud and Labor, seemed to be making a conscious effort to avoid confrontation. One of Labor's important goals was to win votes of former Likud supporters who had become disillusioned with the party's economic program and the severe economic crisis. Labor candidates made few attacks on personalities and almost no mention of Begin. Instead, it charged Likud with administrative and bureaucratic mismanagement and economic failures. Labor called itself the "party of hope" in contrast to Likud's self-designation as the "national camp." Likud still attempted to instigate Oriental feelings of deprivation vis-à-vis Labor by portraying the Alignment as the party of privilege, corruption, and dovish extremism, hinting that security would be undermined by Labor schemes to pacify the Arabs with concessions including surrender of the West Bank and Gaza.

But Labor avoided Likud's trap by steering clear of definite policy statements about the occupied territories, other than to state that the Jewish settlements would not be removed, that no security positions would be abandoned, and that it opposed establishment of a Palestinian state in Israel-held territory or recognition of the PLO as a negotiating partner. Since it concentrated on statements about what it would not do, it was difficult to determine where Labor differed from Likud on these issues. There was some hint that greater efforts would be made to involve Jordan in the peace negotiations and that this might entail Jordanian government participation in West Bank autonomy discussions. As for the Golan Heights and Jerusalem, Labor had supported their annexation in the Knesset.

The Labor Alignment[22] was constrained from taking clear-cut positions on the West Bank and Gaza by the great diversity of opinion within its leadership and constituency. The Alignment represented a foreign policy spectrum from hawk to dove, from those whose desires about the future of the occupied territories were little different than Begin's to those who would give up all but Jerusalem in exchange for a satisfactory peace settlement. On most foreign policy issues Alignment positions were moderated or checked by Mapam, its left wing whose leaders were still motivated by the ideal of Arab-Jewish rapprochement and coexistence in former mandatory Palestine. Even the Labor party, the backbone of the Alignment, contained doves like Abba Eban who warned that Israel's acquisition of the West Bank and Gaza would be a demographic threat to the Jewish state.

One foreign policy area where Labor and Likud differed was Lebanon. Even though Labor supported the initial invasion during June 1982, it had since opposed many of Likud's follow-up policies. When it became clear that the invasion was to penetrate much farther north than the Litani River, the Alignment became restive. Many Labor MKs were highly critical of the Beirut siege, the pursuit of Palestinian forces into the North and the combat involvement with Syria. As casualties began to mount and public opinion segmented over the invasion, Labor became more openly critical, and during the campaign Peres promised that he would withdraw Israeli forces within six months after taking power. By election time in July 1984, even Likud promised to make "every effort" to leave Lebanon when Israel's security could be assured.

Economic Issues

Polls showed that voters were as concerned about bread-and-butter issues as they were about the continued occupation of Lebanon.[23] Labor linked the two, charging that continued occupation wasted over a million dollars a day. Voters indicated that they believed Likud's greatest shortcomings were its economic policies, or lack of them. The deteriorating economy and Likud's failures to keep its original 1977 campaign promises had led pollsters to predict that Begin would be defeated in 1981, a prediction that failed. But Begin was not running in 1984, and the economy was in tighter straits than ever before. Most economists believed that the country was on the verge of economic disaster. In the three years since 1981 inflation tripled, from 100 to more than 400 percent. As the election drew nearer, there were predictions that it would reach 800 percent by 1985.

Inflation was only an outward measure of the economic crisis and Likud's failure. Half the economy was still in the public sector, which contained 40 percent of the workers. During its seven years in office Likud sold off only eighteen minor state corporations in contrast to the previous two Labor governments, which had sold fifty-four large enterprises including the country's largest shipping company, Zim, and its major oil refineries in Haifa.[24] External debt increased to over $23 billion, and internal debt grew by $30 billion. The country's foreign reserves were rapidly being depleted below the red line set by economists at $3 billion.

The serious economic downturn began as a result of the billions spent during the 1973 war; it was intensified by the high costs of moving military bases from Sinai to the Negev and the loss of Egyptian oil fields, components of the 1979 Egyptian-Israeli peace treaty. Military expenditures shot upward again with the 1982 invasion of Lebanon. But military defense expenditures were only part of the reason for Israel's economic crisis.

The country also had to maintain a very high level of social services and a large public sector because of its commitment to Jewish immigration, one of the fundamental credos of Zionist ideology. It often took years for new immigrants to become economically self-sufficient. There were many newcomers in development towns who remained charges of the state or of the Jewish Agency, an arm of the World Zionist Organization responsible for promoting immigration.

State responsibility for attracting and integrating new immigrants contributed to establishment of one of the largest public-sector bureaucracies in the West. It also was a major factor in low worker productivity in many economic sectors. Although Israel could boast some of the most advanced establishments in electronics, the aircraft industry, and other high-tech fields, as well as high-quality agricultural exports, low worker productivity was a major problem. One analyst showed that the average Israeli worker received 47 percent of the American worker's salary, but produced only 31 percent as much. Whereas American wages comprised 44 percent of production costs, in Israel they were 66 percent.[25]

Most Israelis were protected against the ravages of inflation by institutional arrangements to which all political parties were committed. The powerful trade unions negotiated contracts that indexed wages and salaries, linking them to the constant rise in prices. Middle-class Israelis further protected their savings by placing them in dollar-linked accounts, by purchasing government and bank shares linked to the dollar, and by other financial schemes. Even these devices were no longer as successful as before because the gap between wages and inflation kept growing. However, working-class Israelis still benefited from government subsidization of many basic commodities including bread, milk, chicken, and other food items.

Huge amounts of foreign aid helped to avoid collapse. Foreign debt, although large, was not too pressing because most of it was owed to the U.S. government and to Western Jewish purchasers of Israel bonds. Only 23 percent was owed to private banks. Since the 1973 war, Israel was the largest recipient of American government economic and military assistance, averaging over $2 billion a year. Although bleak, the crisis was unlike that facing many Third World countries whose international debts threatened bankruptcy.[26]

While everyone talked about the economy, neither Likud nor Labor did much about it. On election eve both parties supported special legislation to protect citizens' savings accounts and to increase benefits for army veterans. These "election economic measures" resembled those sponsored by Likud before the 1981 election, when taxes were reduced on consumer durables such as television sets, private cars, and other sought-after import items. Some Likud MKs pressed their finance minister in 1984 for a drastic cut in the income tax, or even for its abolishment, but such blatant election economics were rejected.

By July it was evident that inflation was so out of control that indexation would no longer protect the average worker. Therefore Likud finance minister Yigal Cohen-Orgad now promised to slash all government expenditures, including defense and welfare, and to freeze wages at the 1982–83 level. Subsidies would also be cut and the tax system reformed.

Labor's economic platform was more an echo of Likud's than a challenge. Labor also promised to protect savings, to encourage foreign investment, to restore public confidence in the stock market, and to mobilize capital for "productive" enterprises. Lest it scare off defectors from Likud who it hoped would cast their ballots for Labor, the Alignment candidate for finance minister promised "evolutionary, not revolutionary" changes. It was indeed difficult to identify the Labor Alignment as socialist.

Although all parties agreed that massive budget cuts were essential, there were differences over where. Labor promised to save $1 million a day by withdrawing from Lebanon and another $1 million by suspending Jewish settlement on the West Bank. It also stated that it would halt "political expenditures," that is, payments to various types of educational and social welfare institutions affiliated with the Orthodox religious parties. All the promised cuts would diminish inflation to 85 percent within a couple of years, according to Labor's spokesmen.[27]

Election Results

Voter dissatisfaction with the performance of Likud on economic issues and recognition that Labor's program seemed like more of the same were probably the major reasons for election results demonstrating lack of confidence in both parties. In 1984 the voters elected a larger number of tiny factions than in any election since the second in 1951, and Labor and Likud lost together a total of ten seats. The loss was reflected in election of five more parties in the eleventh Knesset than in the tenth (ten parties in 1981, fifteen in 1984).

Likud was a bigger loser than Labor. It lost seven of its forty-eight seats; Labor lost only three of its forty seven. More than 2 million ballots were cast, about eighty-six thousand more than in 1981, but Likud received over fifty-seven thousand fewer votes in 1984. Labor, on the other hand, received fifteen thousand more. But Labor's lead over Likud by 3 percent (34.9 to 31.9 in 1984; in 1981: 36.47 to 37.11) was insufficient to form a new government.

Labor and Likud remained the dominant parties by far; the election wiped out any third large faction with which one or the other of the big two could form a working coalition. Up until 1981 the NRP emerged as the third faction to which the party with a plurality could turn when it required a coalition partner. Now fragmentation of the Orthodox bloc into five factions undermined its political clout even though its total strength remained approximately the same.

Political splintering of the Orthodox parties resulted in emergence of the militantly nationalist Tehiya party as number three, with five seats. Tehiya was formed during the late 1970s by former members of Begin's Herut who opposed his concessions to Egypt in the Camp David peace negotiations. They continued to oppose territorial concessions and were adamant supporters of unrestricted Jewish settlement in the West Bank. Many Tehiya supporters and some of its leaders were members of Gush Emunim (Bloc of the Faithful), a movement to Judaize the occupied territories.

Likud lost most of its votes to parties on the Right including Tehiya, Morasha, and Meir Kanane's Kach. These three represented a more militant version of the territorial Zionism espoused by Begin and his Herut party. Labor's losses were accounted for in part by increased representation of liberal and left-of-center factions including Shinui (Change—a remnant of the former DMC) and the Citizens' Rights Movement (CRM), a small coalition of former Labor dissidents and other independents. Labor also lost many of its Arab supporters, a shift that was evident in the surprising success of the new Progressive

List for Peace (PLP), which obtained two seats (1.8 percent of the votes) in its first run for the Knesset.

Overall, the Left was more successful than the center, the Right, and the religious bloc because parties to the left of Labor won an additional five seats. They included Shinui, three; CRM, three; PLP, two; and the Communist-backed Democratic Front for Peace and Equality (DFPE), four. The left-of-Labor factions further increased their strength after the election when Mapam with six seats left the Alignment to become part of the opposition and another MK deserted the Labor party to join the CRM. After the election Shinui merged in a Knesset bloc with the Labor party.

Another election surprise was the relatively poor showing of Ezer Weizman's Yahad (Together) party. In polls before the election, Weizman had obtained much more backing than indicated by the three seats (2.2 percent) that he won. Weizman, a former air force commander, defense minister, and leader of the Herut movement, now represented the liberal center—those willing to make concessions for peace and sacrifices to improve the economy. His platform, neither nationalist nor socialist, was closer to Labor's than to Likud's. The center was also represented by Yigal Hurvitz's Ometz (Effort), a one-man faction advocating drastic economic reforms. Hurvitz also had served in Begin's cabinet as a finance minister and was formerly an associate of Moshe Dayan and a Labor party man. After the election, both Yahad and Ometz with their four seats also realigned with the Labor party in the new coalition.

NATIONAL UNITY GOVERNMENT

The reduced strength of Labor and Likud, the disappearance of a strong third party, and the division of the Knesset's 120 seats among fifteen parties or factions made coalition building more difficult than before. After the election, it took nearly two months for the Labor party and Likud to realize that neither could form a government without the other. For weeks, each of the big two attempted to make deals with smaller factions, hoping it could rally enough support to form a new government. Labor was willing to negotiate with all but Meir Kahane's Kach, the DFPE, and the PLP; Likud worked on getting support from all but left-of-Labor factions. But neither could rally the sixty-one MKs required for an effective coalition. As the negotiations dragged on, the economy continued to deteriorate, inflation soared well over 400 percent, foreign reserves were running out at an alarming rate, and the casualties mounted in Lebanon. In desperation, Peres and Shamir finally agreed to form a National Unity Government (NUG).

Peres had initially spurned Shamir's offer for a NUG made during the last days of the election campaign when it became clear that Likud was about to suffer major losses. But weeks of unsuccessful attempts to form a Labor coalition changed his mind, and in September the two parties agreed on a novel arrangement. The idea of coalition was not itself novel. There had been a wall-to-wall coalition from 1967 to 1970 including Likud and most other main-line parties. The new NUG, however, included an agreement that Peres and Shamir would alternate as prime minister. During the first twenty-five months Peres would serve as prime minister and Shamir as foreign minister; during the second twenty-five months they would change places.

The NUG included seven other parties with a solid Knesset majority of almost ninety. Because it was necessary to create new cabinet posts to accommodate the nine coalition parties, the cabinet was enlarged to twenty-five, but an inner cabinet of five Labor and five Likud leaders was to make crucial decisions.

The coalition agreement devised by Labor and Likud showed how small the ideological gap between them had become despite campaign rhetoric. Likud was now forced to abandon many of its ambitious plans for extending Jewish settlement in the West Bank, and Labor called for drastic cuts in the amenities that made Israel a model welfare state.

The new government program emphasized withdrawal from Lebanon and continuation of the Camp David peace process with emphasis on resumption of talks on autonomy for the West Bank and Gaza. A special appeal was made to both Egypt and Jordan to join the peace negotiations. Further West Bank settlement was to be agreed on by both parties, and both underscored opposition to establishment of a Palestinian state in the occupied territories and negotiations with the PLO. After signing the coalition agreement, Peres and Shamir agreed to cut the number of new Jewish settlements to four or five rather than over two dozen planned by Likud. The unity agreement laid out the broad plans for austerity and cuts in the public sector that Likud had first proposed seven years before.[28]

A New Austerity

Peres proposed across-the-board cuts of about $1 billion in the $23 billion budget, but these were considered inadequate and there was pressure for cuts of at least $2 billion. A variety of fees were imposed on government services including education, which had been free, and on child allowances, medical care, and pensions. To control consumer expenditures on luxury items, a six-month ban was placed on fifty imports. The common man's pocket was hit by removal of government subsidies on basic foods, including frozen meat, cooking oil, and margarine, and on gasoline, heating oil, electricity, and water. An initial result was a 55 percent increase in prices. Despite efforts to soak up purchasing power, inflation continued at its unprecedented rate. According to Peres, it would take a year before Israelis could see the light at the end of the tunnel, and along the way inflation was likely to reach 1,000 percent or more.

To facilitate implementation of plans, Peres formed committees of government, employers, and the powerful Histadrut. After much bickering, a three-month freeze on prices, wages, and taxes was accepted. Peres was left with little room for maneuver because Israelis were already squeezed by the world's highest tax rates. Despite the high rates, the government's net income from taxes is lower than in other countries because of transfer payments, subsidies, and inflation. Another limitation is commitment of over 40 percent of the budget for repayment of debts and another 44 percent for the military (this represents 35 percent of the GNP).[29]

Shortly after announcing the economic program, Peres visited Washington to obtain increased American assistance. Israel had already received about $28 billion in U.S. aid since 1948. U.S. help, only $1 million in 1951, reached an all-time high of over $4 billion in 1979. The quantum leap resulted both from the 1973 war when the United States sent massive arms replacement to the embattled country and from U.S. promises to Israel related to the 1979 peace treaty.[30]

All members of the NUG agreed on the necessity to end Israel's occupation of southern Lebanon, but there were nuances of disagreement over the terms of withdrawal. Likud and its allies were reluctant to leave without binding assurances for Israel's future security. Although Peres found it impossible to keep his campaign promise to have Israel's forces out within six months, he succeeded in persuading his Likud colleagues to reverse their previous positions. Begin's government had asserted that Israeli troops would remain in Lebanon as long as Syrian forces were there. Now Syrian withdrawal was no longer a condition, provided it kept out of areas evacuated by Israel and prevented Palestinian attacks from Syrian bases.

Another about-face was the request for increased United Nations forces to replace the Israelis. In the past, Israel suspected the UN of bias and accused the Interim Force in Lebanon (UNIFIL) of hostile acts. But the NUG proposed that UNIFIL take over areas to be evacuated between the Awali and Litani rivers and that border regions south of the Litani be turned over to the South Lebanon Army (SLA). In negotiations that opened between Israeli and Lebanese military officers at the end of the year, Israel was insisting that UNIFIL and the SLA police the areas it would leave.

The SLA was headed by Antoine Lahud, a former Maronite general known for close ties with the deceased Maj. Sa'd Haddad, a deserter from the Lebanese army who had formed his own Israel-supported antigovernment militia in the south. Most of Haddad's forces were Maronite, although it also contained a small number of Shiites and he himself was Greek Orthodox. But Haddad had been so closely allied with Israel, from where he received arms, equipment, uniforms, military training, and so on, that the Shiite majority in South Lebanon regarded him and the successor SLA as renegades. Giving the SLA authority and responsibility for the Israel-Lebanon border would probably help diminish Palestinian penetration into Israel, but it would also alienate much of the Shiite population and several members of the Lebanese cabinet; therefore, no progress was made in the negotiations with Lebanon.

The West Bank

The ideological gap between Labor and Likud over the West Bank was negated by deep budget cuts, which made it impossible to implement Likud's grandiose schemes for integrating the region with Israel. The new government avoided specific commitments in the coalition agreement stating that "during the period of the unity government, no sovereignty, Israel or other, will be applied to Judea, Samaria and the Gaza District."[31]

Many in the Labor party, like ex-foreign minister Abba Eban, opposed further Jewish settlement and integration of the West Bank because addition of more than a million West Bank and Gaza Arabs to Israel's 650,000 Arab citizens would create a breeding ground for future ethnic tensions and undermine Israel's Jewish character. Zionism could succeed only if Palestine were partitioned betwen Jews and Arabs, argued Eban.

The ambiguity of Labor's position on the West Bank was demonstrated by its own policies between 1967 and 1977, when it laid the groundwork for the first Jewish settlements and initiated the integration process. Labor's defense minister at that time, Moshe Dayan, stated that the government would "create new facts" in the occupied areas, by establishing Jewish settlements in strategic areas, but avoid heavily populated Arab regions. Most of these new Jewish settlements were planted in the sparsely settled Jordan Valley. Later, when Gush Emunim set up illegal settlements close to Arab towns like Hebron, the Labor government was ambivalent. On the one hand it scolded Gush Emunim for going ahead without official sanction, but on the other, it refrained from taking action to remove the illegal settlements or to prevent additional ones.

The process of integration was stimulated by development of the West Bank road network and its union with Israel and by the linkage of the electricity grid, the water supply system, and agricultural production with those in Israel. Jewish commercial and business enterprises were not only permitted but encouraged with government loans and special legislation to obtain a foothold in the West Bank. Arab nationalist opposition was put down with severity by the military government, although Labor did permit local authorities to hold elections. However, attempts to create a political network of West Bank or Gaza Arab political leaders were banned.[32]

These integration efforts were greatly intensified and speeded up during the seven years of Likud administration between 1977 and 1984. Under Begin, the number of Jewish settlements was tripled, from thirty-six to over a hundred; the number of Jewish settlers increased from about five thousand to some thirty thousand (excluding former Jordanian Jerusalem, which was annexed). Likud removed all restrictions on Jewish settlement and development in the West Bank, discarding Labor's policy of limiting settlement to sparsely inhabited regions. Instead, Likud emphasized the right of all Jews to settle anywhere in the occupied territories and assisted those who moved into Arab cities like Hebron and Nablus. A new facet of Likud settlement policy was development of urban housing estates on the West Bank only minutes from such major Jewish centers as Jerusalem and Tel Aviv. Many settlers seized the opportunity to purchase this inexpensive housing since similar apartments in the Jewish cities were scarce and costly. Long-term plans of the Begin government called for ten-year expenditures of $1.5 billion and construction of new housing for ten thousand to fifteen thousand new settlers in the next decade.[33]

Under Likud, every effort was made to weed out Arab nationalist organization in the occupied territories. Because so many Arabs had voted for pro-PLO mayors in West Bank municipal and local elections under Labor, new elections were canceled. Nationalist sympathizers were removed from their posts and replaced with Israeli military government officers, and many well-known Arab officials were exiled. Within the West Bank and Gaza, severe measures were initiated to quell demonstrations in schools, universities, and refugee camps. The number of arrests and expulsions was increased, and curfews and other martial law measures were intensified. During 1982 unrest on the West Bank almost reached the point of rebellion; one reason for the invasion of Lebanon was to crush the PLO, perceived as instigator of West Bank unrest.

Many observers perceived Likud policies as an obstacle to the Middle East peace process; they were one cause for deterioration in relations with Egypt. After establishment of the NUG, U.S. secretary of state George Shultz encouraged Peres to "improve the quality of life" for West Bank Arabs. By the end of 1984, the NUG had initiated no bold new programs, but Peres hinted that private foreign investment would be permitted in Arab enterprises and that Israeli military officers in municipal posts might be replaced with Arab officials found acceptable to the NUG. In most cases, they would be notables known for sympathies with the Hashemite regime in Jordan.

JEWISH VIGILANTES

One reaction to growing Arab nationalist sentiment in the West Bank was organization of Jewish vigilante groups among the settlers. On the eve of the 1984 election, twenty-five Jews were charged by the Israeli police with organizing terrorist activity. They were accused of a conspiracy to blow up mosques on the Temple Mount in Jerusalem, of attempting to murder West Bank Arab nationalist mayors, of planting bombs in five Arab-owned buses, and of an attack on the Hebron Islamic College in which three students were killed. Many of the twenty-five were leaders of West Bank settler movements; some were Israeli army officers.

The accused found few supporters in the Hebrew press or among the political leadership, although several officials of nationalist factions including Tehiya compared their activity to the Jewish underground that fought the British before independence. One Tehiya leader asserted that reprehensible as their acts were, the twenty-five saved Jewish lives by aborting Arab terrorist plans. On the other hand, several Likud and Gush Emunim members castigated the activities of the accused for the blemish they placed on the righteousness of the Jewish cause. Exposure of the ring and trials of its members stirred public debate about national goals and the means acceptable to achieve them. The trials also highlighted another result of the 1984 election, the unexpectedly large vote for Meir Kahane's Kach party.

In previous elections Kahane's party failed to win the 1 percent of votes necessary for a Knesset seat, but in 1984 he broke the barrier with nearly twenty-six thousand, five times as many votes as in 1981. His election was not only a surprise to the pollsters but a media event of far larger proportions than the significance of his single seat in parliament would seem to indicate. Because of his bizarre campaign tactics, his blatant disregard for the political norms of Israeli society, and his minor charisma, he succeeded in attracting more attention than leaders of most large parties. Kahane openly supported the Jewish terrorist ring when it came to trial. The essence of his campaign was to seek purification of the Jewish state by deporting all Arabs and introducing legislation to prevent marriage, sexual relations, and other contacts between Jews and non-Jews. Kahane acknowledged that a purely Jewish state was hardly compatible with a democratic one. Thus, he argued, it would be necessary to dispense with democracy if democracy meant equal rights for Arabs.

During the campaign, Labor and parties to its left called on the Central Election Committee to ban Kach from the ballot. Party representatives of the Right in the committee either abstained or voted against the ban. Although the committee majority voted in favor, Israel's Supreme Court decided that a ban on Kach, or the new PLP perceived by some as pro-PLO, would establish a precedent that might limit political activity in the future.[34]

The 1.2 percent of the vote received by Kach was less significant than the debate it stirred in Israeli society. Kahane seemed to represent views of a far larger constituency than voted for him. He raised questions that many hesitated to debate openly. Would it really be possible to maintain a Western-type democracy with citizenship rights for all if Israel annexed the West Bank and Gaza with their million Arabs? How "Jewish" could Israel remain with its 17 percent of citizens who are not Jewish? Should Jews and Arabs be permitted to marry or intermingle socially, and should Arabs be given equal employment and economic and social opportunity within the mainstream of Israel life? Kahane's solution to these dilemmas was clear and unambiguous—expel all Arabs from the Jewish state or the Jewish state would no longer remain Jewish! Although no other political faction openly espoused such blatantly racist doctrine, it had many sympathizers on the Right. His views and platform represented in the extreme ideas of many in Tehiya, Morasha, and Gush Emunim who were reluctant to express them openly.

The extent to which political ideology was moving toward the right was revealed in results of a survey conducted by one of Israel's leading polling organizations, Dahaf, among 651 youths between the ages of fifteen and eighteen during the last six months of 1984. In summary the survey concluded that about a third of the youth interviewed had consistent democratic attitudes, about a quarter held consistently antidemocratic views, and two-fifths held democratic views on certain subjects, but not on others. "Usually, with regard to non-Jews in general and to Arabs in particular, the percentage of those holding anti-democratic views increases to about half of those interviewed."[35]

Specific data indicating ambivalent attitudes toward Israel's democratic institutions follow: 21 percent thought that censorship of the Israeli media should be increased above the current level, 50 percent thought the current level was adequate, and about 28 percent thought the current level should be reduced. Some 27 percent thought it permissible to restrict democracy to prevent those who disagree with the government from expressing their views publicly. Forty-four percent favored a law to prohibit criticism of the government in the media in all matters connected to Israel's relations with the Arabs. Over half those interviewed favored restricting freedom of trade unions to strike. Over 40 percent favored reducing the rights on non-Jewish citizens of Israel, and 47 percent agreed that both Muslims and Christians should be prevented from attaining high positions in the civil service; 47 percent wanted to reduce the rights of Israeli Arabs, 42 percent favored restricting democracy if necessary to deny civil rights to Arabs, and 60 percent agreed that Israeli Arabs are not entitled to full equal rights with Jews.

Only 30 percent were willing to return most of the territories in exchange for a peace settlement with security arrangements satisfactory to Israel, while 62 percent supported annexation. Some 64 percent opposed granting Arabs in the occupied territories the right to vote for the Knesset if the territories were annexed. While most opposed granting occupied Arabs the right to vote, 57 percent agreed that those in the territories who refused Israeli citizenship should be expelled. Thirty-eight percent indicated support for actions by private groups whose goal is to take revenge on Arabs for any attack on Jews, and about a quarter of these (9 percent of the total) were prepared to join such organizations.

A substantial minority seemed to yearn for a stronger central government and more powerful leadership. Over 28 percent wanted a strong regime of leaders who would not depend on political parties, and 18.6 percent preferred a government with whose views they agree if it were not democratic, a third had no opinion on this matter, and 47 percent could support a democratic government even if its views were contrary to theirs. Seventy-three percent opposed a death sentence for any Jew in any circumstance, no matter what the crime, but only 15 percent opposed death sentences for Arab terrorists.

Results of the survey showed a correlation of generally antidemocratic attitudes, support for annexation of the occupied territories, and general opposition to political compromise. The survey concluded that "different views on the issue of the future of the territories cannot be explained by differing perceptions of security. . . . If the difference were only in the perception of security and not a difference in democratic outlook, we would not find a difference between the supporters of compromise plus the right to vote and the supporters of annexation plus the right to vote."[36]

ISRAELI ARABS

Other surveys by Israeli scholars also indicated the dilemmas presented by presence of a large Arab minority. A study by Haifa University sociologist Sammy Smooha of Israeli Arab and Jewish attitudes and perceptions underscored how deep the social separation was between the two communities. It was reinforced by political divisions resulting from widely different definitions of national aspirations, legitimate rights, and acceptable concepts of identity.[37]

On the social plane few Jews (less than 40 percent) had frequent contacts with fellow citizens who were Arab, but nearly two-thirds of the Arabs had contacts with the Jews, largely as a result of their employment in the Jewish economy. Over 50 percent of the Arabs, but fewer than a quarter of the Jews, were willing to have members of the other community as friends; only 18.6 percent of the Jews, but 40.3 percent of the Arabs, were willing to live in a mixed neighborhood. More than 70 percent of the Jews believed that "Arabs will never reach the level of progress of Jews," 59.5 percent believed that "every Arab hates Jews," 96.6 percent, that "it would be better if there were fewer Arabs in Israel," 83.1 percent, that "it is impossible to trust Arabs in Israel."[38]

At the political level, differences between the two communities in perceptions of legitimate national aspirations were so great that they subverted attempts to diminish the social gap. There were few Israeli Arabs who accepted the Jewish consensus on national issues, although an overwhelming majority accepted Israel's legitimacy, wanted to be loyal citizens, and strove to enter the economic and social mainstream.

The Israeli Arab consensus on questions of identity and national aspirations was generally identical to the international operative consensus perceived by mainstream Israel as subversive. Smooha observed that Israel Arabs were becoming increasingly Palestinianized: more than two-thirds called on Israel to accept the PLO, and nearly half considered the organization a true representative of Israel's Arabs. Increased identification with the Palestinian national movement and recognition of the PLO as its principal spokesman did not necessarily imply disloyalty. On the contrary, writes Smooha, "as more

Arabs conceived of their identity in Palestinian terms . . . so more of them also acknowledged Israel's right to exist without reservation . . . or believed that Arabs could be equal citizens in Israel as a Jewish-Zionist state and could identify themselves with it. . . . Thus, the anguish Israeli Arabs experienced with regard to the Israeli war in Lebanon and their general strike on September 22, 1982, in the aftermath of the Sabra and Shatila massacre should be seen as genuine and legitimate concerns by Israel's national minority rather than as signs of extremism or disloyalty."[39]

Growing Israeli-Arab politicization in terms of more persistent, overt, and activist demands for social and economic equality was evident in voting patterns during the 1984 election. At 72 percent, the level of participation compared favorably with voting in the Jewish community. Seven of the twenty-six parties competed for Arab votes, and seven Arabs were elected as representatives of six different parties, four of them Zionist. The Communist (Rakah) party supported the Democratic Front for Peace and Equality (DFPE), most of whose supporters are Arab, and maintained its Knesset strength with four seats (two Arab and two Jewish). During the past several elections, DFPE or Rakah competed with the Labor Alignment for Arab votes. Rakah represented antiestablishment Arabs, and Labor, those who felt more secure in voting for the establishment. Rakah's strength peaked in 1977 when it captured nearly half the Arab vote, but by 1981, it declined to 37 percent and to 33 percent in 1984. Since 1977, the Alignment was in second place, but it too dropped by 5 percent in 1984, winning a quarter of the Arab vote. Still, the forty-seven thousand Arab votes received by Labor were invaluable, providing it with more than two Knesset seats. The importance of Arab votes was not overlooked by the Jewish parties. Many Jewish campaigners worked the Arab sectors of the country. Ezer Weizman was a popular figure and his Yahad list received nearly a quarter of its votes from Arabs and Druzes. Even Likud played to the Arabs, giving one of its Knesset seats to a Druze. The seven Arab MKs also represented Mapam, one; Shinui, one; Labor party, one; DFPE, two; and PLP, one.

Arab politicization was marked by election with mostly Arab votes of two PLP members in the eleventh Knesset. The list was headed by a political activist, Muhammed Miari, whose platform included demands of the new Arab consensus. They were reinforcement of the status of Arabic as an official language, a change in Israel's national anthem and symbols, appointment of an Arab high court judge, elimination of the necessity for military service as a requirement to receive extra National Insurance payments, and no compulsory military service for Arabs without a peace settlement. Symbolic of PLP's orientation toward the world consensus on national issues was designation of reserve general Mattityahu Peled as second on its list. Peled, a former member of the Israel general staff and now professor of Arabic literature at Tel Aviv University, is a key figure in efforts to seek accommodation through direct negotiations between Israel and the Palestinians. He had met with PLO chairman Yasir Arafat and other PLO leaders on several occasions, stirring a political furor in the Jewish community. Election of Miari and Peled was a victory for non-Communist Arab nationalists who were loyal to Israel but insisted that loyalty be recognized through equal political, economic, and social rights. Many in the establishment misperceived the PLP as militantly anti-Zionist, but it was more radical insistence on Arab rights than an antistate program that earned the PLP hostility from the Zionist right wing.

An article in the Tel Aviv monthly *New Outlook* stated that if Israel's Arabs "want to express a strong protest against the inequities of the current system that discriminates against them and to express their clear-cut support for the Palestinian right of self-determination, their only current options are to vote for Hadash [DFPE] or the Progressive List. However, if they want to be taken into account as potential sharers of political power at the governmental level, and if they want to have a direct impact on the struggle for primacy between the Religious-Right and the Center-Left blocks in Israel politics, they have to vote for one of the Zionist parties."[40]

CONCLUSION

Returns from the 1984 election, the political developments following it, and results of recent public opinion polls showed how the Zionist credo of Israeli society was being transformed, but also that the society was divided into two broad camps, a nationalist-Orthodox alliance and a Labor-center coalition.

After the election when the Labor party joined the NUG, the Alignment came to an end because Mapam with six Knesset seats became part of the left opposition; another MK deserted the Labor party to join the CRM, giving it four seats. Labor now had only thirty-seven instead of forty-four seats (it was compensated by the loss with support from Yahad, Shinui, and Ometz totaling seven seats). The left-wing opposition included Mapam, CRM, PLP, and DFPE with a total of sixteen seats, but it was unlikely that the four factions would unify in a cohesive parliamentary block. The right-wing opposition included Tehiya, which refused to join the NUG, and Kach, which the NUG rejected.

What was significant about the two large camps was how much the ideological gap closed between them since 1977. Labor and Likud with their respective NUG supporters devised plans for social and economic policies closer to supply-side economic doctrine than to the socialism of Labor Zionism. It was certainly questionable whether supply-side economics and World Bank–type austerity programs could salvage Israel's economy. It would be difficult to substantially diminish the large public sector, the extensive social security network, and the wide-ranging bureaucracy required to support Israel's social-economic infrastructure. Even increased American aid was no panacea, for it would only buy time for the NUG rather than enable it to alter the country's economic structure.

Ever since Israel's victory in the 1967 war and acquisition of Gaza and the West Bank, the Labor party and public opinion generally moved closer to the goals of territorial Zionism represented by Begin's nationalist ideology. True, many Labor Zionists still rejected territorial Zionism, some for pragmatic (mainly demographic) reasons, others from concern about compromising traditional humanitarian concerns of the Labor movement. However, diversity within Labor stymied new decisions and forced its leaders to accept de facto territorialist policies. Still, Labor's lower-keyed rhetoric enabled it to reopen the dialogue with Egypt, closed by Begin's militant policies, and to make friendly gestures toward Jordan.

Peres's decision to step up efforts for evacuation from Lebanon, the suspension of highly visible settlement activity on the West Bank, and his lower-keyed rhetoric elicited a response from Egypt that it might be prepared to renew the Camp David peace negotiations. Although talks with Egypt would no doubt be prolonged and precarious, especially with Likud's Yitzhak Shamir as foreign minister, they offered hope for extending the peace process. If Egypt were readmitted to the Arab League, the Islamic Conference, and the Third World bloc, possibilities would be greatly strengthened of its becoming an intermediary between Israel and other Arab nations that have not yet found the road to peace.

NOTES

1. Other terms for Jews from Asia and Africa include *Easterners* and *Sephardi*. The latter is not accurate, since *Sephardi* originally was the term for Jews whose descendants were exiled from Spain during the Inquisition.

2. The Likud bloc was formed before the eighth Knesset election in 1973 from nationalist factions opposed to return of Arab territory seized during the 1967 war. It included Herut, the Liberal party, the Free Center, the State party, and the Land of Israel movement.

3. Labor Zionism included several factions, the largest of which was the Mapai party. The Mapam party was the left wing of Labor.

4. The DMC was constituted in 1977 by ex-general Yigal Yadin from a spectrum of "liberals" belonging to nonreligious Zionist groups from Labor to Herut who advocated electoral reform and "clean government." Many were former generals, leaders of Labor, and others opposed to the decline of the Labor movement and its entrenchment in the establishment.

5. The religious bloc at the time included the National Religious party, Aguda Israel, and Labor Aguda Israel (Aguda Israel Workers).

6. Gahal formed in 1965 from a fusion of Herut, Liberals, and General Zionists.

7. Begin adamantly opposed any territorial compromises, especially as proposed in the 1970 Roger's Plan and UN Resolution 242, both of which Golda Meir's government agreed to consider.

8. See Don Peretz, "The Earthquake—Israel's Ninth Knesset Elections," *Middle East Journal* 31, no. 3 (Summer 1977): 251–66.

9. See Don Peretz and Sammy Smooha, "Israel's Tenth Knesset Elections—Ethnic Upsurgence and Decline of Ideology," *Middle East Journal* 35, no. 4 (Autumn 1981): 506–26.

10. See Sammy Smooha, *Israel: Pluralism and Conflict* (Berkeley and Los Angeles: University of California Press, 1978).

11. See Nissim Rejwan, "The Two Israels: A Study in Europocentrism," *Judaism* 16, no. 1 (Winter 1967): 97–108.

12. Don Peretz, "Israel's 1969 Election Issues: The Visible and the Invisible," *Middle East Journal* 24, no. 1 (Winter 1970): 31–46.

13. See Don Peretz, "The War Election and Israel's Eighth Knesset," *Middle East Journal* 28, no. 2 (Spring 1974): 111–25.

14. Peretz and Smooha, "Tenth Knesset Elections."

15. *Jerusalem Post* (hereafter cited as *JP*), 12 June 1981.

16. *JP*, 22 May 1984.

17. *Progressive Israel* (New York), special issue, 1984. Americans for Progressive Israel.

18. *JP*, 13 July 1984.

19. By the end of 1984 Israeli casualties reached over 600 dead and more than 3,500 wounded.

20. *JP*, 1 August 1984.

21. The Kahan Commission was appointed by the Begin government to investigate the massacre of Palestinian refugees by Phalangist militia in the Sabra and Shatilla refugee camps in September 1982. See *The Beirut Massacre: The Complete Kahan Commission Report.* (New York: Karz-Cohl Publishing Co., 1983).

22. The Labor Alignment was formed after the 1967 war from the Labor party (Mapai, Achdut Avoda, Rafi) and the left-wing Mapam.

23. Israel's two major polling organizations are Dahaf and Modeen Ezrachi. On polling in Israel, see Gabriel Weimann, "Every Day is Election Day: Press Coverage of Preelection Polls," in *The Roots of Begin's Success: The 1981 Israel Elections,* ed. D. Caspi, A. Diskin, and E. Gutmann (New York: St. Martin's Press, 1984).

24. *JP*, 21 May 1984.

25. Ibid., 11 July 1984.

26. Ibid., 10, 15 Aug. 1984.

27. Ibid., 4, 10 June 1984.

28. "National Unity Government Agreement" (abridged), *JP*, 12 Sept. 1984.

29. *JP International Edition,* 20 Oct. 1984; 8 Dec. 1984.

30. See Thomas R. Stauffer, *U.S. Aid to Israel the Vital Link,* Middle East Problem Paper, no. 24 (Washington, D.C.: Middle East Institute and U.S. General

Accounting Office, 1983); *U.S. Assistance to the State of Israel* (Washington D.C.: U.S. Government, Printing Office, 1983).

31. *JP*, 12 Sept. 1984.

32. See Don Peretz, "Israeli Approaches to a Solution," in *Alternative Approaches to the Arab-Israeli Conflict: A Comparative Analysis of the Principal Actors*, ed. Michael C. Hudson (Washington, D.C.: Center for Contemporary Arab Studies, Georgetown University, 1984).

33. Meron Benvenisti, *The West Bank Data Project: A survey of Israel's policies* (Washington, D.C.: American Enterprise Institute for Public Policy Research, 1984).

34. *JP*, 18, 20 June 1984.

35. Mina Tzemach and Ruth Tzin, "Attitudes of Adolescents with Regard to Democratic Values: Findings of a Survey of Attitudes Conducted Among Adolescents by the Dahaf Research Institute" (Jerusalem: Van Leer Jerusalem Foundation, 1984), mimeo., 2.

36. Ibid., 41.

37. Sammy Smooha, *The Orientation and Politicization of the Arab Minority in Israel*, Monograph Series on the Middle East, no. 2 (Haifa: University of Haifa Jewish-Arab Center Institute of Middle Eastern Studies, 1984).

38. Ibid., 78.

39. Ibid., 5.

40. *New Outlook* (Tel Aviv), Aug./Sept. 1984, 36.

ADDITIONAL READINGS

Ball, George W. *Error and Betrayal in Lebanon: An Analysis of Israel's Invasion of Lebanon and the Implications for U.S.–Israel Relations*. Washington, D.C.: Foundation for Middle East Peace, 1984.

Elon, Amos. *The Israelis' Founders and Sons*. Rev. ed. New York: Penguin, 1981.

Freedman, Robert O., ed. *Israel in the Begin Era*. New York: Praeger, 1982.

Indyk, Martin. *"To the Ends of the Earth": Sadat's Jerusalem Initiative*. Harvard Middle East Papers Modern Series, no. 1. Cambridge, Mass.: Center for Middle Eastern Studies, Harvard University, 1984.

The Jerusalem Quarterly. All issues, 1–33. Jerusalem: Middle East Institute, 1976–84.

Keren, Michael. *Ben Gurion and the Intellectuals: Power, Knowledge, and Charisma*. Dekalb: Northern Illinois University Press, 1983.

Liebman, Charles S., and Eliezer Don-Yehiya. *Religion and Politics in Israel.* Bloomington: Indiana University Press, 1984.

Oz, Amos. *In the Land of Israel.* New York: Vintage, 1984.

Peretz, Don. *The Government and Politics of Israel.* 2d ed. Boulder, Colo.: Westview, 1983.

———. "Israel Confronts Old Problems." *Current History* 84, no. 498 (Jan. 1985): 9–12, 36–38.

Peretz, Don, and Sammy Smooha. "Israel's Eleventh Knesset Election." *Middle East Journal* 39, no. 1 (Winter 1985): 86–103.

Peri, Yoram, and Amnon Neubach. *The Military-Industrial Complex in Israel: A Pilot Study.* Tel Aviv: International Center for Peace in the Middle East, 1985.

Reiser, Stewart. *The Politics of Leverage: The National Religious Party of Israel and Its Influence on Foreign Policy.* Harvard Middle East Papers Modern Series, no. 2. Cambridge, Mass.: Center for Middle Eastern Studies, Harvard University, 1984.

Libya: Internal Developments and Regional Politics

Marius Deeb and Mary-Jane Deeb

This is a survey of Libya's policies and activities in the internal sphere as well as in the regional context. In the first part, we will attempt to trace Muammar Qaddafi's background and rise to power, his strategies to remain in power, and his policies of social and economic development. The second part will analyze Libya's relationship to its neighbors in the region—Egypt, the Sudan, Chad, and the Western Sahara—and will trace Libya's foreign policy toward the United States.

BACKGROUND OF THE REVOLUTIONARY ELITE

According to Qaddafi, the planning for the military coup of 1969 began a decade earlier in 1959. As a fifteen-year secondary school student in Sebha (in the Fezzan), he formed his earliest study cells among his fellow students to discuss Nasir's speeches and his military coup in Egypt. It was that coup that was to provide the inspiration for the Libyan revolution. Many of those who were members of those study groups were expelled from schools in the Fezzan; they finally graduated from secondary schools in Misrata and then entered the military academy in Benghazi in 1963. It was probably there that Qaddafi formed the central committee of the Free Unionist Officers, whose members included among others Muhammad Abu Bakr Maqarif, Muhammad Najm, and Khuwaylidi al-Humaydi, who played very important roles later on in Libya's new government under Qaddafi. In 1965, he and several members of his group were appointed to the army as its lowest ranking officers.

The Free Officers, who made up the core group around Qaddafi and were actively involved in the coup, were recruited from among those who were in military school with him and were junior officers in the army between 1965 and 1969. There was another group, however, that lent its support to the coup; this was the group of civilian auxiliaries, who had been close to Qaddafi in his school days in Sebha and Misrata, but had not entered the military academy.

Most of them had attended the University of Libya in Benghazi, but shared Qaddafi's Nasirite convictions.

On 1 September 1969 the coup d'état took place: "It had been a copy book putsch. In a matter of hours a small group of audacious young men had overthrown [the] government and seized control of the state, with a minimum deployment of forces and almost no bloodshed. For all claims of a long and continuous conspirational history, there were signs of hurried last-minute preparations."[2]

Fathaly and Palmer analyzed the background of those who beside Qaddafi himself held the reins of the revolution. The first salient feature that appears from this analysis is that all the eleven members of the elite in 1971 belonged to the original cells set up by Qaddafi either in high school at Sebha and Misrata or at the military academy. He appointed them to various positions in the new government: Jallud was appointed prime minister; Maqarif, military commander of Benghazi and minister of housing; Hawadi, chairman of the Arab Socialist Union; Yunis, chief of staff; Humaydi, minister of the interior and commander of the Special People's Militia; Kharrubi, director of military intelligence; Muhayshi, minister of planning; Qurwi and Hamza, Revolutionary Command Council members; Huni, minister of foreign affairs; and Najm, minister of municipalities and later of education and housing.[3]

The second salient feature noted by Fathaly and Palmer is that this new governing elite had few ties to the previous prerevolutionary elite. Only Muhayshi, Yunis, and Maqarif could be said to have been related to the old or notable families of Libya. Most came from rural or bedouin families who had recently settled in urban centers; some were poor, whereas others are classified by the authors as middle class.[4] Qaddafi himself came from a poor seminomadic family from Sirte. Many of his later ideas on religion, as well as on social and economic reforms, have their roots in his early and somewhat austere and puritan background, typical of the milieu in which he grew up.[5] Finally, all twelve of them, including Qaddafi, were graduates of the military academy. Qaddafi, Jallud, and Huni were the only three who had had some training abroad, Qaddafi having spent six months in England receiving military training after he graduated in 1965.[6]

QADDAFI'S ECONOMIC POLICIES

Qaddafi's policies for social and economic development have evolved over the decade and a half since he took power. The first four years of the revolution (1969–73) were characterized by two major processes in the economic sphere—nationalization and Libyanization. Nationalization in part or in whole of the international petroleum companies operating in Libya began taking place in the late months of 1971. British Petroleum, for instance, was completely nationalized in December 1971, Bunker Hunt in June 1973, Occidental Oasis in August 1973, and Shell in March 1974. The Libyan government's share in other companies such as Exxon, Mobil, Texaco, and Chevron increased to 51 percent by September 1973.[7] Furthermore, Libya took the lead in OPEC in securing new rights from the oil companies and taking control of its oil production. The process was completed by and large by 1975.

Libyanization of the property of Italian settlers also took place during that phase. Their land (38,000 hectares), farms, agricultural equipment, and livestock were taken over. The government was to remain in control of that land for fifteen years and lease it to farmers, after which it would be made available to Libyans for purchase.[8] All industrial plants owned by Italians (which amounted to between 75 and 80 percent of all such plants in Libya) were also taken over by the government. Furthermore, the Revolutionary Command Council (RCC) Libyanized the branches of all foreign banks operating in the country; by the end of 1970, "the number of commercial banks was reduced to five, three state owned (National Commercial Bank, the Jumhuriya Bank, and the Umma Bank) and two state controlled (Wahdi Bank and the Sahara Bank)."[9]

Insurance companies were completely nationalized by 1971 and were merged into two companies. Large-scale and medium-sized industries were also taken over by the state. Libyanization of many forms of trade took place, and the National Organization for Supply Commodities (a state organization) was set up as the sole importer of certain consumer goods.[10] Finally basic infrastructural facilities, including electric power plants, airlines, and communication facilities, became state owned and state operated.

The small-business sector prospered in those early years, because the RCC followed a policy of giving governmental contracts to Libyan firms and lending up to 95 percent of the capital needed to finance indigenous commercial enterprises. Workers were given larger shares of the economic profits made by the firms that employed them. They became part owners and were eligible to receive up to half of their company's profits. In fact, their shares sometimes exceeded their annual salaries.[11]

It was not until 1973, however, that the new regime made any serious effort at centralized planning. With the First Three-Year Plan for 1973–75, the government set out its development policies. The aims of this plan were threefold: (1) to consolidate the power of the new regime and create a popular base of support by redistributing the oil wealth among the largest possible number of Libyans, (2) to diminish the dependency of the Libyan economy on the oil sector, and (3) to diversify and improve the industrial and agricultural production of the country.

The service sector of the economy was allocated the largest share of the budget during this period. Expenditures on housing, health, education, transportation and communications, electricity and water, and public services constituted 67.3 percent of the total budget for 1973–75. Agriculture was allocated only 16.6 percent, and industry, only 11.8 percent of the budget.[12] Thus, in terms of priorities, it is obvious that the principal aim of the Qaddafi government during this period was to create a popular base of support for the new regime, and that political imperatives dictated the major decisions made in planning for the economic development of the country.

The three years between 1973 and 1975 saw the implementation of a government policy to stimulate Libyan entrepreneurship. The aim was to encourage local initiative and develop a strong indigenous middle class, which would form a popular base for the new regime. When local businesses began to emerge they were virtually assured of receiving government contracts. Very soon, however, they were depending on foreign labor and technicians, and many became mere fronts for foreign business concerns.

But these development policies failed in the long run to bring the expected results. In the agricultural sector, for instance, many of the projects were doomed to failure because of water shortages or the remoteness of the areas where land was reclaimed. In the industrial sector, also, diversification of production was not feasible at such an early stage and with such a weak infrastructure and limited natural resources (apart from oil). In terms of trade, Libya became even more dependent on the West during those three years. The United States was the leading exporter of agricultural technology and, with other Western nations, sold the bulk of food, textiles, and raw materials that Libya imported.[13] Thus, the aims of attaining self-sufficiency in food and of reducing dependency on oil revenues were not achieved during that period.

But it is perhaps in his effort to develop a middle class supportive of the regime that Qaddafi encountered his greatest challenge. Those Libyan entrepreneurs who held government contracts reaped huge profits, which they then more often than not invested abroad. In fact, the process that was taking place was not so much the formation of a new middle class as the consolidation of the economic power of the traditional urban notability, who, because of their skills, experience, and connections, were best able to take advantage of government-sponsored programs.[14] Thus the regime, instead of finding in that class the support it sought, began to perceive it as a major challenger to its own power.

The most significant feature of the next five years (1975–80) was the issuance of Qaddafi's al-Kitab al-Akhdar (Green Book), the first part of which appeared either at the end of 1975[15] or in early 1976,[16] the second part in 1977, and the third in 1978. In this book, he set down his political and social philosophy, which was to become the foundation of many of the economic policies implemented during that period and the next. In the second volume, Qaddafi's "natural socialism" is fully expounded. We shall present here only some of the major "reforms" he proposed and point out their social and political implications.

Workers, for instance, were no longer to be employed by others but were to become "partners, not wage earners." A law was promulgated in May 1978 (based on the Green Book's philosophy concerning property ownership) that stipulated that tenants could take immediate possession of their rented homes and that those who owned more than one house had to relinquish their property. Furthermore, foreign trade pursued by the private sector was abolished in the late 1970s and was taken over by public corporations. In early 1979, internal wholesale trade was abolished, and retail trade was replaced by government cooperatives. Finally, the role of the industrial bank, as the major financial agency for the private sector for industry and construction, declined in importance. As more and more industrial and commercial enterprises come under direct government control, state investments moved to large industrial enterprises and away from private small-scale industries.

These policies had tremendous repercussions on Libyan society. It was undoubtedly the urban notability and the burgeoning class of small businessmen who were most severely affected by these changes. The law in real estate, for instance, undermined their economic power, for, by some estimates, the private sector had invested 41 percent of its capital in real estate between 1973 and 1975.[17] Moreover, much of the rest of its capital investment was either in foreign trade, which was taken over by the state, or in commercial and industrial enterprises for the domestic sector. By the end of 1978, a large number of these businesses, having been taken over by employees, were being administered by the workers and supervised by committees elected from among their ranks.[18] The state subsidies extended to the small businessmen were either reduced or no longer available. This left that group paralyzed by its lack of capital and its incapacity to carry on with business in the domestic sector, as government cooperatives replaced retail trade.

The overall result for the Libyan economy was negative. Sizable amounts of private capital continued to leave the country. There were serious shortages of a number of consumer goods, including foodstuffs and nonluxury commodities. But, perhaps most significant for a country attempting to develop rapidly, "many of the skills of the new capitalist class were removed from the productive sector of the economy [while] the poorer classes remained in a subsidized state of non-productivity."[19]

QADDAFI'S SOCIAL POLICIES

Women

Under Qaddafi, the issue of women's role in society was brought to the forefront for the first time in Libya's history. Under the Sanusi monarchy, the first step had already been taken when, in the 1951 constitution, Article 30 stated that elementary education was compulsory for both sexes.[20] But it was only after 1969 that the state began taking an active interest in the issue of women. This was primarily due to the realization that women constituted an untapped source of labor in a country that was suffering from a serious manpower shortage. The second reason may have been political: the new government was seeking to broaden its political base, and by increasing the rights of women in numerous areas, it expected active support from that sector of the population to boost its legitimacy.[21]

It was according to these two premises that reforms were introduced. First, it was imperative that women become educated in order both to acquire the skills necessary to become productive members of the labor force and also to absorb the political and social values of the new regime. Thus in the first eight years of the revolution, the absolute number of women in secondary schools quadrupled. The number of women at the university level also increased significantly, and they began entering such fields as medicine, engineering, agriculture, chemistry, and physics.[22] The number of schools increased enormously, too, but, most significant, the majority of the schools, as early as the academic year 1974–75, were mixed schools, where both girls and boys studied together.[23] This was a major reform for a society that had traditionally kept the two worlds of men and women well apart.

The second major reform, which aimed at giving women more independence from their families, dealt with personal status law and, in particular, with the issue of divorce. The right of men to divorce was significantly curtailed, while women were given more rights to ask for separation or divorce. One such measure, termed *al-tatliq li-idrar*, was instituted to permit a woman to obtain a divorce when she could prove that her husband had maltreated or abandoned her.[24]

Women were also encouraged to seek employment in various fields. Laws were passed to ensure that women would receive pay equal to that of men for equal work,[25] paid leave when they gave birth,[26] free time to nurse their infants, day-care centers for their preschool children, and a number of other benefits to induce them to remain employed even after they had married and had children.

But perhaps the most controversial of Qaddafi's reforms has been the conscription of women into the Libyan army. This was preceded in the early 1980s by the creation of the Nuns of the Revolution, a kind of small police force and an auxiliary body of the revolutionary committees.[27] On 13 March 1984, a law for the conscription of women was passed amid very strong opposition from all sectors of Libyan society.[28] A military academy for girls has been set up and women have been coerced to attend it, according to opposition newspapers.[29]

The issue of women is very much alive in Libya. As we have pointed out elsewhere, "The political and social institutions are each pulling women in opposite directions, each for its own ends—the social institutions in order to keep the status quo, the government in order to be able to use women as a political basis, both active and vocal, to boost its legitimacy."[30]

Islamic Reforms

Qaddafi's conception of Islam has been rooted in the Sanusi tradition, but over the past decade it has gradually transcended it. As a Muslim reformer he has rejected *tazammut*, the rigid interpretation of religion, insisting on a progressive role for Islam in society. Although at a certain stage (in the early seventies) he tied his social and political ideology to Islam, he later changed. A protagonist of his regime put it succinctly: "Islam is not the ideology of the Mass Republic of Libya; what we are saying is that our understanding of Islam and of the Qur'an are [forever] changing and renewing themselves."[31]

Qaddafi's emphasis on the Qur'an as the only source of *shari'ah*, and his explicit belief that those parts of the *hadith* that do not tally with the Qur'an ought to be rejected make him a kind of protestant reformer of Islam. On the other hand his insistence on the transcendence of God and on the purely human nature of the Prophet, whose role is only that of an intermediary between God and man, can be compared to the views held by the Hanbalite and other fundamentalist schools of thought. However, both his reformism and his fundamentalism were brought about, in part at least, by a practical consideration, namely, his desire to undermine the religious establishment that had become quite vocal in its criticism of the regime.

Qaddafi maintained in early 1976 that the Qur'an ought to be the only source of legislation, as all other sources were liable to human error. He also began criticizing the role of the '*ulama*' and *fuqaha*', claiming that there was no need for any intermediary between the believer and his God. By 1978 he was launching a full-fledged attack on the men of religion and the Islamic jurists. "The Qur'an is in the Arabic language and we can therefore comprehend it ourselves without the need for an *imam* to interpret it for us."[32] Between April and May 1978, mosques were seized and their imams replaced by more compliant ones. It is in his attack on the religious establishment that Qaddafi reveals his true colors as a pragmatic politician who has used religion as a means of undermining the opposition among this powerful sector of Libyan society. In fact, one of Qaddafi's major critics was the grand mufti of Libya, al-Shaykh al-Tahir al-Zawi, who eventually resigned in January 1984.[33] It was understood that his resignation was a protest against the persistent attacks by the state and government supporters on himself personally as well as on *Dar al-Ifta'* (the office of the Mufti of Libya).[34]

It is interesting to note here that Shaykh al-Zawi's major criticisms of Qaddafi had not been primarily religious, but economic. In 1977 he had issued a *fatwa* against the taking over of private property (following the housing law of that year), against the policy of dealing with interest on loans or in banking, and against the levying of taxes on individuals when the government already had an external source of income. We can thus see that one of the main pillars of the opposition against Qaddafi's policies in Libya, especially after 1976, was the religious establishment. This had not been the case in the early years of the revolution, however, when the non-Sanusi 'ulama' were restored to positions of preeminence, while the power of the Sanusi *zawiyas* was curtailed by the RCC.[35]

As Fathaly puts it, however, "There was an inevitable association between family prominence and religious leadership. The fact served to intensify the concentration of religious leadership within small groups of families throughout the country."[36] It is not surprising, then, that the religious establishment shared the views of the traditional urban notability, who were already being undermined by Qaddafi's economic and political reforms. It is not surprising either that Qaddafi reacted as he did and tried to discredit and weaken the religious establishment, not because of its stand on religious issues, but because of its opposition to him on economic and political issues.

INSTITUTION BUILDING

Early on, Qaddafi realized he needed to build institutions to replace those he was undermining, primarily in order to obtain the legitimacy the military coup had not automatically given him. There were other reasons as well: "(1) to establish a direct link with the masses that would facilitate their mobilization in support of the regime; (2) provide the masses with the opportunity to express their support for the regime; (3) preclude political parties or the building of coalitions that might threaten the regime."[37]

The earliest effort at institution building was the creation in July 1971 of the Arab Socialist Union (ASU), a mass party controlled by the state. This was an attempt by Qaddafi to duplicate the ASU of Egypt and in so doing to acquire some legitimacy by assuming the role of the recently deceased Nasir. But the ASU in Libya was a failure, for it did nothing to enhance Qaddafi's legitimacy nor did it meet the needs of the Libyans for a more effective channel for political participation.

In 1973 Qaddafi introduced another form of political institution, the popular committees. Selected by elections, some replaced local administrators, and others were expected to run state corporations and universities. The aim was to increase mass participation in the political process and by so doing increase support for the regime.

Although more appropriate than the ASU for Libya's sociopolitical environment, the popular committees nonetheless faced major difficulties. The inexperience of many of the elected members, combined with the fact that the committees were used in many cases to settle personal scores, rendered them ineffective.[38] Furthermore, they soon came into conflict with the ASU over their roles and duties. By the end of 1975 the ASU was formally abolished, and in its stead basic people's congresses were formed; they could vote on all major issues and elect a delegate to the General People's Congress. Each basic people's congress also elected its own popular committee to administer local affairs. Some of its members could rise to higher echelons and even reach the General Popular Committee, equivalent to a cabinet. In most cases, however, instead of congresses affecting the decision-making processes of the state, they became the instruments of state policies, implementing them passively.[39]

In 1977 Qaddafi resorted to the formation of revolutionary committees (Lijan thawriyah) who were to be the watchdogs of the popular committees. These committees have become "an undeclared political party through which the government implements and enforces its policies."[40]

The army is yet another institution that Qaddafi has spent much time and effort to build, although in 1973 he created a counterweight to it, namely, the people's militia, headed by his colleague Khuwaylidi al-Humaydi. This organization has recently been replaced by the mass republican guards (al-Haras al-Jamahiri), who are the armed members of the revolutionary committees.

LIBYAN OPPOSITION

Libyan opposition to Qaddafi's regime did not really crystallize until the 1980s for three basic reasons. First, as long as Qaddafi was closely allied to, or at least not at loggerheads with, the major Arab states and in particular Egypt, opposition to his regime was insignificant. There were two unsuccessful military coups in the first year of Qaddafi's rule—in December 1969 and in August 1970—but he was able to survive them. The third and most serious attempt to topple him was the attempted coup of August 1975 led by 'Umar al-Muhayshi, a colleague of Qaddafi and a leading Free Officer. This military coup coincided with the deterioration of Libya's relation with Egypt in the wake of the October War of 1973 and the signing of the first disengagement agreement between Egypt and Israel.

The second reason for the slow emergence of an organized Libyan opposition to Qaddafi's regime was the fact that until the late 1970s when all the Green Book had been published his socioeconomic program was not clearly spelled out. The implementation of the second part of the book during 1978–79, which could be regarded as a watershed in Qaddafi's rule, led to the rise of a strong and well-organized opposition to his regime.

The third reason is that the tremendous growth of an opposition was a reaction to the policy he pursued after 1980. He demanded the return of Libyan residents abroad and threatened that he would send hit squads after them if they refused to comply. But his campaign of terror against some leading Libyans, coupled with his socioeconomic policies, only augmented the number of Libyans who stayed in the major European countries and the United States (an estimated fifty thousand in all), making them less willing to return. In this way he performed a service for the Libyan opposition, which became more effective and well organized.

Perhaps the most prominent opposition organization is the National Front for the Salvation of Libya (NFSL) (al-Jabhah al-Wataniyah li-Inqadh Libya) established on 7 October 1981; its secretary-general, a former diplomat, is Muhammad Yusuf Maqarif. It was reported that when it was founded it was subsidized by Saudi Arabia with 12 million pounds and that it has had the support of the Muslim Brothers since.[41] The NFSL has issued a bimonthly magazine called al-Inqadh since 1982 and other publications such as Akhbar Libya, a monthly leaflet dealing with internal political developments in Libya. Other opposition organizations share with the NFSL the objective of overthrowing Qaddafi's regime. There is the Libyan Constitutional Union (al-Ittihad al-Dusturi al-Libi),[42] the Libyan National Movement (al-Harakat al-Wataniyah al-Libiyah), the Libyan Liberation Organization (Munazzamat Tahrir Libya), the Islamic Group (al-Jama'ah al-Islamiyah) of Libya, as well as the asociations of Libyan students, women, or of Libyans residing in Egypt.[43] A secret organization that emerged in 1984 and is engaged in counterterror against Qaddafi's regime is al-Burkan (volcano); this group claimed responsibility for the assassination of the Libyan ambassador in Rome in January 1984[44] and assassinated the head of the Libyan Information Bureau in the same city in January 1985.[45]

The most interesting development among the Libyan opposition has been its use of armed struggle. Perhaps the most dramatic instance of this was the attack on Qaddafi's residence and headquarters at Bab al-'Aziziyah on 8 May 1984, when eight guerrillas of the NFSL tried to penetrate the barracks, hoping to assassinate Qaddafi himself.[46] The reaction of most of the opposition groups to the Bab al-'Azizayah operation was positive, except for the Libyan Constitutional Union, which depicted the attack as suicidal and counterproductive. They feared it could harm the cause of the opposition and make Qaddafi more oppressive in his measures against the Libyan people.[47]

The Bab al-'Aziziyah operation was supposed to have been led by the head of the military branch and a founding member of the NFSL, Ahmed Ibrahim Ahwas, who was a former diplomat and army officer. Ahwas was killed, however, in an armed clash with Libyan security forces near Zawara on 6 May 1984. Consequently, the attack was hastily organized and executed because it was feared that Qaddafi would discover the presence of NFSL's guerrillas who managed to infiltrate back into Libya.[48]

The NFSL hailed the Bab al-'Aziziyah operation as the first guerrilla action planned and organized by Libyans since 1942, when Italian forces evacuated Libyan territory. It was also the first time that Qaddafi had to pay with the lives of his armed men since he had come to power in 1969.[49] Whatever the immediate effect of the incident on the internal situation in Libya (and in fact Qaddafi's countermeasures have been more repressive), the Bab al-'Aziziyah operation ushered in a qualitative change in the means used by the Libyan opposition to overthrow Qaddafi's regime. It also demonstrated that Qaddafi could be vulnerable in the very barracks where he lives and from which he operates.

The ideology of the Libyan opposition varies from one group to another. The Islamic Group (al-Jama'ah al-Islamiyah) represents the Muslim fundamentalists, whereas other opposition groups tend to be more secular in their outlook, seeking the establishment of a free democratic political system. The NFSL's ideology centers on the rejection of all forms of military rule and advocates free elections and plebiscites as the method most appropriate "to determine the legitimate Bay'a."[50] The only guarantee for the realization of the objective of social justice and economic prosperity, according to the NSFL, is through free elections; the drafting of a constitution; the formation of councils and institutions to maintain separation of powers among the executive, legislative, and judiciary bodies; and the establishment of permanent traditions for the new state.[51] In the fourth congress of the General Union of Libyan Students held in the United States, Ibrahim 'Abd al-'Aziz, a leading member of the NFSL, called for the establishment of "a national constitutional and democratic" rule in Libya, rooted in Islamic doctrines and the cultural legacy of the Libyan people.[52] Other objectives that the opposition press frequently refers to and that are lacking in Libya under Qaddafi are freedom of thought and the sanctity of private property.[53]

FOREIGN POLICY: THE EGYPT SYNDROME

The key to understanding Qaddafi's policy toward the West and in particular toward the United States lies in his conception of Libya's role in the Arab world and the bordering region of West Africa, and in the actual relationship between Libya and its neighbors, especially Egypt. The paramount importance of Libyan-Egyptian relations cannot be overemphasized for two basic reasons. First, Egypt was, especially under Nasir, the pivotal power in the Arab world, being the most populous and powerful Arab state. Libya always looked up to Egypt, and the ties between the Libyans of the Cyrenaican regions and Egyptians were strong even before its independence in 1951. Second, Qaddafi himself emulated Nasir in forming a secret Free Unionist Officers' Movement, which managed to take power in 1969. Nasir had been Qaddafi's hero, and as long as Nasir was alive Qaddafi followed his policies. Except for his uncontrollable outbursts against King Hussein when he had his showdown with the PLO in September 1970, Qaddafi toed the line behind his charismatic hero.

During the first four years of his rule, when his ties with Egypt were good, Qaddafi's relations to many of the Arab states and the West were not characterized by conflict or tension. It was only after parting company with Egypt in the immediate aftermath of the October War of 1973 that he embarked on a new course in his foreign policy.

The Arab-Israeli war of 1973 constituted a watershed in Libyan-Egyptian relations. Even before the war, the relationship between Egypt and Libya had shown signs of strain. Qaddafi attempted in February 1972 to force the hand of Sadat for a merger unity of the two countries. This culminated in July 1973, when Libyan marchers, sent by Qaddafi, arrived in Cairo and submitted to Sadat a petition demanding the complete and integrative unity of Libya and Egypt. More significant was the fact that Qaddafi was not consulted and therefore was not privy to the momentous decision to launch the 6 October 1973 attack against Israeli forces in Sinai and the Golan Heights; this further estranged him from Sadat and other Arab leaders. Qaddafi felt that he had been slighted and was regarded only as a junior partner of the loose Federation of

Arab Republics (FAR) formed in April 1971 by Egypt, Syria, and Libya.[54] Neither Libya's army nor its arsenal (the French Mirage planes notwithstanding) had qualified Libya to be on an equal footing with its partners in the FAR. This affront to Qaddafi probably determined to a large extent his attitude toward the October War and toward Egypt since then. While Sadat, Assad, and King Faisal of Saudi Arabia capitalized on the prestige gained from the October War, Qaddafi was left out in the cold and could hardly claim, with any credibility, that he had played a role in the war. His ambition to be treated on a par with Sadat and Assad had been thwarted, as their newly acquired charisma put Qaddafi in a position inferior to theirs.

The disengagement agreement between Egypt and Israel of January 1974 complicated the relations between Libya and Egypt. Although Qaddafi in his public utterances had been consistently against the peaceful settlement of the Arab-Israeli conflict, he had allied himself to countries, such as Egypt under Nasir and Syria under Assad, that accepted the UN Resolution 242 of November 1967. Qaddafi's stand on the Arab-Israeli conflict was never really the bone of contention between him and Sadat in the aftermath of the October War of 1973 and until Sadat visited Jerusalem in November 1977.

Only Nasir was able to keep Qaddafi under his control. Consequently, Qaddafi was able to establish a special relation between Libya and Egypt during Nasir's lifetime, but it was not sustained for long after Nasir's death. Qaddafi's aspiration to play a role in Arab and regional affairs greater than Libya's military, demographic, or political capabilities would allow was a major cause of the rift between Qaddafi and Sadat. Knowing Libya's limitations, Qaddafi had sought unsuccessfully to reestablish the special relationship between Libya and Egypt.[55] Qaddafi wanted Libya to be regarded by the major Arab states as a principal actor in Arab affairs. It was this ambition that led to the series of political setbacks from which he has suffered since the mid-1970s.

Because Qaddafi realized that Libya was not being taken seriously, for one thing, because of its weak military capability, he embarked upon an armament program. Ironically, the war that Libya had not been particularly enthusiastic about led to the quadrupling of the price of oil, and Libyan oil revenue soared from approximately $1.5 billion in 1972 to $6.6 billion in 1974.[56] Thus Qaddafi could afford sophisticated arms, which he sought to buy from both Western Europe and the Soviet Union. As Egypt moved closer to the West, thanks to Kissinger's shuttle diplomacy and the Egyptian-Israeli disengagement agreements of 1974 and 1975, culminating in the abrogation of the Egyptian-Soviet treaty of friendship in 1976, Libya moved in the opposite direction—closer to the Soviet Union.

In the post–October 1973 period Libya's foreign policy underwent a qualitative change, which could be aptly described as interventionist in character. His intervention, especially in the states bordering Libya, reflects at once an obsession with the exaggerated role he feels Libya should play in the Arab world and West Africa and his unwillingness (perhaps because of his bedouin roots) to draw clear lines of demarcation between what belongs to him and what belongs to other states. Being geographically far from the arena of the Arab-Israeli conflict and bordering the most powerful Arab state, Egypt, Qaddafi had to resort to intervention elsewhere. The Sudan because of its endemic instability has been a major target of Qaddafi's meddling through various Sudanese opposition groups and parties dating from the first unsuccessful attempts in September 1975 and July 1976 to the latest Libyan raid on the Umm Durman Radio in March 1984. The joint defense pact between Sudan and Egypt signed in July 1976 has warded off the Libyan threat against Sudan, but Qaddafi since 1983 has singled out Ja'far Numayri as a target for his wrath.[57]

WESTERN SAHARA AND CHAD

Libya's support for the Polisario Front in Western Sahara began in 1976, which antedates its direct military intervention in Chad, beginning June 1980. During the period 1976–81, Qaddafi's support for the Polisario put Libya at loggerheads with Morocco, and diplomatic relations were broken in April 1980.[58] The failure that characterized the first Libyan military intervention in support of Idi Amin's regime in Uganda during the period February–April 1979 did not deter Qaddafi from intervening in Chad; this would be the most successful Libyan intervention in any Arab or African state.

The first Libyan military intervention began when Goukouni, who presided then over the Transitional Government of National Unity (GUNT), signed an agreement with Libya in order to strengthen his position vis-à-vis his minister of defense Habré. Libyan troops moved into Chad at the end of 1980, culminating in a declaration by Goukouni and Qaddafi of the union of Libya and Chad in January 1981. Habré, who was relegated to the eastern region of the country, began receiving U.S. military aid through Egypt and Sudan. But this intervention was short-lived, for Goukouni asked for the withdrawal of Libyan troops, which took place by November 1981.[59]

The second military intervention was primarily rooted in Qaddafi's African aspirations: "In the attempts to hold an OAU summit in 1982, the Chadian question was kept alive by Libya, and when the Summit was finally held in Addis Ababa in June 1983 and Mengistu of Ethiopia was chosen to preside rather than Qadhdhafi, the Libyan leader left in a huff and stormed back to Tripoli to unleash Goukouni's forces."[60] The Libyan offensive, which began in July 1983, led to French intervention in August after the United States and many African states put strong pressure upon France to move into action.

There was another dimension to the second Libyan military intervention in Chad, which was related to a series of events that took place in 1983 in the Middle East as a whole: the Soviet rearmament of Syria during the winter; the discovery of an unsuccessful plot to topple the regime of Numayri in Sudan in February; the bombing of the U.S. embassy on 18 April; and the beginning of a Syrian offensive against the multinational force in Lebanon. Perhaps both Libya and Syria in alliance with Iran felt the need to strike against the region's pro-Western states in order to regain the upper hand they had lost in the aftermath of the Israeli invasion of Lebanon in 1982. Cognizant of the distribution of power in the Middle East, Qaddafi was apprehensive that if Syria were totally defeated by Israel, it would weaken his own position in the whole region. Consequently, during the Israeli invasion of Lebanon Qaddafi told Assad "that Syria only has to be steadfast and not throw itself into an unequal battle."[61] Since the late 1970s, Libya's alliance with Syria has become a permanent feature of the two states. They spearheaded the anti-Egyptian Front of Steadfastness and Confrontation formed in December 1977, which included South Yemen, Algeria, and the PLO (although the last two have drifted away since).[62]

The second Libyan military intervention in Chad was prevented by the French from achieving its objective of occupying the country and toppling Habrés government. In September 1984 Libya and France reached an agreement "that provided for French withdrawal from the country, Libyan withdrawal to the Aouzou strip, and the maintenance of Zairean troops in the country."[63] Although the French left, the Libyans did not, and half the country is still occupied by Libya. "France was hoodwinked in the process, . . . and Libya showed itself to be as untrustworthy as many suspected."[64]

The Libyan-French agreement in Chad was not entirely unrelated to developments elsewhere. The discovery of mines in the Red Sea, which Egypt accused Libya of planting, pushed Qaddafi for tactical reasons to be more conciliatory in respect to Chad and to the Western Sahara. Hoping that his association with King Hassan II of Morocco would give him some respectability, Qaddafi formed the African-Arab Union in August 1984. This included Libya and Morocco and is less a union than a temporary alliance to counterbalance the recently formed alliance by Algeria, Tunisia, and Mauritania. The deal between Hassan II and Qaddafi included the ending of Libya's support for the Polisario in exchange for the handing over to Qaddafi of three leading members of the Libyan opposition.[65]

LIBYA AND THE UNITED STATES

Qaddafi's attitude toward the United States has been a function of his policies toward his major Arab rivals. During the first four years of his rule, Qaddafi was anti-imperialist in the Nasirite tradition. But as long as his ties with Egypt were strong, his anti-imperialism remained within the confines of the pan-Arab nationalism of the 1950s and 1960s. When Egypt moved closer to the United States after 1974 and Qaddafi was left out in the cold by Sadat, Libya moved closer to the Soviet Union, and its anti-Western posture became more virulent. The second phase of Libyan-U.S. relations, during the period 1975–79, was characterized by tensions and strain epitomized by the Billy Carter affair. In 1979, after the signing of the Israeli-Egyptian peace treaty and, more significant, the successful overthrow of the pro-Western shah regime in Iran, Qaddafi adopted a new radicalism. This accompanied the implementation of the socio-economic components of his Green Book in Libya itself and rendered his regime more unpopular than ever. The use of terrorism to liquidate Qaddafi's enemies abroad has coincided with the rising use of terrorism and violence the Iranian revolution has inspired since November 1979. It was not accidental that on 2 December 1979, only a few weeks after the takeover of the U.S. embassy in Tehran on 4 November, Qaddafi allowed Libyan demonstrators to sack and burn the American embassy in Tripoli; it was as though he wanted to steal the thunder from Iranian militants. Since then Libyan-U.S. relations have entered a third phase characterized by threats and counterthreats, including the downing of two Libyan planes by the United States in the Gulf of Sidra on 19 August 1981.

A recent study on Libyan-U.S. relations concludes that "the policy of calculated hostility and stern retribution adopted by the Reagan administration is more effective in curbing al-Qaddafi than the previous approaches of the U.S. government, which were based on friendship and indifference."[66] This statement lumps together the three distinct phases of Qaddafi's foreign policy: 1969–74, 1975–79, and 1979 to the present. During the first phase Qaddafi's anti-imperialist stand was not unlike Nasir's and therefore in methods and objectives Libyan policies were not necessarily inimical to U.S. interests in the region. In the second phase it was still possible to have correct relations between Libya and the United States, but these were primarily economic and trade relations and, to a lesser degree, political. But in the last phase, since late 1979, for domestic as well as for regional purposes, Qaddafi has been pushed to ride the anti-Western and particularly anti-U.S. wave inspired and led by Khomeini's Iran, which both Libya and Syria (in a more subtle but more effective manner) have managed to exploit to keep their narrowly based ruling elements in power. U.S. policy toward Libya, then, has been a reaction to Libyan policy and a function of Libya's rivalry with pro-Western Arab states in the region as a whole. One wonders if it is effective to pursue the U.S. policy of "calculated hostility" and "stern retribution," for any U.S.-Libyan confrontation plays into Qaddafi's hands and tends to enhance his prestige.

Qaddafi's foreign policy until the early 1970s contained a modicum of idealism rooted in the pan-Arab nationalism of the 1950s and 1960s, but as his power base became very narrow indeed by the late 1970s and the 1980s, the survival of his regime became his uppermost concern. Conseqently he has pursued a foreign policy that is devoid of any ideology, siding with Iran against Iraq, for example, because his alliance with Syria has become indispensable and he fears that if Saddam Hussein wins the war he could become the new Nasir. Similarly, even when Syria condemned the attendance of an Israeli delegation at a conference of Moroccan Jews held in Rabat in May 1984, Qaddafi pursued his alliance with Morocco by forming the African-Arab Union in August—a clear indication of the triumph of realpolitik over ideology in Qaddafi's mind.

NOTES

1. See Omar I El Fathaly and E. Monte Palmer, *Political Development and Social Change in Libya* (Lexington, Mass.: Lexington Books, 1980), 38–44. Also Ruth First, *Libya, the Elusive Revolution* (New York: Africana Publishing Co., 1974), 101–4.

2. First, *Elusive Revolution*, 110.

3. Fathaly and Palmer, *Political Development*, 43, table 3–1.

4. Ibid.

5. Marius Deeb and Mary Jane Deeb, *Libya Since the Revolution: Aspects of Social and Political Development* (New York: Praeger, 1982), 98.

6. Fathaly and Palmer claim he spent these six months in Sandhurst (p. 39),

whereas First writes that "he attended an army school for education at Bovington Hyltre in Beaconsfield" (p. 265n7).

7. Yves Gazzo, *Petrole et developpement: Le cas Libyan* (Paris: Ed. Economics, 1982), 59.

8. First, *Elusive Revolution*, 165.

9. Andrew W. Green and Phillip de Mass, "The Money and Banking System of Libya: Its Structure, History and Relationship to the Libyan Economic System" (Paper delivered at the Eastern Economic Association, Hartford, Conn. Apr. 1977) 11.

10. Harold D. Nelson, ed., *Libya: A Country Study* (Washington, D.C.: American University, 1979), 133.

11. Fathaly and Palmer, *Political Development*, 68–69.

12. *The Three-Year Plan, 1973–75* (Libya, Ministry of Planning, n.p., n.d.), 90.

13. "Libya Still Looks West for Technology," *Business Week*, 20 Sept. 1976, 35.

14. Fathaly and Palmer, *Political Development*, 158.

15. Ibid., 149.

16. Herve Bleuchot, "The Green Book: Its Context and Meanings," in *Libya Since Independence: Economic and Political Development*, ed. J.A. Allan (London: Croom Helm, 1982), 146.

17. Timothy C. Niblock, "Homes Policy Aids Families and Worries Private Investors," *Middle East Economic Digest*, 1 Sept. 1978, 5.

18. Deeb and Deeb, *Libya Since the Revolution*, 115–16.

19. Fathaly and Palmer, *Political Development*, 159.

20. See Majid Khadduri, *Modern Libya: A Study in Political Development* (Baltimore: Johns Hopkins University Press, 1963), 344.

21. Deeb and Deeb, *Libya Since the Revolution*, 86.

22. *Lamhah 'an al-Wadi' al-Iqtisadi wal-Ijtima'i lil-Mar'ah fi al-Jumhuriyah al-'Arabiyah al-Libiyah* (Benghazi: University of Benghazi, 1975), 15.

23. Of a total of 2,394 schools in 1974–75, 1,805 were mixed-sex. Figures based on LAR, Ministry of Culture and Education, Department of Planning and Development, *Ihsa'at al-Ta'lim fi al-Jumhuriyah al-'Arabiyah al-Libiyah 'an al-'Am al-Dirasi 1394–1395 AH, 1974–75 AD* (Tripoli: Government Press, n.d.), tables on pp. 39, 67, 95.

24. Chapter 2, "al-Tatliq lil-Idrar," an explanation of law no. 176 of 1972, in a pamphlet with no title published by LAR, Ministry of Justice, on laws no. 112 of 1971, no. 176 of 1972, and no. 18 of 1973.

25. Siba al-Fahoum, *La femme libyenne en dix ans 1965–1975* (Beirut: Lebanese Branch of the World Feminine League for Peace and Freedom, n.d.), 52.

26. *Lamhah 'an al-Wadi'al-Iqtisadi wal-Ijtima'i lil-Mar'ah*, 14.

27. Monte Palmer and Omar El Fathaly, "The Transformation of Mass Political Institutions in Revolutionary Libya: Structural Solutions to a Behaviorialist Problem," in *Social and Economic Development of Libya*, ed. E.G.H. Joffe, and K.S. McLachlan (Boulder, Colo.: Middle East and North African Press, 1982), 251.

28. *Akhbar Libya*, no. 31 (Mar. 1984): 3.

29. *al-Inqadh*, no. 8 (Apr. 1984): 15.

30. Deeb and Deeb, *Libya since the Revolution*, 86.

31. U.S. Department of Commerce, Office of Technical Services, JPRSO7332, "The Religious Principles of the Ideology of al-Jamahiriya," translated from *al-Usbu' al-Siyasi*, 2 Mar. 1979, 14.

32. *al-Fajr al-Jadid*, 21 Feb. 1978, 4.

33. *al-Inqadh*, no. 8 (Apr. 1984): 60.

34. Ibid.

35. Lisa Anderson, "Qadhdhafi's Islam," in *Voices of Resurgent Islam*, ed. John L. Esposito (New York: Oxford University Press, 1983), 140.

36. Fathaly and Palmer, *Political Development*, 26.

37. Palmer and Fathaly, "Transformation of Mass Political Institutions," 241.

38. Fathaly and Palmer, *Political Development*, 120.

39. Palmer and Fathaly, "Transformation of Mass Political Institutions," 245.

40. Deeb and Deeb, *Libya since the Revolution*, 121.

41. *Akhbar Libya* no. 32 (July 1984): 5.

42. Ibid.

43. *Watha'iq Tudin al-Qadhdhafi*, n.d., 5.

44. *al-Inqadh* no. 8, (Apr. 1984): 104–5.

45. *al-Nahar*, 15 Jan. 1985, 1, 8.

46. *al-Inqadh*, no. 9 (Jan. 1984): 12–17.

47. *Akhbar Libya*, no. 32 (July 1984): 5.

48. *al-Inqadh,* no. 9 (June 1984): 12–13.

49. Ibid., 56.

50. *al-Inqadh,* no. 8 (Apr. 1984): 52.

51. Ibid., 53.

52. *al-Inqadh,* no. 11, (Nov. 1984): 57.

53. Ibid., 64.

54. Deeb and Deeb, *Libya since the Revolution,* 131–32.

55. Ibid., 133–34.

56. Wilfrid Knapp, *North West Africa: A Political and Economic Survey* (Oxford: Oxford University Press, 1977), 213.

57. *al-Inqadh,* no. 8 [supp.] (Apr. 1984): 19–22, 24–26.

58. John Damis, *Conflict in Northwest Africa: The Western Sahara Dispute* (Stanford: Hoover Institution Press, 1983), 110–12.

59. I. William Zartman, "Conflict in Chad," in *Conflict Resolution in the Third World,* ed. Arthur Day, forthcoming.

60. Ibid.

61. Foreign Broadcasting Information Service (FBIS), 4 Sept. 1984, Q5.

62. Deeb and Deeb, *Libya since the Revolution,* 136.

63. Zartman, "Conflict in Chad."

64. Ibid., 17. For Qaddafi's interests in Chad and beyond, see I. William Zartman, "What's at Stake in Chad," *Worldview* 26, no. 11 (Nov. 1983): 4–5.

65. *al-Inqadh,* no. 11 (Nov. 1984): 20.

66. P. Edward Haley, *Qaddafi and the United States since 1969* (New York: Praeger, 1984), 322.

Terrorism in the Middle East: The Diffusion of Violence

John W. Amos II

The 23 October 1983 bombings of the U.S. Marine and French headquarters in Beirut, with resulting large numbers of casualties, focused world attention on the ability of small groups with limited technological resources to inflict major damage. The use of truck bombs driven by suicidal volunteers seemed to hark back to earlier patterns of terrorism in the Middle East wherein extremist Shiite assassins fanned out from mountain hideouts to strike their victims. Although it may be true in a romantic sense that some Shiite terrorist groups do in fact use traditional organizational and ideological techniques, this obscures a larger pattern of violence that has emerged in the Middle East in the last decade.

EVOLUTION: FROM PROFESSIONALS TO AMATEURS

Modern international terrorism dates from the 1968 hijacking of a Tel Aviv–bound airliner by the Popular Front for the Liberation of Palestine (PFLP). This was the first such attack on an aircraft and represented the introduction of a strategy of conflict designed to exploit both the destructive power and the vulnerabilities of Western technology. In the 1960s and 1970s, Middle Eastern terrorists (principally Palestinian in origin) sought to exploit a number of political and technological trends: (1) the development of air transport systems, which offered easy targets for spectacular terrorist attacks; (2) the emergence of global communication facilities, which facilitated the transmission of terrorist demands; (3) the creation of sophisticated weaponry, which gave small groups the ability to inflict enormous destruction; and (4) the appearance of multiple sources of political and financial support (Beres 1974; Weisband and Roguly 1976).

The original Middle Eastern terrorist organizations were largely secular (e.g., nationalist or Marxist) in organization and orientation and Westernized in terms of education and training. Most of the terrorists were pragmatic professionals in the sense that they had discernible career patterns and a commonality of outlook, and were careful to provide for their own safety. Carlos was the prototype of the Middle Eastern terrorist of the 1960s and 1970s (Dobson and Payne 1977).

In the 1970s, Sunni-Muslim terrorism emerged and nationalistic violence was paralleled by religious violence. In the 1980s, terrorism has become a minority (either ethnic or religious) phenomenon. Existing terrorist groups are now complemented by Christian and Shiite groups. The professional terrorist has given way to the amateur: Terrorists of the 1980s are less well trained (with the exceptions of the Armenians and the Abu Nidal group members) and more extreme in their willingness to risk their own lives. Suicide volunteers now compete for headlines.

The willingness and means to resort to terrorist violence have become more diffuse. Existing Middle East conflicts—for example between the Lebanese, between Iraq and Iran, and between the Palestinians and Israelis—have been increasingly metasticized in scope and impact. The transnational quality of Middle Eastern violence has been accentuated, as has its unfocused quality in the sense that much contemporary terrorist targeting appears randomly directed.

This diffuse and unfocused nature is reflected in the common practice of referring to all of it as "terrorism." In a technical sense, terrorism is any act that in itself is a crime, specifically a violent crime, and that is conducted for psychological purposes. External terrorism, or transnational terror, is terrorism conducted across national boundaries or against citizens of another state. Beyond these generalized observations, there is no agreement on what constitutes terrorism. For example, Israeli spokesmen routinely refer to any Palestinian activity as "terrorism"; similarly, the term *terrorist* has been used by opponents to describe a number of governments in the Middle East and it has been used also to identify combatants in the Lebanese conflict.

Part of the difficulty in defining a person or an act as "terrorist" (aside from propagandistic differences) has to do with the motives, political or otherwise that are associated with the violence. (See Murphy 1975; Jenkins 1981; and Hacker 1976 for attempts to distinguish among the sorts of violence perpetrated by terrorists, criminals, and psychopaths.)

Given the already complex pattern of political and sectarian conflicts within the Middle East, the added problem of distinguishing terrorist from nonterrorist violence becomes almost impossible. But for our purposes here, this article utilizes the following working definition: a terrorist act is an act that is perpetrated for discernible political purposes and that employs more or less identifiable terrorist techniques—assassination, bombing, kidnapping, hijacking, and hostage-taking.

CONFLICT PATTERNS: THE SOURCES AND LINKAGES OF VIOLENCE

Contemporary Middle Eastern terrorism (including even random interpersonal violence) has its roots in the multiplicity of conflicts that characterize the Middle East as a system of politics. At least three sources or levels of conflict are discernible: (1) intracommunal conflicts, that is to say, conflicts between individual cliques, factions, or parties, conflicts that grow out of small groups or organizational structure (an example would be the conflict among factions in the PLO); (2) intercommunal conflicts, which are larger and more inclusive conflicts between ethnic and sectarian groups, conflicts that originate in the relations between these communities (the Lebanese war is an example of a series of these conflicts); and (3) intracultural conflicts, which are more pervasive conflicts between value systems (for example, conflicts that occur between religiously defined communities—Christians and Muslims, or Sunnis and Shi'as) (LeVine 1961; Snyder 1979). Each of these three levels is worked into a fourth level, that of interstate conflict—conflict among the Middle Eastern states themselves or between these states and non–Middle Eastern states: Arab-Israeli, Iraq and Iran, Libya and the United States.

These various levels of conflict are linked by a complex web of shared interests and strategies. The result is a series of cross-cutting coalitions on the part of governments and communal and organizational leaders, which leads to a pattern of violence that not only cross-cuts existing conflicts, but ties in previously unrelated conflicts. For example, Shiite militants in southern Lebanon receive aid from the Iranian government. Aid to these militants, in turn, is a function of conflicts within the Iranian elite. Aid also comes from Syria and Libya. Similarly, Armenian militancy is tied into the Iraq-Iran war by Iranian and Syrian contacts and into European politics by European contacts.

Terrorist linkage politics is not new. Palestinian groups in the early 1970s created linkages with a variety of non–Middle Eastern groups (Sterling 1981). Given the emergence of successive waves of terrorist groups, however, the linkage phenomenon has taken on added dimensions as a device for surrogate conflict: the use of terrorist groups by Middle Eastern governments as an adjunct to regular intelligence and clandestine activities. This use is the product of a realization that conventional violence is far too dangerous; in a sense, it also represents a realization on the part of certain governments that their conventional military capabilities are clearly no match for those of their neighbors. Terrorism, if the responsibility can be mediated through other groups, is a cost-effective way of engaging in violence against both domestic and foreign opponents. Libya and Iran have become the major transnational terror brokers of the early 1980s. The Syrians train (or permit training on Syrian-controlled territories) a number of groups. However, Syrian sponsorship of terrorist groups appears to be limited to groups operating in Lebanon or in countries immediately adjacent to Syria. Iraq, which used to be a major source of support for terrorism, has sharply reduced this activity. Since 1980, Iraqi support appears limited to groups operating against Iran, Syria, and Kurdish nationalists.

VIOLENCE BY SUBMERGED MINORITIES: SHI'A AND ARMENIANS

In contrast to earlier decades when violence was the prerogative mainly of regular governments and/or predominantly Sunni groups, violence in 1984 was mostly a minority phenomenon. Both Shi'a violence and Armenian violence are responses, albeit in a different manner, to the Muslim trend, which accelerated after the 1967 war and brought in its train an intensification of the sectarian aspect of Middle Eastern politics. (On the Muslim trend, see, for example, Lewis 1976; Dekmejian 1980; Dessouki 1973; Ajami 1981; Cudsi and Dessouki 1981; and Esposito 1983.)

Shiite communities were mobilized by the twin impact of the Lebanese conflict and of Khomeini's call for a revolution among the oppressed, meaning a revolution among Shiite populations. This heightened sense of identity has occurred throughout the Gulf region but it is particularly intense in Lebanon where Shiite communities in the south have suffered enormous casualties and destruction of property as a consequence of Israeli-Palestinian military activities in that area. The result on the part of Shiite communities has been to organize in their own defense and articulate their own specifically Shiite interests.

Armenian violence is part of a larger trend of Christian militancy in the Middle East. Heretofore submerged Christian communities have become politically mobilized as a consequence of the Islamic resurgence. The conflict in Lebanon again has accelerated this trend. For a number of Christians, the issue presented by Lebanon is that of the survival of a distinct Christian identity.

Like the Shiites, the position of Christians in the Middle East has been anomalous. The Islamic trend, however, with its emphasis on Muslim-ness, has made the situation of non-Muslims much more visible and much more uncomfortable. Christian communities are progressively more alienated and are suffering their own identity crisis. The rise of nongovernmental Islamic militancy, along with regular governmental repression, have forced Christians into an agonizing reappraisal of their situation. The choice seems to be one of submerging themselves as Christians and losing their identity or seeking a new identity through some form of nationalism. Those Christians who choose the nationalist route have become increasingly more militant in response to the rising tide of violence around them. (For an overview, see Joseph 1983, especially 129ff; Hovannisian 1974; and Joseph and Pillsbury 1978.)

SHIITE ORGANIZATIONS: OLD STRUCTURE, NEW TECHNIQUE

Geographically, Shiite communities stretch in a belt from the east coast of the Gulf through southern Iraq into Iran, parts of northern Syria and southern Lebanon, and up into Azerbaijan. Historically, these communities were religiously distinct from the dominant Sunni communities, relatively isolated both sociologically and geographically from the intellectual and political mainstreams of the area, and relatively disadvantaged in economic terms (Mortimer 1982, 360ff). But even though their religion, sociology, and standard of living would have predisposed them toward revolutionary violence, Shiite communities by and large remained quiescent. (Some Shiite militancy was expressed by young political parties opposed to Sunni establishment.) Shiite quietism took the form of an inward-turning practice of religious study and meditation, al-taqiyah, a system of religious study engaged in by Shiite youth in private. The essence of this training was development of an inward sense of identity hidden from public view. Over the years Shiite communities had developed an organizational structure that would support the Shiite religious identity. The basic unit of this structure was the *husayniyah,* a cadre of Shiites concerned with religious and educational activities. By the 1970s, hundreds of husayni-yahs were in operation in Iraq and the Gulf area (*Arab Press Service,* 19–26 Sept. 1979); *Arab Press Service,* 28 Dec. 1983). Thus, Shiite communities were, in a structural sense, capable of organized militancy, and in an ideological sense, the tenets of Shiism contained a messianic element that could provide a possible ideological justification for violence (Sachedina 1981). In spite of this, however, Shiite communities remained relatively quiescent until the events in Lebanon and Iran mobilized them.

The emerging Shiite sense of identity (and alienation) was intensified by the Iraq-Iran war, which accentuated Shiite-Sunni tensions throughout the Middle East. In Iraq, the extensive internal security apparatus was particularly concerned to suppress any potential Shiite uprising; in Syria, the minority Shiite elite found itself targeted by Sunni Islamic fundmentalists (in turn, partly organized by the Iraqis). In the Gulf region, both Iranian and Iraqi orga-nizational activities contributed to the mobilization of these populations.

The impulse to convert traditional Shiite social organizations into po-litical organizations with terrorist potential came from both within and without the Syrian community. In Lebanon, the original impetus came from the Amal (hope) movement. Amal was founded by Imam Musa al-Sadr in the middle 1970s. The movement provided military training in Lebanon for Shiites, its main thrust being to organize a force capable of protecting Shiite communities. As such, it became the mainstream movement among Shiites in Lebanon (*al-Watan,* 20 June 1980). (Musa al-Sadr disappeared in 1978 while visiting Libya.)

The Amal maintained its own militia, which participated in the Le-banese National Resistance Front, along with other groups. The Amal militia has carried out a number of attacks against Israeli troops in southern Lebanon. Its members operate in three-man cells using light weapons, basically Kalash-nikov rifles, Soviet RPG launchers, and German submachine guns (*Borneo Post,* 9 Sept. 1984). In 1984 these attacks escalated and became a major factor in the Israeli decision to withdraw their forces from southern Lebanon.

However, a number of splinter and more radical Shiite groups rapidly emerged, many of them under the aegis of Iran and Syria. Radical groups within the Amal umbrella now include the Islamic Jihad organization, the Islamic Amal, and the Hizb Allah (Party of God). The Islamic Jihad organization orig-inally had both Syrian and Libyan support, but Libyan links were severed in early 1984 because of a conflict between Qaddafi and the Islamic leadership of the Jihad over Libyan aid to Lebanese Sunni militant groups. The Islamic Amal and Hizb Allah are said to be sponsored by the Iranians, more specifically the radical faction within the Iranian elite headed by the speaker of the Iranian parliament, Hashemi Rafsanjani. Both also have Syrian backing (*Arab Press Service,* 20–27 Aug. 1984; *Arab Press Service,* 26 Nov. 1984).

In Lebanon, Shiite volunteers for the more radical groups are trained at husayniyahs in Shiite-inhabited suburbs in the Beirut area, and in military bases in the Shiite-inhabited parts of the Bekaa Valley. The training centers recruit young volunteers between the ages of seventeen and twenty and put them through a course that is a variation on the traditional taqiyah training. The curriculum is said to take between six and eight weeks to complete. Trained militants are sent to other military camps for training in explosives and other specifically military weaponry and are then assigned targets (*Arab Press Service*, 28 Dec. 1983).

Of the Lebanese Shiite groups, the Islamic Jihad party is the most aggressive in its terrorist activities. It was responsible for the truck bombing of the U.S. embassy in West Beirut in April 1983 (*Washington Post*, 25 Oct. 1983), the bombing of the U.S. and French military headquarters in October 1983, a bombing of a hotel and French military court command post in West Beirut in December 1983, and the bombing of the U.S. embassy in East Beirut in September 1984. The 1983 bombings were one of the major factors in influencing the United States to pull its Marine contingent out of Lebanon (*New York Times*, 24 Oct. 1983; *New York Times*, 22 Dec. 1983). In August 1984, the Islamic Jihad group threatened to "purify" Lebanese territory of American presence and indicated that the July 1984 attack on the Soviet embassy in Beirut was also carried out by it. In December 1984, Jihad gunmen hijacked a Kuwaiti airliner to Tehran. Three passengers were killed before Iranian security forces stormed the plane.

Shiite militancy outside of Lebanon was promoted by Iranians and Syrians. In Iraq, for example, al-Hizb al-Da'wah al-Islamiyah (Party of the Islamic Call) was founded in 1968–69 under the leadership of Imam Muhammad al-Sadr (who was executed by the Iraqi government in 1980.) Hizb al-Da'wah is currently headquartered in Tehran; it has Syrian as well as Iranian support. This was the group responsible for blowing up the Iraqi embassy in Beirut in December 1981, and it has claimed responsiblity for a number of attacks on Iraqi officials both before and after the embassy bombing. Hizb al-Da'wah also claims it made an unsuccessful attempt to assassinate Saddam Hussein himself (*al-Nashrah*, Dec. 1983, 23–25; Batatu 1981).

The group currently is said to be active in Iran, Iraq, Syria, Kuwait, and other Gulf countries. According to its spokesman, its goal is to change the ruling regimes in these countries and set up Islamic republics along the lines advocated by the Khomeini regime (*al-Watan al-'Arabi*, 17–23 Feb. 1984). In this regard, its most spectacular attack was the bombing in December 1983 of the American embassy along with other American, French, and Kuwaiti buildings in Kuwait. At that time, some six bombs were detonated. Twenty-five people were apparently involved, and the weapons and explosives were smuggled into Kuwait from Iran. The personnel themselves moved into Kuwait from Iran via Syria, where they were trained in the use of weapons and explosives.

ARMENIAN TERRORISM: ASSERTION OF A CHRISTIAN IDENTITY

Contemporary Armenian militancy is part of a long tradition of Armenian concern with ethnocultural survival. Historically Armenian communities were both closely integrated internally and isolated from surrounding Muslim society externally. Armenians as a rule did not share the customs or language of majority populations. (The same is true of Assyrian communities in the area.) Armenian nationalist organizations, the Hunchak and Dashnak parties, were founded as early as the 1880s and were concerned with defending the Armenian identity. In this sense, contemporary Armenian terrorist groups are the heirs of these earlier parties.

Armenian militancy today is a specific reaction to the massacre of Armenians carried out by the Young Turks in 1915. The Armenian populations were dramatically and brutally mobilized by the violence. At that time, most of the Armenian community in Turkey was either killed or deported, and survivors were relocated in camps. As a consequence, the Armenian community as a whole became even more alienated from its surrounding populations. (For detailed accounts, see Toynbee 1916; Morgenthau 1918.)

The Armenian Secret Army for the Liberation of Armenia (ASALA) and the Justice Commandos of the Armenian Genocide were formed in 1975. The Armenian Revolutionary Army (ARA) began operations in 1983. Some sources indicate as many as ten to twelve Armenian terrorist organizations may have been active at one time. All these groups share a similar goal of avenging the Turkish genocide of the Armenians. In their formative stages, many of these groups had linkages with Palestine organizations: Armenians received training in PLO camps in Lebanon until 1982. According to some sources, ASALA split with the PLO, specifically Fatah, in the 1980s but remained in contact with Abu Nidal's faction (al-Nashrah, 31 Oct. 1983). After the Israeli invasion of 1982, ASALA moved its training camps to Cyprus and Syria (Perera 1984; Marmara, 24 Apr. 1984). Apparently some ASALA camps remain in Syrian-controlled areas of the Bekaa Valley.

ASALA is organized in a cell structure along the lines of the Irish Republican Army. The apex of this structure is the General Command of the People of Armenia (VAN). Specifically military policy is drawn up by a political bureau. Each cell is self-sufficient and its members are given only enough information to attack their targets; cell members ordinarily do not know even who their leaders are. This cell structure parallels that of the old Palestinian Black September organization (ALIK, 24 Oct. 1983).

ASALA claims to have cadres in a number of countries, including Switzerland, France, West Germany, Italy, the United States, Cyprus, Greece, Australia, Spain, Portugal, and Iran. In addition, the group has had contacts for some time with Kurdish insurgents (Arab Press Service, 30 Apr.–7 May 1980), specifically the Kurdish Workers party (PKK) of Turkey, a contact probably mediated by the Palestinians who also trained Kurdish groups (Van Bruinessen 1984). In Lebanon, ASALA was said to have five bases and to be headquartered in Beirut. After 1982, it was headquartered in Paris, and Turkish sources claim that ASALA is now in the process in moving its headquarters to either Spain or Italy (Marmara, 25 Sept. 1984).

ASALA is alleged to have a number of ties with other groups—Abu Nidal's Palestinians and the Red Brigades, for example, and through them to still others (Marmara, 17 Sept. 1984). The group appears to receive some Syrian training, Greek support via Cyprus, and Iranian assistance (Marmara, 31 Mar. 1984). Armenian communities in Iran have been subject to governmental surveillance, and pressure has been put on Armenian schools to teach their curricula in Farsi (ALIK, 23 Oct. 1983). Iranian support is said to include target selection; the threat of increased harassment of Armenian communities in Iran is cited probably as an inducement to secure Armenian cooperation.

In 1982, following the loss of its Lebanese base, ASALA is said to have split into two wings, a military and nationalist wing, which stresses terrorism, and a more political wing known as ASALA– Revolutionary Movement, which stresses political action (Perera 1984).

Unlike their Shiite counterparts who employ techniques designed to kill as many as possible, members of ASALA (along with other Armenian organizations) operate in a more classic terrorist tradition. Their main tactics have been the assassination of Turkish diplomatic personnel and the occupation of Turkish embassies. Accordingly, ASALA has been implicated in approximately fifty murders, including twenty-nine Turkish diplomats or their dependents. ASALA in all organized some one hundred attacks on Turkish targets in over fifteen countries. (Again unlike Shiite counterparts, ASALA operates on an international rather than a Middle Eastern scale.)

Extremely sophisticated weapons are used, including antitank rockets, Soviet-made guns, grenades, and other explosives. Also in the classic Western terrorist tradition, ASALA uses a series of safe houses in major cities (Wilkinson 1983).

Not all ASALA attacks have been limited to single individuals. In August 1982, members machine-gunned passengers at the Ankara airport; in June 1983, ASALA terrorists killed two and injured twenty-three people in a bazaar in Istanbul; the next month, a suitcase bomb was exploded at the Orly airport (*New York Times*, 18 July 1983). In 1984, ASALA attacked two Turkish diplomats in Tehran (*Marmara*, 29 Mar. 1984) and claimed responsibility for the shooting of a Turkish businessman in the same city in May (*Tehran Times*, 1 May 1984).

Two other Armenian organizations are also active. The Justice Commandos of the Armenian Genocide is apparently headquartered in California and employs the same tactics as ASALA. In March 1983, the Justice Commandos assasinated the Turkish ambassador in Belgrade, Yugoslavia (*Aztag*, 23 Apr. 1983). The group's first attack occurred in 1975 when it assassinated Turkish ambassadors in Vienna and Paris.

The Armenian Revolutionary Army (ARA) is the newest group. Its first known attacks were the assassination of a Turkish diplomat in Brussels and the occupation of the Turkish embassy in Lisbon. Both of these events took place in July 1983 (*ALIK*, 30 June 1984). Since then it has been extremely active in attacking Turkish officials. In 1984, ARA assassinated two Turkish diplomats in Vienna (*Marmara*, 20 Nov. 1984).

Armenian activities have occasioned great concern in the United States, where it was felt that Armenians might attempt to attack Turkish team members during the 1984 Olympic Games, much as the Black September organization attacked the Israeli team in Munich in 1972. Planning for Olympic security was said to have started as early as 1979, some five years before the games were held (*Los Angeles Times*, 19 Oct. 1983; Charters 1983). Elsewhere, governments have cracked down on Armenian activities, notably Spain, France, and Iran. In Turkey, Armenian communities have been subjected to official surveillance and governmental harassment. Authorities there arrested a group of Armenian goldsmiths; accusations were made under the pretext that they were financially supporting ASALA (*Zartonk*, 7 Dec. 1984).

In addition, it appears that some counterterror operations have been organized allegedly by Turkish intelligence. In 1983 a bomb exploded in the Armenian Cultural Center at Alfortville, France, and in March 1984 a second bomb exploded in the Marseilles Cultural Center (*Le Monde*, 5 May 1984). Other bombs were exploded at Alfortville in May of 1984 and in Paris in November 1984 (*Le Monde*, 5 May 1984; 27 Nov. 1984).

PALESTINIAN TERRORISM: FACTIONALISM AND PROFESSIONALISM

Palestinian terrorist activities in 1983–84 were dominated by the Abu Nidal group. Abu Nidal (code name of Sabri al-Banna) broke with the Fatah establishment in 1972 and formed Fatah–The Revolutionary Command. From the beginning, the Abu Nidal group opposed any diplomatic solution of the Arab-Israeli conflict and accused Yasir Arafat of being too soft on the Israelis. It followed up these accusations with the assassination of PLO moderates. This, in turn, provoked a Fatah riposte in the form of a special counterinsurgency squad organized by Fatah's Salah Khalaf. Both sides train and operate in the old Black September tradition. The Abu Nidal group is relatively small, with about two hundred to five hundred members, and is organized in cells. Most of these cells are in Kuwait and the Gulf states, although there are a number in European cities as well.

Originally the Abu Nidal group was supplied by the Iraqis; since 1980 it has received Libyan and Syrian aid. After 1982, the group joined the Syrian-sponsored anti-Arafat rebellion. Most of the group's training bases currently are located in Libya (*Arab Press Service*, 16–23 Jan. 1984).

Organizationally, the Abu Nidal group is said to be one of the most professional of all terrorist groups. It presently recruits from Arab students studying in Europe. Tactically, terrorist operations are normally carried out by three-man assassination squads. These squads spend some time in advance of the planned attack familiarizing themselves with the city in which the attack is to take place and acquiring weapons. Most of the attacks are aimed at pro-Arafat Palestinians, but the group has carried out a number of attacks on Jordanian officials as well (*Arab Press Service*, 16–23 Nov. 1983; *Arab Press Service*, 3 Sept. 1984; see also a series by Nadim Nasir in *al-Majallah*, 24–30 Mar. through 28 Apr.–4 May 1984). In 1984 the attacks continued in the form of bombings, and Arab sources indicated that the group had received Syrian as well as Libyan support in carrying them out (*Arab Press Service*, 3 Sept. 1984).

In January 1984, Libyan, Iranian, and Abu Nidal representatives met in Tripoli to coordinate a strategy designed to "punish all those regimes which have backed Egypt's return to the Arab fold and the union plans between Jordan and the PLO." According to Arab sources, the punishment objectives were set by the Libyans and Abu Nidal's representatives, while Iran insisted on the inclusion of those regimes supporting Iraq in the war (*Arab Press Service*, 16–23 Jan. 1984).

Abu Nidal himself is said to have died in November 1984 of a heart attack (*al-Watan al-'Arabi* 1984); thus the group's future is uncertain. Arab sources indicate that the group had planned (with Syrian and Libyan encouragement) to infiltrate Palestinian communities throughout the Gulf area and create a broad-based anti-Arafat movement there. The Abu Nidal group also planned to infiltrate pro-Arafat guerrillas who are currently languishing in camps throughout North Africa and the Middle East.

SURROGATE TERRORISM: LIBYA AND IRAN

The major terrorist brokers in the Middle East are Libya and Iran. (Iraq, a strong supporter of terrorism in the 1960s and 1970s, sharply reduced its support for such groups as part of a major policy shift prior to the 1980 war.) Both Libya and Iran support terrorist groups as part of their overall foreign policy objectives of exporting revolution and eliminating expatriate sources of opposition (*Arab Press Service*, 20–27 Aug. 1984).

In line with these general foreign policy objectives, both Iran and Libya have sponsored a number of groups and provided training facilities for others. Although their overall outlines of strategies are the same, their operationalization is different. Libya, for example, is said to maintain thirty-four camps for the training of various revolutionaries. The camps are specialized in terms both of personnel (e.g., special camps set aside for North Africans, as against Palestinians, as against Africans), and of military training techniques. Some camps are devoted to training for desert warfare, others are for training frogmen, and still others teach demolition techniques (*Arab Press Service*, 30 Apr. 1984, contains a list of these camps). Frogmen trained in Libyan camps were thought to be the men who placed mines in the Red Sea; the Islamic Jihad claimed responsibility for the operation (*Kayhan*, 23 Aug. 1984). According to Egyptian sources, training is given to Egyptians, Tunisians, Sudanese, Yemenese, Palestinians, Iraqis, Algerians, Moroccans, Omanis, Iranians, Italians, Japanese, Latin Americans, and others. Instructors come from the U.S.S.R., East Germany, Cuba, and other Communist bloc states (*Arab Press Service*, 7 May 1984; see also Weber 1978).

The Libyan terrorist infrastructure relies heavily on the People's Bureaus. These bureaus function as centers for purchasing arms (particularly in London, Brussels, Paris, Berne, Istanbul, Athens, and Rabat) and for coordinating terrorist activities. According to *Africa Confidential* (1984), key terrorist coordinating centers are the bureaus in Berne, Switzerland, and Madrid, Spain. They apparently coordinate, supply, and dispatch Libyan hit teams, six-member squads whose chief function is the assassination of Libyan expatriates.

In 1983, these teams conducted assassinations in the United States, Italy, France, and West Germany. In April 1984, a series of incidents involving Libyan personnel—a gunman firing from the Libyan embassy in London; a bomb exploding at Heathrow airport; the British embassy besieged in Tripoli—led to a break in relations between Libya and Britain (*Washington Post*, 18 Apr. 1984; New York Times, 22 Apr. 1984). Both sides began deporting the other's nationals. Libyan hit team activities were also directed against members of the National Front for the Salvation of Libya (NFSL) after they attempted a coup against Qaddafi in May of 1984. The NFSL itself was made up of members of the Muslim Brethren and received support from the Sudan (al-Mukhtar 1984). People's Bureaus' activities are supplemented by a series of front groups and private individuals who operate in Europe, the Middle East, Asia, Africa, and Latin America (Tariq 1984).

Whereas Libyan activities are more or less standard terrorism, the Iranians have opted for a much more exotic symbiosis of modern and traditional forms of violence. On the one hand, Iranian embassy personnel throughout Europe, and particularly in Spain, have been accused of sponsoring terrorist cadres in several countries. In late 1983, Spanish police arrested a number of Iranians who confessed that they were planning to attack expatriate Iranian opponents of the Khomeini regime (*Arab Times*, 13 Oct. 1984, 5).

In December 1983, the French government expelled several Iranian diplomats. According to French sources, the Iranian embassy in Paris served as a center for the organization of cadres of terrorists, whose main function was the listing, location, and assassination of anti-Khomeini Iranians. Regular embassy resources were supplemented by cultural and student organizations.

The Iranian strategy here was to train terrorists in Syrian and Libyan camps and then send them abroad with diplomatic cover. In France, 150 to 300 such "students" were said to be supervised by embassy personnel (*Liberation*, 30 Dec. 1983). Iranian liquidation squads are suspected to be operating as far afield as the Philippines (*Bulletin Today*, 3 Dec. 1983, 6) and Indonesia (*Asiaweek*, 4 Nov. 1983).

Iranian-conducted terrorism, however, has been directed at other targets as well. In August 1984, Spanish police arrested four Iranians, members of the Martyrs of the Iranian Revolution, in connection with a plot to hijack a Saudi airliner. The Iranian press attaché was said to be in contact with the Martyrs. In the same month, a French airliner was hijacked to Tehran. The hijackers demanded the release of Iranians jailed in France following an attempt to assassinate Shapur Bakhtiari in 1980 (*Washington Post*, 2 Aug. 1984). Following the hijacking, Iranian spokesman described it as a "lesson for France" because of French policies toward both Iraq and Iranian expatriates living in France (*Le Quotidien*, 6 Aug. 1984).

On the other hand, Iranian activities in the Middle East have also utilized Shiite husayniyahs and other traditional Shiite organizations. In Lebanon, for example, Iranian volunteers began training with the Amal movement as early as 1979. These volunteers later returned to Iran to become part of the Pasdaran (Mortimer 1982, 372).

The introduction in 1982 of Iranian Revolutionary Guard units in Lebanon enabled the Iranians to penetrate the Shiite community. Iranians helped organize Amal splinter groups, the Islamic Amal, the Hizbullah (Partisans of God), and the Islamic Jihad. The Guards, the Hizbullah, and Syrian intelligence all cooperate in organizing terrorism (*Newsweek*, 7 Nov. 1983, 90; *Arab Press Service*, 26 Nov. 1984; *al-Majallah* 1983).

Terrorist training in both Iran and Syria began in early 1983 (*Arab Press Service 3*, 20–27 Aug. 1984). In Iran, two camps are maintained for the training of "suicide" volunteers. According to Arab sources, the number being trained in these camps rose sharply following the attack on the U.S. embassy in April 1983. The largest camp, outside of Qum, is said to have about two thousand personnel (*Liberation*, 30 Dec. 1983). Volunteers for the training are selected by Iranian embassy officials in the Middle East and Europe. The programs, which last approximately three weeks, involve training in truck bombing and the use of weapons and explosives, and attendance at ideological indoctrination sessions. Palestinian, Cuban, Syrian, and Polisario personnel are said to serve as instructors. After graduation, the trainees are then given their assignments (Nurizadah 1983). Some of them go into the Basij forces, which are used in suicidal attacks against the Iraqis (*Arab Press Service*, 27 Feb. 1984).

CONCLUSION: THE SYMBIOTIC USE OF VIOLENCE

Violence in the Middle East in the middle of the 1980s has taken on a new dimension. The old pattern of conventional warfare is being increasingly replaced by violence predicated upon small-scale operations involving small numbers of individuals using sophisticated weaponry. Violence, which used to be the prerogative of governments or majority populations, is now increasingly filtering down to minorities. The use of terrorism as a political technique for inducing governmental change and/or symbolically expressing minority grievances has become more and more widespread. Professional terrorism is being augmented by suicidal amateur terrorism. Random violence has increased; any limitation that pragmatism may have placed on terrorist violence is rapidly eroding.

In addition, however, a more profound trend is occurring: that is the amalgam between traditional social structure and twentieth-century weapons technology. This trend started in the 1960s and 1970s when Palestinian groups utilized traditional social organization and kinship structure as the basis for a sophisticated terrorist organizational format. Similarly, Sunni fundamentalist organizations in the 1970s, or more specifically, offshoots of the Muslim Brethren made use of existing kinship linkages as a basis for organized revolutionary violence. What is new is that this particular symbiosis has been adopted by a succession of groups, predominantly the Shiites and, to a lesser extent, the Armenians. As a long-term trend in the region, the diffusion of the technology of violence will produce long-term instability.

REFERENCES

Africa Confidential 1984. No. 9 (Apr.): 1–4.

Ajami, Fouad. 1981. *The Arab predicament: Arab political thought and practice since 1967.* Cambridge: Cambridge University Press.

Batatu, Hanna. 1981. Iraq's underground Shi'a movement: Characteristics, causes, and prospects. *Middle East Journal*, Autumn.

Beres, Louis Rene. 1974. Guerrillas, terrorists, and polarity: New structural models of world politics. *Western Political Science Quarterly* 27 (Dec.): 624–36.

Charters, David A. 1983. Terrorism and the 1984 Olympics. *Conflict Quarterly*, Summer, 37–47.

Cudsi, Alexander S., and Ali E. Hillal Dessouki, eds. 1981. *Islam and power.* Baltimore, Md.: Johns Hopkins University Press.

Dekmejian, R. Hrair. 1980. The anatomy of the Islamic revival: Legitimacy crisis, ethnic conflict, and the search of Islamic alternatives. *Middle East Journal* 34, no. 1 (Winter): 1–12.

Dessouki, Ali E. Hillal. 1973. Arab intellectuals and al-Nakba: The search for fundamentalism. *Middle Eastern Studies* 9, no. 2 (May): 187–96.

Dobson, Christopher, and Ronald Payne, 1977. *The Carlos complex: A study in terror.* New York: C. Putnam & Sons.

Esposito, John L., ed. 1983. *Voices of resurgent Islam.* New York: Oxford University Press.

Hacker, Frederick J. 1976. *Crusaders, criminals, crazies: Terror and terrorism in our time.* New York: W.W. Norton & Co.

Hovannisian, Richard G. 1974. Ebb and flow of the Armenian minority in the Arab Middle East. *Middle East Journal* 28 (Winter): 19–32.

Jenkins, Brian M. 1981. The study of terrorism: Definitional problems. In *Behavioral and quantitative perspectives on terrorism*, edited by Yonah Alexander and John M. Gleason, 3–10. New York: Pergamon Press.

Joseph, John. 1983. *Muslim-Christian relations and inter-Christian rivalries in the Middle East: The case of the Jacobites in an age of transition.* Albany: State University of New York Press.

Joseph, Suad, and Barbara L.K. Pillsbury, eds. 1978. *Muslim Christian conflicts: Economic, political and social origins.* Boulder, Colo.: Westview Press.

LeVine, Robert A. 1961. Anthropology and the study of conflict: Introduction. *Journal of Conflict Resolution* 5:3–15.

Lewis, Bernard. 1976. The return of Islam. *Commentary* 61, no. 1 (January): 39–49.

al-Majallah. 1983. No. 195 (5–11 Nov.): 10–12.

Morgenthau, Henry. 1918. *Ambassador Morgenthau's story.* New York: Doubleday.

Mortimer, Edward. 1982. *Faith and power: The Politics of Islam.* New York: Random House.

al-Mukhtar, Omar. 1984. The struggle for Libya. *Arabia, the Islamic World Review,* no. 34 (June): 6–13.

Murphy, John F. 1975. International legal controls of international terrorism: Performance and prospects. *Illinois Bar Journal,* Apr. 444–52.

Nurizadah, 'Ali. 1983. The Gulf: An exciting investigation of a 'base' for launching terrorists. *al-Dustur,* nos. 318–19 (26 Sept.): 14–15.

Perera, Judith. 1984. Who can heal Armenian wounds? *Middle East Magazine,* no. 116 (June): 29–30.

Sachedina, Abdulaziz Abdulhussein. 1981. *Islamic messianism: The idea of the Mahdi in twelver Shiism.* Albany: State University of New York Press.

Snyder, Lewis W. 1979. Minorities and political power in the Middle East. In *The political role of minority groups in the Middle East,* edited by R.D. McLaurin, 240–65. New York: Praeger Publications.

Sterling, Claire. 1981. *The terrorist network.* New York: Readers Digest Publications.

Tariq, Abi. 1984. The terrorists' intelligence agencies and the policy of fronts. *al-Inqadh,* no. 8 (Apr.): 37–39.

Toynbee, Arnold. 1916. *The treatment of Armenians in the Ottoman Empire, 1850–1860.* London: His Majesty's Stationery Office.

Van Bruinessen, Martin. 1984. The Kurds in Turkey. *MERIP Reports,* 6–12 Feb., 14.

al-Watan al-'Arabi. 1984. No. 405 (16–23 Nov.): 26–30.

Weber, Tom. 1978. The strange capital of world terrorism. *San Francisco Chronicle,* 9, 11, 19 Oct.

Weisband, Edward, and Damir Roguly. 1976. Palestinian terrorism: Violence, verbal strategy and legitimacy. In *International terrorism: National regional and global perspectives,* edited by Yonah Alexander, 258–319. New York: Praeger Publishers.

Wilkinson, Paul. 1983. Armenian terrorism. *World Today,* Sept. 344–50.

Bibliography:
The Year's Publications in Middle Eastern Studies, 1984

Mark Tyler Day
David H. Partington

The bibliography lists monographs and serials in English, French, and German that appeared in 1984 on the modern Middle East, including major historical works that provide the background necessary to understand contemporary events. Some entries are included for materials published before 1984 which could not be included in earlier volumes of *The Middle East Annual*; in these cases, the imprint date is included in the entries.

So as not to overburden the bibliography with redundant titles, French and German translations of works that either originally appeared in English or are available in English-language versions have not been included, nor have reeditions and reprints of English-language works unless they are studies that have been revised extensively, have long been unavailable, or have particular relevance to contemporary events. On the other hand, an attempt has been made to include English, French, or German editions and translations of non-English-language publications, particularly those originally written in a Middle Eastern language.

Annotations in brackets are based on information derived from such secondary sources as publishers' catalogs, national bibliographies, and reviews; other annotations are based on examination of the books themselves. The alphabetical arrangement disregards the Arabic article *al* in its various permutations (*al, Al, el, El, etc.* etc.); thus, al-Morayati will be found under M, El Sheik under S, and so on.

Monographs

Abdrabboh, Bob. *Saudi Arabia: The Uniqueness of the Country and Its Heritage.* Annandale, Va.: Mike O'lwan & Co. 109 pp. Bibl.; append.
[This work is a basic study of Saudi values, contemporary society, and economic growth in the post-oil-boom era, written for foreigners new to the

country. The author's analysis of the role of oil and religion in the modernization process is not systematically developed.]

Abdulghani, Jasim. *Iraq and Iran: The Years of Crisis*. Baltimore, Md.: Johns Hopkins University Press. 288 pp.

Abdullah, Yahya Taher. *The Mountain of Green Tea*. Translated by Denys Johnson-Davies. London: Heinemann; Washington, D.C.: Three Continents Press. 113 pp.
Abdullah was one of the most promising young Egyptian authors when he was killed in a car accident in April 1981. He was a self-taught monolingual writer whose short stories, such as those collected here, give us a uniquely inspired vision of what it is like to be a modern Egyptian. Johnson-Davies's introduction, written before the author's unfortunate accident, provides the Western reader with the cultural background information necessary to interpret these very personal stories.

Abdulrahman, A.J., comp. *Iraq*. World Bibliographical Series, no. 42. Oxford, England, and Santa Barbara, Calif.: Clio Press. 161 pp. Bibl.; illus.; map; index.

Abdul-Razzak, Fatimah H. *Marine Resources of Kuwait: Their Role in the Development of Non-Oil Resources*. London and Boston: Kegan Paul International in association with the University of Kuwait. 300 pp. Bibl.; index.

Abou, Selim. *Bechir Gemayel ou l'esprit d'un peuple*. Paris: Anthropos. 461 pp.
[This book aspires to be not just a biography; rather it attempts to be a reminder that leads us to rediscover at their source the causes of the Lebanese conflict and some reasons for hope.]

Abou Bakr. Yahya, Saad Lahib, and Hamdy Kandil. *Le développement de l'information dans les pays arabes: Besoins et priorités*. Etudes et documents d'information. Paris: Unesco. 62 pp.
[A report focused on those organizations that are interested in communication in regard to the study of equipment and the necessity for the planning of information in Arab countries.]

Abraham, A.J. *Lebanon: A State of Siege (1975–1984)*. Notre Dame: Foundations Press. 69 pp.

Abu Nabaa, Abdel A. *Marketing in Saudi Arabia*. New York: Praeger Publishers. 228 pp. Bibl.; maps; index.

Abu Saud, Abeer Salah. *Qatari Women: Past and Present*. London: Longman. 192 pp. Illus.
[Based on interviews with a representative section of Qatari women as well as on the few available literary sources, this book probes such issues as marriage, divorce, women's rights, traditional crafts, and the clouded question of veiling.]

Achour, Mouloud, and Joachim H. Thielemann. *Algérie*. Photographs by Hed

Wimmer. Paris: Bibliothèque des Arts. 194 pp. Illus.; maps.
[Attempts to capture in words and pictures the ethnic, historical, and
regional diversity of this ancient land.]

Adams, James. *The Unnatural Alliance: Israel and South Africa*. London and
New York: Quartet Books. 218 pp. Index.

Agasi, Yehudit, and Yoel Darom, eds. *The Alternative Way of Life*. Proceedings
of the First International Conference on Communal Living, 1981. Kib-
butz Studies Book, vol. 9. Norwood, Pa.: Norwood Editions. 139 pp.
["Organized by the two main kibbutz movements in collaboration with Yad
Tabenkin Institute at Efal and the Haifa University Department for Kibbutz
Research."]

Aït Sabbah, Fatna. *Femme dans l'inconscient musulman: Désire et pouvoir*.
Paris: Le Sycomore, 1982. 203 pp.

———. *Woman in the Muslim Unconscious*. Translated by Mary Jo Lakeland.
New York: Pergamon Press. 200 pp.
[The author attempts to illuminate the perception of women in Muslim
society by analyzing the cultural documents that condition and perpetuate
that perception. She quotes extensively from classical texts that continue
to be read and that contain both descriptions and prescriptions for
relations between the sexes—including practical genres such as marriage
manuals as well as the more general erotic, chivalric, and religious genres.
She then puts this literature in the broader context of economics and
politics in order to show how certain culturally pervasive descriptions and
prescriptions for women are reflected in lifelong attitudes and behaviors.]

Aleichem, Sholom. *Why Do the Jews Need a Land of Their Own?* Translated by
Joseph Leftwich and Mordecai S. Chertoff. New York: Cornwall Books;
Hertzl Press Publications. 242 pp.
[Most of the author's work concerning the need and desire to return to the
land of Israel is gathered here. Essays, fiction, sketches, and political
journalism mirror the period (c.1880–1910) when organized return and
rebuilding began.]

Aliboni, Roberto, Ali H. Dessouki, Saad E. Ibrahim, Giacomo Lucinai, and Pier-
carlo Padoan. *Egypt's Economic Potential*. London: Croom Helm. 239
pp. Bibl.; index.

Alkhozai, Mohamed A. *The Development of Early Arabic Drama 1847–1900*.
London: Longman. 160 pp.
[The author discusses the embryonic and indigenous forms of drama in
Arab culture and how the link between these primitive forms of true Arab
theater was broken, before going on to describe the extant works of four
playwrights to whom the theater owes a great debt: Marun al-Naqqash, al-
Shaikh Ahmad Abu Khalil al-Qabbani, Yaqub Sannu, and Muhammad
Uthman Jalal.]

Amahan, Ali. *Peuplement et vie quotidienne dans un village du Haut-Atlas
marocain: Abadou de Ghoudjama, étude socio-linquistique*. Paris: Librairie Orientaliste Paul Geuthner. 248 pp.

[A native of Abadou, the author presents an abundance of oral testimony that permits him, among other things, to reconstruct the demographic movements of two centuries and the complexity of social life—which life has been transformed by the introduction of new products of consumption.]

American-Arab Anti-Discrimination Committee. *The Bitter War: Arabs under Israeli Occupation in 1982: A Report on Israeli Violations of Human Rights in Occupied Lebanon, West Bank/Gaza, and the Golan Heights, and a Conclusion on Israeli Failure to Comply with International Conventions and Treaty Obligations and Agreements with the U.S. Government*. Washington, D.C.: American-Arab Anti-Discrimination Committee. 276 pp. Map.

Amin, Ahmad. *Orient and Occident: An Egyptian's Quest for National Identity*. Translated by Wolfgang H. Behn. Berlin: Adiyok.

Amin, Samir. *The Arab Economy Today*. Introduction by Aidan Foster-Carter. London: Zed Press. 128 pp.

Arian, Asher, ed. *The Elections in Israel, 1981*. Tel Aviv: Ramot, 1983. 300 pp. Index.

Arjomand, Said A., ed. *From Nationalism to Revolutionary Islam: Essays on Social Movements in the Contemporary Near and Middle East*. Albany: State University of New York Press. 256 pp. Bibl.; illus.; index. [This study of dominant social movements in the Middle East is the first to bring nationalism and the contemporary Islamic movements into a unified thematic perspective. The process of national economic and political integration supplies the unifying context for analyses of the various social movements to which it gives rise.]

———. *The Shadow of God and the Hidden Imam: Religion, Order, and Societal Change in Shiite Iran from the Beginning to 1890*. Publications of the Center for Middle Eastern Studies, no. 17. Chicago: University of Chicago Press. 356 pp. Illus.

Arnaud, Jacqueline, and Françoise Amacker. *Répertoire mondial des travaux universitaires de la littérature maghrébine de lanque française*. Paris: Centre d'Etudes Littéraires Francophones, Université Paris XIII; Edition Diffusion L'Harmattan. 78 pp. Bibl.; indexes. [This index aims to supply the most complete list possible of studies conducted on the topic of North African literature in French. It complements the references that, for France alone, are given in the central card index of Nanterre, which is updated daily.]

Aroian, Lois A., and Richard P. Mitchell. *The Modern Middle East and Northern Africa*. New York: Macmillan. 455 pp. Bibl.; maps; index.

Atighetchi, Abolghassem. *Industrialisierungspolitik als Versuch der Überwindung ökonomischer Unterentwicklung im Iran*. Frankfurt: Haag & Herchen, 1983. 219 pp. Bibl.

Awret, Irene. *Days of Honey: The Tunisian Boyhood of Rafael Uzan.* New York: Schocken Books. 256 pp.
[The rituals, excitement, and tragedies that made up Rafael Uzan's Jewish childhood in North Africa were relayed to the author over her kitchen table in Israel. Uzan's early life in Tunisia makes an intrinsically dramatic saga and proves a fascinating contrast to the more familiar tales of European shtetl life.]

Awwad, Hanan. *Arab Causes in the Fiction of Ghāda al-Sammān, 1961–1975.* Sherbrooke, Quebec: Editions Naaman, 1983. 120 pp. Bibl.
[One thing modern Arab authors cannot possibly be accused of is disregard for the unjust conditions and just causes of the Arab woman in modern times. Ghāda al-Sammān's claim to fame. the author shows, rests upon the distinction between heightening or merely approving of the causes and actually championing them. al-Sammān's favorite and most successful form of literary expression has been fiction. Given al-Sammān's large corpus of twenty-one works, Awwad has performed a very useful function in summarizing and analyzing them.]

El Azhary, M.S., ed. *The Iran-Iraq War: Historical, Economic and Political Analysis.* New York: St. Martin's Press. 144 pp. Bibls.; maps; index.
[Chiefly papers presented at a symposium entitled "Shatt al-Arab," held at the University of Exeter in July 1982.]

———. *The Impact of Oil Revenue on Arab Gulf Development.* London: Croom Helm; Boulder, Colo.: Westview Press. 203 pp. Illus.; index.

Azmaz, Adviye. *Migration and Reintegration in Rural Turkey: The Role of Women Behind.* Socio-Economic Studies on Rural Development, vol. 51. Göttingen: Edition Herodot. 253 pp. Graphs.
[A 1981 Göttingen University dissertation.]

Bacharach, Jere L. *A Middle East Studies Handbook.* Seattle: University of Washington Press. 160 pp. Bibl.; charts; maps; tables; index.
[A fully indexed handbook full of useful information (publications, terms, dates, etc.) representing a major revision of the author's *A Near East Studies Handbook: 570–1974,* originally published in 1974.]

Badrud-Din, Abdul-Amir. *The Bank of Lebanon: Central Banking in a Financial Centre and Entrepot.* Dover, N.H.: Frances Pinter. 230 pp.
[The author writes with the inside knowledge and authority of one who has been deputy-governor of the bank for many years and concerned daily with central banking problems for about twenty-three years. Thus, he provides insight into both banking in general and the fiscal policies of war-torn Lebanon in particular.]

Bailey, Clinton, *Jordan's Palestinian Challenge, 1948–1983: A Political History.* Boulder, Colo.: Westview Press. 165 pp. Map; index.
[This book examines the thirty-five-year struggle between the Hashimite monarchy and the forces of Palestinian nationalism over the future identity, and perhaps location, of those two-thirds of the Palestinian people who have been Jordanian subjects since 1948. The author bases his study on "open" sources: reports appearing in the Arab, Israeli, and world

press, in addition to academic studies and published memoirs of persons involved in the events described.]

Bakhash, Shaul. *The Reign of the Ayatollahs: Iran and the Islamic Revolution.* New York: Basic Books. Bibl.; index.
[The author presents a chronologically organized narrative of the principal political events in Iran since the collapse of the Pahlavis, ending with Khomeini's eight-point statement of December 1982 that declared the revolution over. Bakhash does not tell us why or how Iran remains a society in turmoil, but uses secondary sources to describe precisely who did what to whom and with what effect in terms of Iran's internal politics. This perspective puts many events, including the so-called hostage crisis, in a new light for most Americans.]

Balázs, Judit. *Die Türkei: Das Phänomen des abhängigen Kapitalismus.* Islamkundliche Untersuchungen, vol. 64. Berlin: Klaus Schwarz Verlag. 262 pp. Bibl.; illus.; index.

Bar, Luc-Henri de. *Le communautés confessionnells du Liban.* Paris: Editions Recherche sur les Civilizations, 1983. 235 pp. Maps; index.
[The author's stated aim is to describe the religious and social organization of Lebanon's confessional communities and to determine the place of each in the political, economic, and intellectual life of Lebanon. In fact, much of de Bar's work concerns itself with sketching the tangled history that brought each community to the position it occupied in 1972.]

Baron, Xavier. *Les Palestiniens, un peuple.* Paris: Editions le Sycomore. 554 pp. Maps.
[This work of the director of the Bureau de l'Agence France-Presse in Beirut, originally published in 1977, has been revised completely in light of recent events.]

Barthel, Günter, ed. *Iran: From Monarchy to Republic.* Asia, Africa, Latin America Special Issue, vol. 12. Berlin: Akademie-Verlag. 1983. 168 pp. Bibl.

Bashiri, Iraj. *The Fiction of Sadeq Hedayat.* Lexington, Ky.: Mazda Publishers. 210 pp. Bibl.
[This volume is the first comprehensive study of the life, learning, and entire corpus of Hedayat's fictional writings. It surveys previous critical literature about Hedayat (considered to be the father of modern Persian short stories) and examines his stories for theme, literary technique, symbolism, style, and humor, in addition to showing how Hedayat developed his career from social commentator in the 1930s to human rights advocate in the 1940s. Includes a comprehensive bibliography of works and critical sources, plus lists of English translations and of Hedayat's letters.]

Bashiriyeh, Hossein. *The State and Revolution in Iran: 1962–1982.* London: Croom Helm; New York: St. Martin's Press. 203 pp. Bibl; index.
[Bashiriyeh analyzes the forces in Iranian society that had the greatest impact on the revolution and the current political structure. He also places the revolution in its historical context, elucidating the sources of political and social conflict within Iran.]

Bates, Darrel. *The Fashoda Incident of 1898: Encounter on the Nile.* Oxford and New York: Oxford University Press. 194 pp. Bibl.; illus.; index.

Bator, Wolfgang, and Angelika Bator, comps. *Die DDR und die arabischen Staates: Dokumente 1956–1982.* Berlin: Solidaritätskomittee d. DDR; Staatsverlag der Deutsche Demokratische Republik. 421 pp.

Bawly, Dan, and Eliahu Salpeter. *Fire in Beirut: Israel's War in Lebanon with the PLO: Prelude to Aftermath.* Briarcliff Manor, N.Y.: Stein & Day. 261 pp. Illus.; maps.

Beblawi, Hazem. *Arab Gulf Economy in a Turbulent Age.* New York: St. Martin's Press. 240 pp.

Becker, Jillian. *The PLO: The Rise and Fall of the Palestine Liberation Organization.* New York: St. Martin's Press. 303 pp. Bibl.; illus.; maps; index.
Presents a factual historical survey of PLO activities since 1963, including the long record of terrorism.

Behr, Vera. *Auswirkungen der Arbeitsemigration auf die wirtschaftliche Entwicklung Tunesiens.* Frankfurt: R.G. Fischer. 353 pp. Map.
[A 1981 Köln University dissertation.]

Bellmann, Dieter. *Arabische Kultur der Gegenwart: Rückblicke, Bestandsaufnahme, Zukunftserwartungen.* Berlin: Akademie-Verlag. 453 pp. Bibl.

Benard, Cheryl, and Salmay Khallizad. *"The Government of God": Iran's Islamic Republic.* New York: Columbia University Press. 240 pp.
[The authors bring a unique combination of specialized, firsthand regional knowledge and theoretical sophistication to the study of Iran. As a result they are able, on the one hand, to critique Western academic writing about the Middle East by showing us what recent events in Iran reveal about both the strengths and the weaknesses of contemporary social science concepts; on the other hand, they are able to utilize these same critiqued concepts in a careful manner to interpret the events leading up to the overthrow of the shah and the consolidation of the Islamic Republic in Iran.]

Benjelloun-Ollivier, Nadia. *La Palestine: Un enjeu, des stratégies, un destin.* Preface by Maxime Rodinson. Paris: Presses de la Fondation Nationale de Sciences Politiques. 378 pp.
[Reviews the unfolding of the political-military strategy that began in 1967 in terms of its internal, regional, and international aspects, while stressing the tragic dimension of this thirty-year war.]

Benvenisti, Meron. *The West Bank Data Project: A Survey of Israel's Policies.* Washington, D.C.: American Enterprise Institute. 97 pp.
[The vast majority of literature on the West Bank is argument about what should or should not be done with the area. Benvenisti's work is an exception, for he concentrates instead on what he believes can and can not be done. He concludes that Israeli withdrawal from the area is impossible. Also, unlike most reports about the West Bank, this one does not simply reproduce statistics of Israel's Central Bureau of Statistics, but uses a variety of official and unofficial sources to supplement and correct CBS figures. Although this makes the book useful as a guide through conflicting

claims, the many citations to unpublished papers written by Benvenisti's researchers make the study less useful to scholars. A more serious problem is that, despite what some Israeli officials have said about Benvenisti "scientifically" proving annexation to be irreversible, such claims simply state the severe constraints that exist upon the processes by which the issue of the West Bank may be settled.]

Ben-Ziv, Abraham. *Alliance Politics and the Limits of Influence: The Case of the U.S. and Israel, 1975–1983.* JCSS Paper no. 25. Tel Aviv: Tel Aviv University, Jaffee Center for Strategic Studies; Boulder, Colo.; West-view Press. 75 pp.
[This paper examines four case studies of pressure placed on Israel by the last three U.S. administrations and draws lessons for the future.]

Berger, Johannes, and Uwe Reichel, comps. *Die Aufrüstung Saudi-Arabiens: Regionalmacht oder Stützpunkt?* Militärpolitik-Dokumentation, no. 36. Frankfurt: Haag & Herchen. 120 pp. Bibl.; illus.; map.

Berque, Jacques. *L'Islam au temps du monde.* Paris: Editions Sindbad. 280 pp.
[Eleven previously unpublished essays on Islamic social history, cultural anthropology, and textual studies by a scholar who has intimate knowledge of the Arab countries, attempt to make Islam better known and to anticipate its place in the world to come.]

———. *Arab Rebirth: Pain and Ecstasy.* Translated by Quintin Hoare. London: Al Saqi Books, distributed by Zed Press. 138 pp.
[Berque, the prominent French Arabist, presents in this extended essay his synthesis of Arab civilization. His view from pre-Islamic Arabia to the twentieth century is an important attempt to provide characterizations and patterns on both the past and the future. The French original, *Les Arabes,* is now in its third edition (1979).]

Bianchi, Robert. *Interest Groups and Political Development in Turkey.* Princeton, N.J.: Princeton University Press. 426 pp. Bibl; illus.; appends.; index.
[Combining a discussion of the emergence of interest groups in modern Turkey with a comparative study of Western Europe, Latin America, and Southeast Asia, Bianchi questions prevailing notions of the role of interest groups at different stages of modernization. He reviews the shifting power balance between pluralist associations, allied with leftist parties, and corporatist associations, allied with the Right.]

Bidwell, R.L., and G.R. Smith, eds. *Arabian and Islamic Studies: Articles Presented to R.B. Serjeant on the Occasion of His Retirement from the Sir Thomas Adam's Chair of Arabic at the University of Cambridge.* London and New York: Longman. 282 pp. Illus.
[Articles are in Arabic and English.]

Bill, James, and Carl Leiden. *Politics in the Middle East.* 3d ed. Boston: Little, Brown & Co. 464 pp. Bibl.; map, index.
[The is the most comprehensive and current work of its kind on the Middle East, whose main theme is that the region is undergoing the most rapid modernization of any area in the world but is slow in its political development. The book is extremely valuable for, among other things,

pinpointing important American misconceptions about the area, which are based on a "painfully inadequate" understanding.]

Bin-Nun, Ariel. *Einführung in das Recht des Staates Israel*. Darmstadt: Wissenschaftliche Buchgesellschaft, 1983. 159 pp.

Black, Edwin. *The Transfer Agreement: The Untold Story of the Secret Pact between the Third Reich and Jewish Palestine*. London and New York: Macmillan. 430 pp. Illus.; index.

Bleuchot, Herué. *Chroniques et documents libyens (1969–1980)*. Extraits de l'Annuaire de l'Afrique du Nord. Paris: Editions du CNRS. 272 pp. Figs.; tables.

Bligh, Alexander. *From Prince to King: Royal Succession in the House of Saud in the Twentieth Century*. New York: New York University Press. 140 pp. Bibl.; index.

Bodurgil, Abraham. *Kemal Atatürk: A Centennial Bibliography, 1881–1981*. Washington, D.C.: Library of Congress; for sale by the Superintendent of Documents. 211 pp. Bibl.

Böhm, Edward, and Sybille Reymann. *Das Wirtschaftliche Engagement der Sowjetunion in Asien: Afghanistan, Indien, Pakistan, Iran und Türkei*. Veröffentlichungen des HWWA-Institut für Wirtschaftsforschung, Hamburg. Hamburg: Verlag Weltarchiv, 1983. 124 pp. Bibl.

Bonosky, Phillip. *Afghanistan Unveiled . . .: The CIA's Secret War*. English language ed. New York: International Publishers. 350 pp. Index.

Bontems, Claude. *La guerre du Sahara occidental*. Perspectives Internationales. Paris: Presses Universitaires de France. 224 pp. Bibl.; map.

Borovik, Yehuda. *Israeli Air Force: 1948 to the Present*. London: Arms & Armour Press. 69 pp. Illus.

Brown, James, and William P. Snyder, eds. *The Regionalization of Warfare: The Falkland Islands, Lebanon, and the Iran-Iraq Conflict*. New Brunswick, N.J.: Transaction Books. 266 pp.

Brown, L. Carl. *International Politics and the Middle East: Old Rules, Dangerous Game*. Princeton Studies on the Near East. Princeton, N.J.: Princeton University Press. 363 pp. Illus.; index.
[This work argues that the political complexities of today's Middle East and the region's enmeshment in great-power politics are best explained in terms of the distinctive international relations subsystem that has evolved over the past two centuries. Brown shows how present tensions grew out of the elaborate diplomatic game in which European states dismembered the Ottoman Empire. The game still goes on, with outside participants neither absorbing the Middle East nor releasing it from their hold. The author describes the rules of this game and their durability in a region otherwise undergoing revolutionary change.]

Bucher, Henry. *Middle East*. Guilford, Conn.: Dushkin Publishing. 150 pp.

Bulliet, Richard. *Gulf Scenario.* New York: St. Martin's Press. 256 pp.

Bunzl, John, ed. *Das andere Israel: Gespräche mit der Friedensbewegung.* Hamburg: Junius, 1983. 150 pp. Bibl.

Burgat, François, and Michel Nancy. *Les villages socialistes de la révolution agraire algérienne, 1972–1982.* Paris: Editions du CNRS. 288 pp. Bibl.; illus.; appends.
[After Houari Boumediene's coup in 1965, a plan was developed to resolve the agricultural crisis by creating one thousand socialist villages. But because the government was afraid to relinquish central control, the reform was doomed. In this book, Nancy presents a historical overview and describes the economy of the project, and Burgat studies the juridical aspects of the failed experiment. Together they show us just how the government of independent Algeria works, or does not work, and provide us with a guide to statecraft in a newly independent one-party state.]

Bürgel, J.C., and U.H. Fähndrich, eds. *Die Vorstellung vom Schicksal und die Darstellung der Wirklichkeit in der zeitgenössichen Literatur islamischer Länder.* Schweizer asiatische Studien: Studienh. Vol. 7. Bern, Frankfurt, and New York: Peter Lang, 1983. 207 pp.
[Papers from an international symposium held at the University of Bern; contributions in German and English.]

Burns, William J. *Economic Aid and American Policy toward Egypt, 1955–1981.* Albany: State University of New York Press. 256 pp. Bibl.
[This study shows how the American government attempted to use its economic aid program to induce or coerce Egypt to support U.S. interests in the Middle East in the quarter century following the 1955 Czech-Egyptian arms agreement. Burns has analyzed recently released government documents and interviews with former policymakers to throw light on the use of aid as a tool of American policy toward the Nasir and Sadat regimes.]

Carter, Barbara L. *The Copts in Egyptian Politics, 1918–1952.* London: Croom Helm. 256 pp.

Centre des Hautes Etudes sur l'Afrique et l'Asie Modernes. *Contestations en pays islamiques.* Paris: La Documentation Française. 120 pp.
[Through the cases of Turkey, Algeria, Senegal, Egypt, and Iran, this volume studies the two principal contesting currents that are placing in question the structures of the state and of society in the Islamic world: the movements inspired by Marxism and the fundamentalist movements.]

Chaabani, Zinelabidine. *Der Einfluss des Französischen auf das Arabische in Tunesien: Zur Beschreibung morphosyntaktischer Phänomene das Neuhocharabischen.* Europäische Hochschulschriften; ser. 21, Linguistik und Indogermanistik, vol. 31. Bern, Frankfurt, Berlin, New York, and Nancy: Peter Lang. 207 pp. Bibl.
[A 1983 Göttingen University dissertation.]

Chafets, Ze'ev. *Double Vision: How America's Press Distorts Our View of the Middle East.* New York: William Morrow. 349 pp. Bibl.; index.
[Chafets, an American-born former head of Israel's Government Press

Office, argues consistently that Israel alone is subject to distorted reporting in the foreign press. Although lowering his credibility by not examining Israel's own news management efforts, Chafets nonetheless raises serious questions about the accuracy of news from the Mideast.]

Chaliand, Gérard, and Yves Ternon. *Le génocide des Arméniens*. La Mémoire du siècle. Brussels: Editions Complexe. 192 pp.

Charnay, Jean-Paul. *Principes de stratégie arabe*. Classiques des stratégie arabe. Paris: Editions L'Herne. 552 pp.
[A variety of materials are collected here—ranging from Qur'an verses to the writings of Nasir and Qaddafi, from Sunni and Shiite texts to the writings of nationalists and progressives—in order to clarify the orientations and contradictions of contemporary Arab strategies.]

Chraibi, Driss. *Mother Comes of Age*. Translated by Hugh A. Harter. Washington, D.C.: Three Continents Press. 121 pp.
[In this novel Driss Chraibi, a Moroccan writer who straddles the Western and Arab worlds in orientation and sympathy, describes the liberation of a traditional Moroccan woman. As her sons are educated and absorb Western culture, she too absorbs modern ways and is transformed.]

Cobban, Helena. *The Palestinian Liberation Organization: People, Power, and Politics*. Cambridge and New York: Cambridge University Press. 261 pp. Bibl.; illus.; appends.
[Cobban, a correspondent in Beirut from 1976 to 1981, has based this analysis on documentary sources and firsthand recollections. She begins with a history of the PLO's predominant member group, al-Fatah, then discusses the interrelations among the Fatah leadership and various factors affecting its performance, and concludes by assessing the sources of the leadership's surprising stability over the past quarter century and its effectiveness in key operations.]

Cooke, Miriam. *The Anatomy of an Egyptian Intellectual: Yahya Haqqi*. Washington, D.C.: Three Continents Press. 188 pp. Bibl; index.
Using themes as an organizing principle for the chapters in the first half, the author analyzes the artistic discourse of a major Arabic writer largely unknown to English readers in order to discover how he has dealt with being a believer, an artist, a man, and an Egyptian in the modern world. The second half is devoted to a study of Haqqi as a literary critic and craftsman. What emerges is a subtle portrait of an Egyptian intellectual attempting, through his writing, to come to terms with a modern world in transition.

Cordesman, Anthony H. *The Gulf and the Search for Strategic Stability: Saudi Arabia, the Military Balance in the Gulf, and Trends in the Arab-Israeli Military Balance*. London: Mansell; Boulder, Colo.: Westview Press. 1,041 pp. Bibl.; illus.; index.

Crabbs, Jack A. *The Writing of History in Nineteenth-Century Egypt: A Study in National Transformation*. Detroit: Wayne State University Press; Cairo: American University in Cairo Press. 230 pp. Bibl.; index.

Critchfield, Richard. *Shahhat: An Egyptian*. Syracuse, N.Y.: Syracuse University Press. 237 pp. Illus.

[The author presents an insightful picture of the social life and customs of contemporary Egyptian peasants through his dramatic narrative of the young adulthood of Shahhat.]

Dann, Uriel. *Studies in the History of Transjordan 1920–1949: The Making of a State*. Boulder, Colo.: Westview Press. 127 pp.

Darwish, Khalil. *Sozioökonomische Struktur und sozialer Wandel der palästinensischen Gesellschaft nach 1948; eine empirischen Untersuchung am Beispiel zweier Flüchtilingslager*. Pfaffenweiler: Centaurus-Verlagsgesellschaft, 1983. 219 pp. Graphs.

[A 1983 Freiburg (Breisgau) University dissertation.]

Dawisha, Adeed, ed. *Islam in Foreign Policy*. Cambridge and New York: Cambridge University Press. 201 pp.

[A collection of ten case studies analyzing the role and influence of Islam in the foreign policies of states with substantial Muslim populations, including Iran, Saudi Arabia, Libya, Pakistan, Egypt, Morocco, Iraq, Nigeria, Indonesia, and the Soviet Union.]

De Felice, Renzo. *Jews in an Arab Land: Libya, 1835–1970*.Translated by Judith Roumani. Austin: University of Texas Press. 448 pp.

[Internationally renowned scholar Renzo De Felice's meticulous pioneering study of the Jews of Libya is, in many ways, a microcosm of the major sources of conflict in the modern Middle East. First published by Il Mulino, Bologna, in 1978, *Ebrei in un paese arabo* is now available in English for the first time.]

Debus, Esther. *Die islamisch-rechtlichen Auskunfte der Milli Gazete im Rahmen des "Fetwa-Wesen" der Turkischen Republik*. Islamkundliche Untersuchungen, vol. 95. Berlin: Klaus Schwarz Verlag. 135 pp.

Dejeux, Jean. *Dictionnaire des auteurs maghrébins de langue française*. Paris: Editions Diffusion Karthala. 400 pp.

[A list of authors and their writings, covering the literature of fiction, essays, history, human sciences, and the arts for Algeria from 1880 to 1982, and the literature of fiction and essays for Tunisia from 1900 to 1982.]

Deschner, Günther. *Saladins Söhne: Die Kurden, das betrogene Volk*. Munich and Zurich: Droemer Knaur, 1983. 351 pp. Bibl.; illus.; maps; index.

Deutschkron, Inge. *Israel und die Deutschen: Das besondere Verhältnis*. Cologne: Verlag Wissenschaft und Politik, 1983. 456 pp. Index.

Dib, Mohammed. *Au café: Nouvelles*. La bibliothèque arabe. Paris: Sindbad. 131 pp.

Dietl, Wilhelm. *Brükenkopf Afghanistan: Machtpolitik im Middleren Osten*. Munich: Kindler. 351 pp. Illus.; index.

Dreyer, Rolf. *Die Arabische Republik Jemen: Zur Verfassung und Verwaltung einer Entwicklungslandes*. Bochumer juristische Studien, no. 36. Bo-

chum: Studienverlag Brockmeyer, 1983. 212 pp. Graphs.
[A 1983 Bochum University dissertation.]

Economic and Social Infrastructure in Qatar. Doha, Qatar: Al Noor Publishing.
107 pp. Bibl.; tables; graphs; index.
[The first four parts of this book break down the economic and social
sectors of the Qatari economy. The fifth part analyzes the economic and
statistical implications of the preceding chapters.]

Efrat, Arie. *Nachbarn im Negev: Ein Kibbuz zwischen Bauern und Beduinen.*
Gerlingen: Bleicher, 1983. 319 pp. Illus.

Efrat, Elisha. *Urbanization in Israel.* London: Croom Helm; New York: St. Martin's Press. 225 pp. Bibl.; illus.; index.

Eickelman, Christine. *Women and Community in Oman.* New York: New York
University Press. Bibl.; index.

Ende, Werner, and Ude Steinbach, eds. *Der Islam in der Gegenwart: Entwicklung und Ausbreitung Staat, Politik und Recht Kultur und Religion.*
Munich: Verlag C.H. Beck. 774 pp. Maps; indexes.
[This book is a reference work for specialists and nonspecialists alike.
Beginning with a historical introduction to Islam as a religion and as a
political system, it covers confessional differences and the various forms of
popular belief within Islam, as well as the current status of Islamic
minorities in Asia, Africa, Europe, and America. The emphasis is on the
Arab world, but considerable attention is paid to Iran, Turkey, Pakistan,
and Indonesia.]

Enfants d'immigrés maghrébins. Paris: Centre National d'Art et de Culture
Georges Pompidou. 72 pp. Illus.
[Surveys the social experience of North African immigrants through the
eyes of immigrant children, illustrating thereby the cultural plurality that
has resulted. Based upon interviews with the children of immigrants and
with social workers.]

Epstein, Lawrence J. *Zion's Call: Christian Contributions to the Origins and
Development of Israel.* Lanham, Md.: University Press of America. 165
pp. Bibl; index.

Ermacora, Felix. *Menschenrechte in der sich wandelnden Welt.* Vol. 2, *Theorie
und Praxis: Die Verwirklichung der Menschenrechte in Afrika und im
Nahen Osten.* Sitzungsberichte Österreichische Akademie der Wissen-
schaffen, Philosophisch-Historische Klasse, vol. 415. Veröffentlichungen der Kommission für das Studium der Menschenrechte, no. 2. Vienna: Verlag der Österreichische Akademie der Wissenschaften, 1983.
708 pp. Bibl.

Escalier, Robert. *Citadins et espace urbain au Maroc.* 2d ed. Fascicules de Recherches, nos. 8, 9. Tours: Laboratoire URBAMA, CNRS, Université de
Tours. Vol. 1, 185 pp.; vol. 2, 199 pp. Bibl.; figs.; tables.
[These volumes, part of a series on the urbanization of the Arab world,
examine Moroccan cities from a demographic perspective. A
comprehensive, highly technical study.]

Eshel, David. *Israeli Armed Forces in Action*. New York: Arco Publications. 224 pp. Illus.

Etemad, Bouda. *Pétrole et développement: Irak, Venezuela, Iran: 1900–1973*. Collection des thèses de la Faculté des Sciences Economiques et Sociales, Université de Genève, no. 291. Bern; Frankfort, New York, and Nancy: Peter Lang, 1983. 490 pp. Bibl.; illus; maps.
[Reviews the nature of petroleum exploitation in the Third World and the effects of investment in the Third World.]

Evin, Ahmet, Ergun Özbudun, et al., eds. *Modern Turkey: Continuity and Change*. Schriften des Deutschen Orient-Instituts. Opladen: Leske & Budrich. 164 pp. Bibl.; index.
[Contributions originally discussed at a seminar held at the University of Pennsylvania in April 1982.]

Fabry, Philipp W. *Zwischen Schah und Ayatollah: Ein Deutscher im Spannungfeld der iranischen Revolution*. Giessen: Damals-Verlag, 1983. 341 pp. Bibl.; illus.; maps; index.

Falk, Walter. *Parallele Ägypten: Die epockengeschichtlichen Verhältnisse in der ägyptischen und deutschen Literatur des 20. Jahrhunderts*. Beiträge zur neuen Epochenforschung, vol. 4. Bern, Frankfurt, Nancy, and New York: Peter Lang. 200 pp. Bibl.
[Written in collaboration with the Kairener Gegenwartsdiagnose project.]

Farid, Abdel Majid, ed. *The Red Sea: Prospects for Stability*. New York: St. Martin's Press; published in association with the Arab Research Centre. 173 pp. Appends.; index.
[A collection of papers of varying quality by various authors.]

Feldman, Lily Gardner. *The Special Relationship between West Germany and Israel*. London: Allen & Unwin. 280 pp.

Feldman, Shai, and Heda Rechnitz-Kijner, eds. *Deception, Consensus, and War: Israel in Lebanon*. JCSS Paper no. 27. Boulder, Colo.: Westview Press. 75 pp.
[The authors give an account of Israel's June 1982 invasion of Lebanon, a war carried out with neither national nor government consensus.]

Fiedler, Ulrich. *Der Bedeutungswandel der Hedschasbahn: Eine historisch-geographische Untersuchung*. Islamkundliche Untersuchungen, vol. 94. Berlin: Klaus Schwarz Verlag. 338 pp.

Findlay, Ann M., Allan M. Findlay, and Richard I. Lawless, eds. *Morocco*. World Bibliographical Series, no. 47. Oxford, England, and Santa Barbara, Calif.: Clio Press. 311 pp. Bibl.; illus.; map; index.
[A general bibliography on Morocco that emphasizes contemporary material published in English, chosen primarily from three collections: the Centre Interuniversitaire d'Etude Méditerranéennes (Poitiers), the Centre National de Documentation (Rabat), and the Scottish National Library.]

Fontaine, Jacques. *Villages kabyles et nouveau reseau urbain en Algérie*. Tours:

Laboratoire URBAMA, CNRS, Université de Tours, 1983. 273 pp. Illus.; figs.; tables.
[A case study of how the Kabylian rural structure is facing the new urban network. Reviews state decisions and how social groups have reacted within the context of both traditional structures and official planning. The emphasis is on methodological approaches.]

Fougerouse, Maurice. *Bahrein: Un exemple d'économie post-pétrolière au Moyen-Orient*. Clermont-Ferrand: Editions de Instant Durable, 1983. 208 pp. Bibl.; illus; index.
[A comprehensive work that describes and analyzes the geographic and historical aspects of the archipelago as well as its institutions, its economy, and its social structure.]

Freedman, Robert O., ed. *The Middle East Since Camp David*. Boulder, Colo.: Westview Press. 263 pp. Bibl.; index.
[In this volume, a group of internationally recognized scholars, many of whom are present or former U.S. government officials, analyze Middle Eastern developments from the perspectives of the superpowers, the region in general, and the five major actors since Camp David: Egypt, Israel, the PLO, Syria, and Iran.]

Gabriel, Richard A. *Operation Peace for Galilee: The Israeli-PLO War in Lebanon*. New York: Hill & Wang. 241 pp. Bibl.; maps; index.

Gall, Sandy. *Behind Russian Lines: An Afghan Journal*. New York: St. Martin's Press. 194 pp. Illus.

Gälli, Anton. *Textil-und Bekleidungsindustrie in den arabischen Ländern*. With a contribution by Michael Breitenacher. Ifo-Forschungsberichte der Abteilung Entwicklungsländer, no. 64. Munich, Cologne, and London: Weltforum-Verlag. 114 pp. Bibl.

Gardet, Louis. *Les hommes de l'Islam: Approche des mentalités*. Collection Historiques, no. 8. Brussels: Editions Complexe. 450 pp.
[A study of the evolution of Islamic values and mentality from the beginning of the seventh century to the present.]

Gavron, Daniel. *Israel after Begin: Israel's Options in the Aftermath of the Lebanon War*. Boston: Houghton Mifflin. 199 pp.
[Gavron confronts the ideological and political struggle being waged in Israel between Judaic "universalism" (represented by Labor and its allies such as the Shinui party, which Rubinstein heads) and Judaic "particularism" (represented by the Likud coalition that Begin forged). As an American immigrant in Israel, Gavron presents a somewhat guarded account of this struggle, but with the others calls for a return to pre-1973 Labor Zionism.] See also Oz; Rubinstein.

Geffken, Rolf. *Die "Demokratie" der Militärs: Analyse der neuen türkischen Verfassung: Zweisprachig*. Introduction by Klaus Thüsing. Rechtspolitik aktuell, no. 5. Cologne: Presseverlag Theurer, 1983. 112 pp.
[In German and Turkish; includes a German translation of the Turkish Constitution.]

Genç, Mehmet. *Die besondere Rolle der Republikanischen Volkspartei beim Transformationsprozess der türkischen Gesellschaft.* Reihe der Forschungen, vol. 12. Rheinfelden: Schäuble, 1983. 506 pp. Bibl.
[A 1983 Heidelberg University dissertation.]

Geyikdaqi, Mehmet Y. *Political Parties in Turkey: The Role of Islam.* New York: Praeger Publishers. 177 pp. Bibl.; index.
[This short but informative volume summarizes historical events and the policies of political parties with respect to secularism and the role of Islam in Turkey between 1950 and 1980.]

Ghanayem, Ishaq I., and Alden H. Voth. *The Kissinger Legacy: American Middle East Policy.* New York: Praeger Publishers. 237 pp. Bibl.; illus.; index.

Gikette, Alain, and Abdelmalek Sayed. *L'Immigration algérienne en France.* 2d ed. rev. Paris: Editions Entente. 284 pp.
[This is a new edition of a classic work, which originally appeared in 1976, that brings up-to-date responses to questions posed by the presence of 800,000 Algerians in France.]

Gillard, David, ed. *British Documents on Foreign Affairs: Reports and Papers from the Foreign Office Confidential Print.* Pt. 1, *From the Mid-Nineteenth Century to the First World War.* Series B. *The Near and Middle East, 1856–1914.* 20 vols. Frederick, Md.: University Publications of America, 1984-.

Gillespie, Kate. *The Tripartite Relationship: Government, Foreign Investors, and Local Investors during Egypt's Economic Opening.* New York: Praeger Publishers. 236 pp. Bibl.; illus.; appends.
[The author analyzes Egypt's open-door policy in terms of a sequence of coalitions that may be applicable to other developing countries. In the last three chapters, Gillespie reports her own survey of Law 43 ventures (documented in Appendix B) and provides new evidence for the oscillation of investment patterns between capitalist and nationalist poles.]

Goldberg, H. *Greentown's Youth: Disadvantaged Youth in a Development Town in Israel.* Assen, The Netherlands: Van Gorcum; Atlantic Highlands, N.J.: Humanities Press. 160 pp.

Golvin, Lucien, and Marie-Christine Fromont. *Thula: Architecture et urbanisme d'une cité de haute montagne en République Arabe du Yemen.* Paris: Editions Recherché sur les Civilisations. 238 pp.

Gordon, Bezalel. *House Divided: Israel in Crisis.* New York: Empire Books.

Gournay, Jean-Francis. *L'Appeal du Proche-Orient: Richard Francis Burton et son temps, 1821–1890.* Lille: Atelier National de Reproduction des Thèses de l'Université de Lille III; Paris: Société Nouvelle Didier Erudition, 1983. 652 pp. Bibls.; indexes.
[A 1979 Université de Lille III dissertation in which the author discusses the fascination of the Orient and of Islam for certain Europeans during the nineteenth century, and more particularly for R.F. Burton, translator of the *Thousand and One Nights.*]

Green, Stephen. *Taking Sides: America's Secret Relations with a Militant Israel.* New York: William Morrow. 370 pp. Index.

[The author relies heavily on public documents made available to him under the Freedom of Information Act. Because many documents were still denied him and he slights many publicly available materials, the book presents a biased and inadequate picture of its subject; its major contribution is a discussion of U.S. Air Force reconnaisance assistance to Israel before and during the 1967 war.]

Gresh, Alain, and Dominque Vidal. *Proche-Orient, une Guerre de cent ans.* Paris: Messidor/Editions Sociales. 208 pp.

[Analyzes the roots of the Arab-Israeli conflict from the massive Jewish immigration to Palestine that began in 1882 up to the Israeli invasion of Lebanon in 1982.]

Grimaud, Nicole. *La politique extérieure de l'Algérie.* Paris: Editions-Diffusion Karthala. 380 pp.

[A professor of political science shows that Algeria had intensive diplomatic activity even before it was recognized as a state and then explains the dynamics of Algerian foreign policy, reviewing its key resources.]

Guecioueur, Adda, ed. *The Problems of Arab Economic Development and Integration.* Boulder, Colo.: Westview Press. 223 pp.

[This is a well-balanced book which considers the possibilities for Arab economic integration. The volume is a report of a symposium held at Yarmouk University, Jordan, in 1981 and contains many excellent papers on all aspects of the topic.]

Gurdon, Charles. *Sudan at the Crossroads.* Outwell, Cambridgeshire, England: Middle East and North African Studies Press. 128 pp. Illus.; map; index.

[Considering the multiple crises that face Sudan in the 1980s, the author puts the current situation into perspective and points the way for future change.]

Gurdon, Hugo. *Iran: The Continuing Struggle for Power.* Outwell, Cambridgeshire, England: Middle East and North African Studies Press. 88 pp. Map; index.

[A journalist based in the Middle East examines the inherent paradoxes within the Iranian political system and points to some of the areas where powerful forces work for change.]

Gutmann, Emanuel, Dan Caspi, and Avraham Diskin, eds. *The Roots of Begin's Success: The 1981 Israeli Elections.* London: Croom Helm; New York: St. Martin's Press. 293 pp. Bibl.; index.

[This book offers an explantion of the unusual 1981 elections, covering such aspects as the new balance of power in the Knesset, the cultural and political background of the Likud coalition, and the role of religious factors. Focusing on the political support the coalition received from the North African immigrant population, the book's demographic analysis shows that this growing sector of the electorate is likely to be increasingly important in coming elections.]

Haag-Higuchi, Roxane. *Untersuchungen zu einer Sammlung persischer Erzäh-lungen. Islamkundliche Untersuchungen*, vol. 92. Berlin: Klaus Schwarz Verlag. 229 pp.

Haddad, Heskel M. *The Jews of Arab and Islamic Countries: History, Problems and Solutions.* New York: Shengold. 167 pp. Bibl.; index.
[Translation of *Yehude artsot 'Arav ve-Islam.*]

Haddad, Yvonne Y., Byron Haines, and Ellison Findly, eds. *The Islamic Impact.* Syracuse, N.Y.: Syracuse University Press. 239 pp. Index.
[A collection of ten essays on politics, economics, education and science, law, women, mystical thought, art, music, Muslims in the United States, and Muslim identity. The book is the result of a conference conceived in the spirit of dialogue and includes contributions from those of both Muslim and non-Muslim background.]

al-Hakim, Tawfiq. *Plays, Prefaces, and Postscripts of Tawfiq al-Hakim.* Vol. 2, *Theater of Society.* Translated by William M. Hutchins. Washington, D.C.: Three Continents Press. 350 pp. Bibl.
This is the second of a two-volume translation series of plays by Tawfiq al-Hakim, who is the doyen of modern Arabic drama. The first volume, published in 1981, contained five plays from the period 1934 to 1965, whose themes were inspired by the religious and literary history of both East and West. In this volume Hutchins has selected six plays from the period 1951 to 1972, whose themes were inspired by contemporary and future conditions in Egypt and the world. Hakim's "prefaces and postscripts" offer the English reader an exceptionally candid insight into the author's methods and meanings.

Halevi, Ilan. *Sous Israël, la Palestine.* Paris: Editions le Sycomore. 247 pp.
[Surveys the creation of the state of Israel, and its expansion, as experienced by Palestinians living there.]

Haley, P. Edward. *Qaddafi and the United States since 1969.* New York: Praeger Publishers. 364 pp. Map; index.
[This book is an exhaustive recitation of the American public record on its topic. The author's system of allocating a theme to each stage of American-Libyan relations, and his almost exclusive reliance on journalistic sources to provide not only the material but the very structure of the narrative, lead to a certain lack of continuity in the story.]

Harik, Elsa Marston, and Donald C. Schilling. *The Politics of Education in Co-lonial Algeria and Kenya.* Papers in International Studies: Africa Series, no. 43. Athens: Ohio University, Center for International Studies. 102 pp.

Hart, David. *The Ait 'Atta of Southern Morocco: Daily Life and Recent History.* Boulder, Colo.: Westview Press. 260 pp. Illus.; maps; gloss.; index.

Hassan bin Talal. *Search for Peace.* New York: St. Martin's Press. 152 pp. Illus.; maps.
The author is crown prince of Jordan.

Hassoun, Jacques, ed. *Juifs d'Egypte*. Paris: Editions du Scribe. 260 pp. Bibl.; illus.; gloss.

[Describes the everyday life of the Jewish community in Egypt, its diversity and its contradictions, and the important intellectuals the community has engendered over the centuries.]

Hawi, Khalil. *Naked in Exile*. Interpretation and translation by Adnan Haydar and Michael Beard. Washington, D.C.: Three Continents Press. 208 pp. Bibl.

This work contains the three poems from Hawi's *Bayadir al-ju'* in Arabic with facing translations in English and extensive interpretive material. An introduction explains the significance of Hawi's life as a poet and teacher in modern Lebanon and the centrality of this book of poems, first published in 1965. Hawi was born into a Greek Orthodox community in 1925, taught at the American University of Beirut for many years—both before and after he wrote a Cambridge University dissertation on Khalil Gibran—and committed suicide in 1982 under the influence of the Israeli invasion of Lebanon. A short bibliography of Hawi's works concludes the volume.

Headley, Lee A., ed. *Suicide in Asia and the Near East*. Foreword by Norman L. Faberow. Berkeley: University of California Press. 375 pp. Bibls.; illus.; index.

Hegazi, Awad. *Zionismus und palästinensische Araber*. Foreword by Erich Fried. Wissenschaftliche Publikationen zur Politik und Ökonomie in der Dritten Welt. Bremen: Edition CON; Lüdinghausen: Periferia-Verlag, 1983. 181 pp. Bibl.

Heine, Peter, and Reinhold Stipek. *Ethnizität und Islam: Differenzierung und Integration muslimischen Bevölkerungsgruppen*. Reihe Islam und Ethnologie, vol. 1. Gelsenkirchen: Müller. 188 pp. Bibl.; maps.

Heller, Mark A. *The Iran-Iraq War: Implications for Third Parties*. JCSS Paper no. 23. Tel Aviv: Jaffee Center for Strategic Studies, Tel Aviv University. 49 pp.

[A discussion of the political and security interests of third parties concerned with the Iran-Iraq war, with particular attention paid to the Arab states of the Gulf.]

Helms, Christine Moss. *Iraq: Eastern Flank of the Arab World*. Washington, D.C.: Brookings Institution. 215 pp. Illus.; index.

[This unconventional study is intended to enlarge our understanding of Iraqi behavior and of the concerns that motivate its leaders. The author focuses on the forces that influence policy formulation in Iraq and evokes the perspective from which the Iraqi government itself views its problems and sets its priorities.]

Henry, Paul-Marc. *Les jardiniers de l'enfer*. Paris: Olivier Orban. 232 pp.

[The French ambassador to Lebanon from November 1981 to August 1983 explains the roots of today's problems in Lebanon and provides personal testimony on the period during which he lived at the heart of the battles and negotiations.]

Heper, Metin, and Raphael Israeli, eds. *Islam and Politics in the Modern Middle East*. New York: St. Martin's Press, in co-operation with the Harry S. Truman Research Institute for the Advancement of Peace. 131 pp. Bibls.; index.

Heydemann, Steven, ed. *The Begin Era: Issues in Contemporary Israel*. Boulder, Colo.: Westview Press. 137 pp.
[Essays explore how Israel changed under Begin, the source of those changes, and how Israel is likely to evolve in a post-Begin era.]

Hirst, David. *The Gun and the Olive Branch: The Roots of Violence in the Middle East*. 2d ed. London and Boston: Faber & Faber, 1983. 475 pp. Index.
[In this new edition the author has added three new chapters and an epilogue that discuss events since 1977; "Peace with Egypt," "The Rape of the West Bank," and "The Invasion of Lebanon."]

Holod, Renata, and O.E. Ahmet, eds. *Modern Turkish Architecture*. Philadelphia: University of Pennsylvania Press. 192 pp. Illus.

Honegger, Claude. *Friedliche Streitbeilegung durch regionale Organisationen: Theorie und Praxis der Friedenssicherungs-Systeme der OAS, der Liga der Arabischen Staaten und der OAU im Vergleich*. Schweizer Studien zum internationalen Recht, vol. 34. Zürich: Schulthess Polygraphisher Verlag, 1983. 199 pp. Bibl.
[A Zürich University dissertation.]

Hoveyda, Fereydoun. *Les nuits féodales: Tribulations d'un Persan au Moyen-Orient*. Paris: Scarabée et Compagnie. 285 pp.
[An autobiographical testimony covering a century of civil wars in Iran and Lebanon.]

Hunter, Shireen. *OPEC and the Third World: The Politics of Aid*. Bloomington: Indiana University Press. 336 pp. Bibl.
[With the Arab oil embargo of 1973, the economic political influence of the OPEC nations increased tremendously. Third World nations were hopeful that OPEC would use its new wealth and influence to improve their condition vis-à-vis the industrialized nations. The author examines the divergence of interests between OPEC and the Third World and explains why these hopes were never realized.]

Idris, Yusuf. *Rings of Burnished Brass*. Translated by Catherine Cobham. London: Heinemann; Washington, D.C.: Three Continents Press. 142 pp.
[Organized thematically, these four short stories explore human love and compassion in the Egyptian city and countryside. The complexities of modern Egyptian politics and their impact on individuals in society are illuminated, as the author attempts to describe the intangible emotional experiences of life.]

Indyk, Martin. *"To the Ends of the Earth": Sadat's Jerusalem Initiative*. Harvard Middle East Papers; Modern Series, no. 1. Cambridge, Mass.: Center for Middle Eastern Studies, Harvard University. 70 pp.
The author believes that previous attempts to explain the unusual event of Sadat's traveling to Jerusalem in November 1977 place undue emphasis on

the man rather than on the political circumstance that surrounded his
actions. Thus, Indyk focuses on the dynamics of Egypt's interaction with
the United States and the U.S.S.R., and shows how its positions as a lesser
power both allowed Sadat to exert leverage on the two great powers and at
the same time circumscribed his options and restricted his leverage.

International Labour Office. *Employment and Manpower Problems and Policy
Issues in Arab Countries: Proposals for the Future.* Papers and Pro-
ceedings of an ILO Regional Symposium held in Geneva, Jan. 1983.
Geneva: ILO. 140 pp.

Ioannides, Christos P. *America's Iran: Injury and Catharsis.* Preface by D.A.
Strickland. Lanham, Md.: University Press of America. 308 pp. Bibl.;
index.

Islam communautaire. Arabiyya. Geneva: Labor et Fides; Paris: Publications
Orientalistes de France. 140 pp.
[The constitution of the first year of the Hegira had proclaimed Islam to be
a "single community, distinct from other peoples." The essays collected
here examine Islam today and illustrate the importance of the concept of
the Islamic community and of the jurdicial reality attached to it.]

Islami, A. Reza S., and Mostam Mehraban Kavoussi. *The Political Economy of
Saudi Arabia.* Near Eastern Studies 1. Seattle: Department of Near
Eastern Languages and Literature, University of Washington, distributed by the University of Washington Press. 124 pp. Bibl.; tables.
[Islami, a political scientist, and Kavoussi, an economist, argue
persuasively against the prevalent view that Saudi Arabia is a stable
"desert democracy." Using carefully researched data, the authors review
the economic forces that are transforming Saudi society in order to predict
the class structure that is likely to emerge and to estimate the ways in
which government policy and oil revenues have affected income and
created potential political discontent.]

Israël entre l'Orient et l'Occident. Combat pour la diaspora, no. 13. Paris: Editions Syros. 94 pp.

Itinéraires et contacts de cultures. Vols. 4–5, *Littératures du Maghreb.* Publi-
cation du Centre d'Etudes francophone de l'Université de Paris XIII.
Paris: L'Harmattan. 386 pp.
[A collection of essays on North African literature, providing guidance to
Arabic and French writings, to national literatures, and to oral literatures
in both Arab and Berber dialects.]

Jablonski, Edward. *A Pictorial History of the Middle East: War and Peace from
Antiquity to the Present.* Maps by Rafael Palacios. Garden City, N.Y.:
Doubleday. 294 pp. Bibl.; illus.; maps; index.

Jaffe, Eliezer D. *Israelis in Institutions: Studies in Child Placement, Practice
and Policy.* Special Aspects of Education Series, vol. 2. New York: Gor-
dan & Breach Science Publishers. 290 pp. Bibl.; index.

Jargy, Simon. *L'Orient déchiré: Entre l'Ouest et l'Est.* Arabiyya, no. 5. Geneva:

Labor et Fides; Paris: Publications Orientalistes de France. 268 pp. Bibl.; index.
[Reviews the role of the United States and the Soviet Union in the recent history of the Near East.]

Johnson-Davies, Denys. *Arabic Short Stories*. London: Quartet Books, 1983. 173 pp.
[This collection of twenty-four stories by authors from around the Arab world complements the translator's earlier collection of twenty stories entitled *Modern Arabic Short Stories* (Oxford University Press, 1967). Both provide the Western reader with a broad range of imaginative views of life in the Arab world as perceived and written by Arabs for Arabs.]

Jureidini, Paul, and R.D. McLauren. *Jordan: The Impact of Social Change on the Roles of the Tribes*. New York: Praeger Publishers. 98 pp.

Kaminsky, Catherine, and Simon Kruk. *Le nationalisme arabe et le nationalisme juif*. Les Chemins de l'Histoire. Paris: Presses Universitaires de France. 256 pp.

Kanafani, Ghassan. *Palestine's Children*. Fifteen Stories translated by Barbara Harlow. Washington, D.C.: Three Continents Press. 142 pp.
[These stories, by one of Palestine's most noted authors and national martyrs, consider the Palestine of the past four decades through the eyes of the Arab children—hardened, sometimes bitterly resigned to their condition under Israeli administration, sometimes committed to change. Includes a sequence of stories about Mansur, a boy who periodically runs away from home to fight in skirmishes, and a short novella, "Return to Haifa," about a young couple who lose their child in the confusion of the occupation, only to be surprised twenty years later.]

Kanovsky, Eliyahu. *Migration from the Poor to the Rich Arab Countries*. Occasional Papers Series, no. 85. Tel Aviv: Dayan Center, Shiloah Institute for Middle Eastern and African Studies, Tel Aviv University. 77 pp. Tables.
[This study focuses on the large-scale labor migration following the oil bonanza of 1973–74. It examines the migration's nature and scale, and concludes that although individuals and families may benefit, the economies of the labor-exporting nations suffer from the manpower loss, despite the added income brought in.]

Karetzky, Stephen. *The Cannons of Journalism: The New York Times Propaganda War against Israel*. Stanford: Calif.: O'Keefe Press. 112 pp. Append.
[This work argues that "the most prestigious and influential newspaper in the United States has been presenting an inaccurate, tendentious picture of developments in Israel and its neighboring territories."]

Kassis, Hanna E. *A Concordance of the Qur'an*. Foreword by Fazlur Rahman. Berkeley: University of California Press, 1983. 1,349 pp. Indexes.
The revolutionary conception of this work provides the non-Arabic reader with a tool by which to understand and appreciate the Qur'an in its own terms. Based upon Arberry's translation, the work is divided into two parts: the concordance and the index. Both are further comprised of two

sections: the Divine Names and the Remaining Vocabulary. The utility of the work derives from its organization of the concordance by transliterated Arabic roots and of the English-language index by all words that occur as translations of the Arabic vocabulary, with multiple roots listed when a single English term has been used for more than one Arabic root. Perhaps the most important work published on the Qur'an for an English-speaking audience.

Kedourie, Elie. *The Chatham House Version and other Middle-Eastern Studies.* New ed. Hanover, N.H.: Published for Brandeis University by University Press of New England. 488 pp. Bibl.; index.
[This edition begins with a new introduction in which the author considers some important historical issues that were raised in the discussions that followed publication of the first edition in 1970. In the twelve studies that follow, Kedourie analyzes what he believes were wrong decisions made by the British government and its representatives and asserts that Britain's disastrous handling of many Middle Eastern problems resulted from what he calls "the Chatham House version" of Middle East history as propagated in the various publications of Arnold Toynbee.]

Kent, Marian, ed. *The Great Powers and the End of the Ottoman Empire.* London and Boston: G. Allen & Unwin. 237 pp. Bibl.; illus.; maps; index.
[Seven essays investigate, in the words of the editor, "the nature and motivation of the Great Powers' interests in the Ottoman Empire and the extent to which these interests and involvement might have contributed to the end of that Empire" (p. 3). For the student, the investigation illuminates the major problems faced by European diplomats prior to World War I; for the scholar, it presents no remarkable discoveries.]

Kepel, Gilles. *Le Prophète et Pharaon: Les mouvements islamiques dans l'E-gypte contemporaine.* Paris: Armillaire-la Découverte. 245 pp. Bibl.; map; index.
[This book treats those Islamic movements in Egypt for whom the mortal enemy is not the West, but the impious princes who govern the Muslim countries. The author utilizes unpublished archives and documents on the evolution, doctrines, and leaders of these movements to explicate the fascination that the so-called Golden Age of the seventh century exerts upon Muslims, and the extraordinary efflorescence of contemporary Islamic movements. The book is also important for its information on the Copts of Egypt and their position vis-à-vis the fundamentalists.]

Khadduri, Majiid. *Islamic Conception of Justice.* Baltimore, Md.: Johns Hopkins University Press. 270 pp.

El-Khawas, Mohamed, and Samir Abed-Rabbo. *American Aid to Israel: Nature and Impact.* Brattleboro, Vt.: Amana Books. 191 pp.
[The authors demonstrate succinctly that American aid to Israel has been exceptional in amount and kind. They also show that the massive private contributions made possible by special privileges support a whole range of Israel state activities that go against official U.S. policy. However, this careful marshaling of facts is diminished, rather than enhanced, by the tendentious nature of the authors' accompanying remarks.]

Khomeini, Ruhollah. *A Clarification of Questions: An Unabridged Translation*

of "*Resaleh Towzih al-Masael.*" Translated by J. Borujerdi, with a fore-word by Michael M.J. Fischer and Mehdi Abedi. Boulder, Colo.: Westview Press. 432 pp. Appends; gloss.; indexes.
[This original source document provides the Western reader with the means to begin viewing the belief structure of contemporary Iranian Shi'ism from within. A compendium of three thousand "problems," Khomeini's treatise is only one of many similar writings, but the first to be translated into English. In it he attempts to guide the layman in all life's questions and needs—from personal hygiene and ritual purity to organ transplants and modern banking. Such guidance presumes a knowledge of dogma and an acceptance of beliefs that most English readers do not possess; the explanatory foreword by anthropologists Fischer and Abedi provides information on the nature of this knowledge and acceptance for these readers.]

Kim, Chong Lim, Joel D. Barkan, Ilter Turan, and Malcolm E. Jewell. *The Legislative Connection: The Politics of Representation in Kenya, Korea and Turkey*. A publication of the Consortium for Comparative Legislative Studies. Durham, N.C.: Duke University Press. 237 pp. Index.

Kislow, A., and R. Zimenkov. *U.S.A. and the Islamic World*. New Delhi: Sterling Publishers. 80 pp. Index.

Kodmani, Bassma, ed. *Quelle sécurité pour le Golfe?* Travaux et recherches de l'IFRI. Paris: Institut Français des Relations Internationales; distributed by Editions Economica. 200 pp.
[Considering the crisis that has shaken the Arab-Persian Gulf region in the course of the last five years, this work illuminates concerns raised by this crisis by attempting to familiarize the Western reader with local perceptions and modes of thought, and with behavior patterns exhibited by the Gulf powers.]

Konzelmann, Gerhard. *Jerusalem: 4000 Jahre Kampf um eine heilige Stadt*. 2d ed. Hamburg: Hoffmann & Campe. 495 pp. Maps; index.

Kostiner, Joseph. *The Struggle for South Yemen*. London: Croom Helm; New York: St. Martin's Press. 195 pp. Bibl.; map; index.
[A revision of the author's master's thesis, University of Haifa.]

Kotobi, Mortéza, ed. *Iran, une première république: Le grand satan et la tulipe*. Preface by Alfred Mahdavy. Etudes et recherches de l'Institut superieur de gestion. Paris: Sponti, 1983. 294 pp. Illus.; maps.

El Koury, Fouad, and Brigitte Legars. *Beyrouth aller-retour*. Paris: Editions de l'Etoile; distributed by Editions du Seuil. 108 pp. Illus.

Kubursi, Atif A. *Oil, Industrialization, and Development in the Arab Gulf States*. London and Dover, N.H.: Croom Helm. Bibl.; index.

——. *The Economics of the Arabian Gulf: A Statistical Source Book*. London: Croom Helm. 206 pp. Tables.

Kuniholm, Bruce R. *The Persian Gulf and United States Policy: A Guide to*

Issues and References. Guides to Contemporary Issues, no. 3. Claremont, Calif.: Regina Books. 220 pp. Bibl.; maps; index.

Lanir, Zvi, ed. *Israeli Security Planning in the 1980's: Its Politics and Economics*. New York: Praeger. 271 pp. Bibl.; illus.; index.
[Based on a symposium on Defense and National Economy in the 1980's, organized in 1981 by the Jaffee Center for Strategic Studies at Tel Aviv University, this book delineates the problems involved in the growing gap between Israel's military needs and the capacity of its economy to provide resources.]

Laoust, Henri. *Pluralismes dans l'Islam*. Revue des Etudes Islamiques, hors série, no. 15. Paris: Librarie Orientaliste Paul Geuthner. 515 pp.
[A collection of articles that appeared in the *Revue des Etudes islamiques* between 1932 and 1980, centered on the fundamental question: how can we define Islam?]

Laqueur, Walter, and Barry Rubin, eds. *the Israel-Arab Reader: A Documentary History of the Middle East Conflict*. Rev. ed. New York: Penguin Books. 704 pp.
This comprehensive set of documents is divided into seven parts, each of which covers a particular period beginning with the late nineteenth century when Arab and Jewish nationalist movements first arose, and ending with the most recent period initiated by the Camp David accords and the Israeli invasion of Lebanon. Each part is introduced by a short essay that puts the documents in context.

Lawless, Richard, and Allan Findlay, eds. *North Africa: Contemporary Politics and Economic Development*. New York: St. Martin's Press; London: Croom Helm. 283 pp. Index.
[This volume attempts to fill the need for a good reader on North Africa. It is divided into two parts, with the first devoting one chapter each to the politics of Morocco, Algeria, Tunisia, and Libya. The second half concentrates on the economic aspects of change for each state.]

Leatherdale, Clive. *Britain and Saudi Arabia. 1925–1939: The Imperial Oasis*. Totowa, N.J., and London: Frank Cass, 1983. 403 pp. Bibl; appends.; index.
[This work surveys relations between Britain and Saudi Arabia from 'Abd al-'Aziz's conquest of the Hejaz to the outbreak of World War II and is evidently the published version of the author's dissertation in international relations. Leatherdale has relied on British official records almost exclusively to produce this basic contribution to the history of British–Saudi Arabian relations.]

Lebrecht, Hans. *Die Palästinser: Geschichte und Gegenwart*. Rev. ed. Berlin: Dietz. 342 pp. Illus.; maps.

Leggewie, Claus. *Kofferträger: Das Algerien-Projekt der Linken im Adenauer-Deutschland*. Berlin: Rotbuch-Verlag. 206 pp. Illus.

Lepanot, Alain. *Maroc*. Guides M.A. Paris: Editions M.A. 504 pp. Maps.
[After presenting useful information about the country, the author studies

each of Morocco's seven regions in detail, concentrating on the daily life of the people as well as on their customs and symbolic life.]

Lesser, Allen. *Israel's Impact, 1950–51: A Personal Record*. Lanham, Md.: University Press of America. 369 pp. Bibl; index.

Levy, Victor C. *Aspects of Efficiency in a Socialist Developing Country: Iraq*. Outstanding Dissertations in Economics. New York: Garland Publishers. 78 pp. Bibl; illus.
[Originally a 1978 University of Chicago Ph.D. dissertation.]

Lewis, Bernard. *The Jews of Islam*. Princeton, N.J.: Princeton University Press. 240 pp. Illus.
Presents the thesis that throughout history, Judaism has been able to survive as a meaningful, flourishing religious culture only in the broader context of its two successor cultures—Christendom and Islamdom. Lewis presents an objective overview of Jewish life in general in the Islamic context as a comparative counterweight to the more extensive Western historical work on Jewish life in Christendom. This then is a study of the Judeo-Islamic tradition from its inception under the early Caliphate to its dissolution in modern times—which was due in particular to the status of Jews as a comparatively uneducated and unprotected minority within weakened Islamic empires under attack by modernizing Western powers.

Libanon: Schlaglichter auf die Geschichte eines Volkes. Schriftenreihe Libanon aktuell, no. 2. Bonn: Osang, 1983. 61 pp.

Liebman, Charles S., and Eliezer Don-Yehiya. *Religion and Politics in Israel*. Jewish Political and Social Studies Series. Bloomington: Indiana University Press. 160 pp. Index.
[This book realistically assesses religion and politics in Israel, analyzing their interrelationship and offering a framework for comparing the situation there with those prevailing in other countries.]

Lillich, Richard B., ed. *The Iran-United States Claims Tribunal, 1981–1983*. Seventh Sokal Colloquium, 1983, University of Virginia. Charlottesville: University Press of Virginia. 250 pp. Index.

Lissak, Moshe, ed. *Israeli Society and Its Defense Establishment: The Social and Political Impact of a Protracted Violent Conflict, 1967–1983*. London and Totowa, N.J.: Frank Cass. 262 pp.
[Israel since its establishment has been engaged in a protracted violent conflict and has developed unusual patterns of civil-military relations. This volume comprises seven papers concerned with different aspects of the interaction between the defense establishment and various civilian sectors, mainly the political and economic.]

Litvinoff, Barnet, ed. *The Letters and Papers of Chaim Weizmann*.Vol. 1, Series B, 1898–1931; Vol. 2, Series B, 1931–1952. New Brunswick, N.J.: Transaction Books, 1983. 700 pp.; 750 pp.

Louis, William Roger. *The British Empire in the Middle East, 1945–1951: Arab Nationalism, the United States, and Postwar Imperialism*. New York: Oxford University Press. 803 pp. Maps; index.

[Based on newly available official records, this is an exhaustive and masterful diplomatic history of Britain's changing role in the postwar Middle East. Substantial bibliographical footnotes throughout compensate for the lack of a general bibliography.]

Luciani, Giacomo. *Oil Companies and the Arab World: The Structure of the International Oil Industry in the 1980s.* New York: St. Martin's Press. 208 pp.
[In contrast to most literature on oil production, this book focuses on the changing role of the international oil companies rather than just the oil producers. Luciani analyzes the strategy of these companies in relation to the Arab world since the momentous changes in their respective positions in the 1970s and examines the policies of oil-importing countries, including the limits of government-to-government deals.]

Lukacs, Yehuda, ed. *Documents on the Israeli-Palestinian Conflict, 1967–1983.* Cambridge and New York: Cambridge University Press. 262 pp.
[This is a compendium of documents relating to a conflict that has generated a vast quantity of written material expressing widely divergent interpretations of events and suggestions for achieving resolution. This volume brings together the material necessary for any serious analysis of the conflict; it begins with UN Security Council Resolution 242 and ends with the joint Jordanian-PLO statement that rejected Jordanian participation in the negotiations proposed by the Reagan peace plan of September 1982.]

Lynch, Patricia D., and Hoda Fahmy. *Craftswomen in Kerassa, Egypt: Household Production and Reproduction.* Women, Work and Development, no. 7. Geneva: International Labour Office. 91 pp.
[Undertaken under the auspices of the Center for Egyptian Civilization Studies and with the financial support of the United Nations Fund for Population Activities, this booklet presents ethnographic data on Muslim women and craftswomen and examines how they contribute to the subsistence economy of Egypt.]

Maachou, Abdel Kader. *OAPEC: The Organization of Arab Petroleum Exporting Countries.* Translated by Anthony Melville. New York: St. Martin's Press, 1983. 198 pp. Bibl.; illus.
[The author outlines OAPEC's structure and its efforts to further the aims of its member countries. The study centers on the newly created juridical branch and on the economic activities of the organization, while also considering its contribution to the general intellectual climate of the Arab world.]

Mackenzie, Kenneth. *Turkey in Transition: The West's Neglected Ally.* European Security Studies, no. 1. London: Institute for European Defence and Strategic Studies. 35 pp.
[This study argues that although Turkey is on the road to democracy and prosperity and is of great strategic importance to the West, it is treated with hostility and condescension by its NATO allies.]

Mahmoud, Fatima Babiker. *The Sudanese Bourgeoisie: Vanguard of Development?* London: Zed Press. 192 pp. Bibl.; index.
[The author presents a social class analysis of Sudanese society and the

role of median groups in civil movements, labor, government, political organization, and the opposition in exile.]

Mahrad, Ahmad. *Bibliographie über die Golfstaaten und ihre Energiepolitik: Unter besonders Berücksichtigung der Energiepolitik Irans und seiner Stellung in der Golfregion.* Europäische Hochschulschriften: ser. 31, Politikwissenschaft, vol. 41. Bern and Frankfurt: P. Lang, 1983. 253 pp.

Makdisi, George. *L'Islam hanbalisant.* Revue des Etudes islamiques, hors série, no. 10. Paris: Librairie Orientaliste Paul Geuthner. 80 pp.
[An introduction to this Sunni juridical school, which was founded in the ninth century and whose principles are presently in force in Saudi Arabia.]

Malik, Hafeez, ed. *International Security in Southwest Asia.* New York: Praeger Publishers. 232 pp.

El Malki, Habib, and Hamid Chabar. *Le Maroc dans l'environnement international et régional.* Cahier 25. Louvain-la-Neuve, Belgium: C.E.R.M.A.C. 106 pp.

Mansour, Antoine. *Palestine: Une économie de résistance en Cisjordanie et à Gaza.* Paris: Edition Diffusion L'Harmattan, 1983. 235 pp.
[The author, a Palestinian and professor of economics at Grenoble, asserts that Israel has implemented a political strategy that utilizes legal and economic means to deny the rights and existence of the Palestinian people.]

Ma'oz, Moshe, and Mordechai Nisan. *Palestinian Leadership on the West Bank: The Changing Role of the Arab Mayors under Jordan and Israel.* Totowa, N.J., and London: Frank Cass. 217 pp. Illus.; index.
[This book examines the West Bank mayors and their transformation since the early 1970s into political-nationalist leaders of their communities. Against the background of the nationalist radicalization in the West Bank, the study analyzes the complex relations between the new Palestinian leaders and the governments of Jordan and Israel, as well as the PLO command.]

Marmura, Michael E., ed. *Islamic Theology and Philosophy: Studies in Honor of George F. Hourani.* Albany: State University of New York. 279 pp. Bibl.; index.
[Hourani has made lasting contributions to the study of Islamic theology and philosophy. A volume honoring this work is doubly appropriate given the fact that the contemporary need to explain Islamic fundamentalism has made the subject of his work so topical. The book presents the current state of scholarship and offers the reader a new respect for the complexity and the persistence of many themes that have arisen in the history of Islamic thought.]

Marquez, Jaime R. *Oil Prices' Effects and OPEC's Pricing Policy: An Optimal Control Approach.* Wharton Econometric Series. Lexington, Mass.: Lexington Books. 206 pp. Bibl.; illus.; index.

Marsot, Afaf Lutfi al-Sayyid. *Egypt in the Reign of Muhammad Ali.* Cambridge

and New York: Cambridge University Press. 320 pp. Map; table.
[The author gives a history of nineteenth-century Egypt as viewed through the leadership and policies of Muhammad ʻAli. Marsot's extensive research, particularly that based upon Egyptian archival sources, presents new views on Muhammad ʻAli's motives and social position that led him toward trade with Europe and modernizing reform, and that resulted in economic changes that revolutionized Egyptian social structures.]

Martens, André. *L'économie des pays arabes*. Preface by M.E. Bénissard. Paris: Economica. 200 pp.
[The author, who has lived in the Near East and North Africa, discusses the political economies of twenty states and the different views of each concerning the role of the state.]

Martin, Lenore G. *The Unstable Gulf: Threats from Within*. Lexington, Mass.: Lexington Books. 256 pp. Bibl.; maps; appends.; index.
[Martin analyzes the effects of the religious, ethnic, and ideological differences in the Arab-Persian Gulf on superpower competition and U.S. energy policy. An invaluable analysis of the international political environment for business in the region.]

Marx, Emanuel, and Avshalom Shmuell, eds. *The Changing Bedouin*. New Brunswick. N.J.: Transaction Books. 197 pp. Bibl.
[Eight essays provide much factual information, but all the authors fail to confront (as British colonialist social anthropology failed) the real systematic political significance of Israeli policies and practices toward the remaining Palestinian pastoralists in Israel.]

Mayer, Thomas. *Egypt and the Palestine Question, 1936–1945*. Islamkundliche Untersuchungen, vol. 77. Berlin: Klaus Schwarz Verlag, 1983. 391 pp. Bibl.; index.

The Middle East in Conflict: A Historical Bibliography. CLIO Bibliographical Series, no. 19. Santa Barbara, Calif.: ABC-CLIO Information Services.
[This bibliography contains more than three thousand abstracts from the international journal literature published between 1973 and 1982 and concentrates on the Cyprus, Israeli-Arab, and Iraqi-Iranian conflicts.]

Miller, Ylana N. *Government and Society in Rural Palestine, 1920-1948*. Modern Middle East Series, no. 9. Austin: University of Texas Press. 264 pp. Map.
[Based largely on archival sources never before used, this work gives the reader a deeper appreciation of the internal life of the rural community, which has received relatively little attention. Understanding the experiences of Palestinians before 1948 helps us comprehend better the continuity of movements for Palestinian statehood as well as today's tensions and problems on the West Bank.]

Minassian, Anaide Ter. *Nationalism and Socialism in the Armenian Revolutionary Movement*. Cambridge: Zoryan. 69 pp.

Monego, Joan P. *Maghrebian Literature in French*. Twayne's World Authors Series, no. 727. Boston: G.K. Hall. Bibl.; map; index.

al-Morayati, Abid A., ed. *International Relations of the Middle East and North Africa.* Cambridge, Mass.: Schenkman. 500 pp. Bibl.; index.

Mousa, Issam S. *The Arab Image in the U.S. Press.* American University Studies, Series XV, Communications, vol. l. New York: Peter Lang. 187 pp. Bibl.

Muhammad, al-Hajj. *The House of Si Abd Allah: The Oral History of a Moroccan Family.* Translated and edited by Henry Munson, Jr. New Haven, Conn.: Yale University Press. 280 pp. Bibl.; index.
[An oral history of a Moroccan peasant family over the past hundred years as told to Munson by two members of this family—Muhammad, a fundamentalist Muslim peddler in Tangier, and Fatima Zohra, a Westernized, educated Muslim woman. More generally, this book is a history of the transformation of an impoverished peasantry into a lumpenproletariat and working class, and a history of colonialism and foreign domination. An introduction outlines Moroccan history and interprets relevant dimensions of the Islamic faith.]

Müller-Serten, Gernot. *Palästinas feindliche Brüder: Der endlose Konflikt am Jordan und seine Geschichte.* Düsseldorf and Vienna: Econ-Verlag. 320 pp. Illus.

Murlakov, Eli. *Das Recht der Völker auf Selbstbestimmung im israelisch-arabischen Konflikt.* Schweizer Studien zum internationalen Recht, vol. 31. Zürich: Schulthess, Polygraphisches Verlag, 1983. 162 pp. Bibl.
[Originally a Zürich University dissertation.]

Muttam, John. *Arms and Insecurity in the Persian Gulf.* New Delhi: Radiant Publishers. 227 pp. Bibl.; index.

Mzali, Mohamed. *Le parole de l'action.* Paris: Editions Publisud. 280 pp.
[Before becoming prime minister of Tunisia, Mzali directed various ministries in his country. He recalls the problems that were posed for his developing land by key social sectors such as education, communication, sanitation, and youth.]

Naba'a, Abdel Aziz M. *Marketing in Saudi Arabia.* New York: Praeger Publishers. 227 pp. Appends.; index.
[This work, based on the author's dissertation, provides a fairly comprehensive summary of previous research as the basis for an analysis via questionnaire of the level of knowledge possessed by a small sample of U.S. businessmen about Saudi Arabia. The analysis, however, provides relatively little guidance for evaluating the role of information in marketing in the kingdom.]

Naccache, Georges. *Un rêve libanais, 1943–1972.* Fiches du monde arabe. Paris: Diffusion Alternative. 277 pp.
[This anthology of articles by a Lebanese journalist—who founded *L'Orient,* was minister of information and of public works, and was ambassador in Paris—helps us evaluate the situation in Lebanon.]

Nafi, Zuhair Ahmed. *Economic and Social Development in Qatar.* Dover, N.H.: Frances Pinter. 146 pp. Bibl.; tables.

[An introduction to the resources, policies, and system of government that have brought about the country's rapid progress since it became a sovereign state in 1971.]

Naficy, Hamid, ed. *Iran Media Index*. Bibliographies and Indexes in World History, no. 1. Westport, Conn.: Greenwood Press. 264 pp. Bibl.; indexes.

Naguib, Mohammad. *Egypt's Destiny: A Personal Statement by Mohammad Neguib*. Garden City, N.Y.: Doubleday, 1955. Reprint. Westport, Conn.: Greenwood Press. 256 pp. Index.

al-Nahari, Abdulaziz Mohammed. *Libraries and Librarianship in the Muslim World*. Vol. 1, *A National Library for the Developing Country, with the Experience of Saudi Arabia*. London: Mansell. 208 pp.
[Defines the functions of a national library and, taking Saudi Arabia as a case study, investigates those functions in terms of setting up such a library in a developing country.]

Narkiss, Uzi. *The Liberation of Jerusalem: The Battle of 1967*. Introduction by Elie Wiesel. London: Valentine Mitchell; Totowa, N.J.: Biblio Distribution Center, 1983. 285 pp. Illus.; map.
[From the age of thirteen, Narkiss participated in the activities of the Hagannah and later joined the Palmach, fighting in Jerusalem and Negev during the 1948–49 war. He tells of the capture of Jerusalem during the six-day war, when he was the commanding officer in charge of Israeli forces.

Nashif, Taysir N. *Nuclear Warfare in the Middle East: Dimensions and Responsibilities*. Princeton, N.J.: Kingston Press. 142 pp.
[The author reviews the state of nuclear proliferation in the Middle East and discusses the danger points in both Israeli and Arab thinking about the possible usefulness of nuclear weapons. After indicating the relative availability of nuclear technology even to small countries and other political groups, Nashif makes a strong case for a nuclear-free zone in the area. UN documents relating to nuclear control are appended.]

Neff, Donald. *Warriors for Jerusalem: The Six Days That Changed the Middle East*. New York: Linden Press. 430 pp. Index.
A sequel to the author's *Warriors at Suez* (Linden Press, 1981), this book tells the story of the 1967 six-day war. Neff presents a detailed diplomatic history written in a dramatic, journalistic style. Although documented by material released under the Freedom of Information Act and personal interviews, Neff's often unflattering portraits of primary actors will be controversial.

Neumann, Stephanie G., ed. *Defense Planning in Less-Industrialized States: The Middle East and South Asia*. Lexington, Mass.: Lexington Books. 336 pp. Figures; tables; index.
[This collection of essays is a seminal contribution to the new field of comparative defense studies. The authors explore the confluence of factors that influence the defense doctrines of Egypt, Iraq, Israel, India, Pakistan, Saudi Arabia, and Turkey—offering insight and describing the policies and strategies of each country. They describe the implications for regional stability and for improved relations between the less-developed countries and the industrialized world.]

Ochsenwald, William. *Religion, Society, and the State in Arabia: The Hijaz under Ottoman Control, 1840–1908.* Columbus: Ohio State University Press. 300 pp. Bibl.; gloss.; index.

Olson, David V. *Badges and Distinctive Insignia of the Kingdom of Saudi Arabia.* Vol. 2, *Royal Saudi Air Force.* St. Paul, Minn.: D.V. Olson. 100 pp.

Organization for Economic Cooperation and Development. *Turquie, 1983.* Paris: OECD. 84 pp.
[A detailed economic analysis of one of the OECD member countries and of its evolution during the previous year.]

Organization of the Petroleum Exporting Countries. *OPEC Official Resolutions and Press Releases, 1960–1983.* 2d ed. Oxford and New York: Pergamon Press. 216 pp. Indexes.

Al Othman, Nasser Mohamad. *With Their Bare Hands: The Story of Oil in Qatar.* Translated by Ken Whittingham. London and New York: Longman. 224 pp. Illus.
[This book arises from articles originally published in the newspaper *al-Rayah*.]

Ouitis, A'issa. *Prophétie, magie, et possession en Algérie.* Paris: Editions Arcantère. 221 pp. Bibl.
[A description and analysis of the practices and symbolic behavior of a rural group in the region of Mansourah, a province of Sétif, Algeria.]

Ouassaïd, Brick. *Le Coquelicots de l'Oriental: Chronique d'une famille berbère marocaine.* Paris: Editions la Découverte. 180 pp.
[The author, born in 1950 in the region of the high plain in the east of Morocco, recalls the landscape and the tastes and smells that marked his early years. This personal account allows us to enter into a community that is poorly known in the West in a way that an abstract, sociological inquiry could not.]

Ovendale, Ritchie. *The Origins of the Arab-Israel Wars.* Origins of Modern Wars Series. London and New York: Longman. 232 pp. Bibl; maps; index.
[This is the second in a series on the origins of modern wars. The author traces the history of the Arab-Israeli conflict from the beginning of Zionism to the present. He also gives an account of how Western imperial history precipitated the conflict and of the roles the superpowers have played in more recent history.]

Oz, Amos. *In the Land of Israel.* Translated by Maurie Goldberg-Bartura. San Diego: Harcourt Brace Jovanovich, 1983; New York: Vintage Books, 1984. 272 pp.
[Oz makes the internal ideological struggle within Israel come to life through interviews with a variety of Israel West Bank settlers, Oriental Jewish development town dwellers, and Arabs living under occupation.]
See also Gavron; Rubinstein.

Pakradouni, Karim. *La paix manquée: Le mandat d'Elias Sarkis (1976–1982).* Beirut: Editions Fiches du Monde Arabe. 273 pp. Index.
[This book reveals that the author, a member of the Phalangist party's Polit-

bureau, was closer to President Sarkis than was widely known at the time. The book, intended primarily as a testimony and document, gives a nonchronological review of events. It emphasizes the problems Sarkis faced and his failures, but neglects the negative role played by the author's party in these failures.]

Pakravan, Karim. *Oil Supply Disruptions in the 1980s: An Economic Analysis.* Stanford, Calif: Hoover Institution Press. 85 pp.
Utilizing the techniques and results of other studies to place in context the problem of the gulf states' vulnerability to internal and external destabilizing forces, Pakravan recommends changes in the policies of nations external to the region—particularly the United States—and of the Gulf states. Long-term solutions needed to avoid disaster require the fostering by the Gulf states of regional economic cooperation, beginning with the vital hydocarbon industries.

Palais et maisons du Caire. Vol. 2, *Epoque ottomane (XVIe–XVIIIe siècle).* Paris: Editions CNRS. 612 pp. Illus.; figs.
[Reviews and illustrates the evolution of architecture, decor, and the utilization of materials for Cairo's palaces, the residences of its notables, and its collective dwellings.]

Pascon, Paul, and Herman Van der Wusten. *Les Beni Bou Frah: Essai d'écologie sociale d'une vallée rifaine (Maroc).*Rabat: Paul Pascon et Herman Van der Wusten; Paris: Diffusion L'Harmattan. 295 pp.

Peck, Juliana S. *The Reagan Administration and the Palestinian Question: The First Thousand Days.* Washington, D.C.: Institute for Palestine Studies. 138 pp.
[An analysis of the Reagan administration's public record on the Palestine question and related developments in Lebanon and the occupied territories.]

Pelcovits, Nathan A. *Peacekeeping on Arab-Israeli Fronts: Lessons from the Sinai and Lebanon.* SAIS Papers in International Affairs, no. 3. Boulder, Colo.: Westview Press with the Foreign Policy Institute, School of Advanced International Studies, Johns Hopkins University. 181 pp. Bibl; illus.
[Three recent events have significantly altered the pattern of peacekeeping in the region, in which the UN had sponsored virtually every third-party mission on Arab-Israeli fronts. These events were the Camp David accord; the June 1982 invasion of Lebanon; and the Sabra-Shatila massacres. Pelcovits analyzes these events to answer the questions they raise about the comparative advantages and successes of different types of peacekeeping missions.]

Pelletiere, Stephen C. *The Kurds: An Unstable Element in the Gulf.* Boulder, Colo.: Westview Press. 220 pp. Map; append.; index.
[This is a survey of the Kurdish nationalist movement, with emphasis on Iraq. The author, a former journalist who witnessed some of the events and interviewed participants, paints a vivid picture of the conflict between Mulla Mustafa al-Barzani, who had an absolute charismatic hold over his traditional tribal followers, and the better educated, left-wing Kurdish Democratic party leaders, who believed in modern organization.]

Pendleton, Madge, et al. *The Green Book Guide for Living in Saudi Arabia.* 4th ed. Washington, D.C.: Middle East Editorial Associates. 253 pp. Bibl.; maps; index.
[The book's four authors have collectively spent twenty-six years in the Arabian Peninsula. Their guide covers such subjects as health, schools and children, and housing. The book includes background information on the country and its people, and describes fourteen cities in which foreigners are likely to live.]

Peress, Gilles, photographer. *Telex Iran: In the Name of Revolution.* Commentary by Gholam-Hossein Sa'edi. Millerton, N.Y.: Aperture. 101 pp. Illus.
[This pictorial work on the 1979–81 Iran hostage crisis is an exercise in semiotics, in which the editors deliberately chose to present directly—in a nonchronological order and with little explanatory text—a collection of images related only by general location and time. In a postscript, the noted Iranian author Gholam-Hussein Sa'edi offers a commentary on the land seen through the lens of Peress.]

Peretz, Don. *The Middle East Today.* New York: Praeger Publishers. 577 pp.

Peters, Joan. *From Time Immemorial: The Origins of the Arab-Jewish Conflict over Palestine.* New York: Harper & Row. 601 pp. Bibl.; illus.; index.

Philipp, Hans-Jürgen. *Saudi Arabia: Bibliography on Society, Politics, and Economics from the 18th Century to the Present = Saudi-Arabien: Bibliographie zu Gesellschaft, Politik, Wirtschaft: Literature seit dem 18. Jahrhundert in westeuropäischen Sprachen mit Standortnachweisen.* Munich and New York: K.G. Saur. 405 pp.
[A comprehensive bibliography of works dealing with Saudi Arabia; it provides over 3,600 titles covering the period from the inception of the country to the present. It includes, besides trade publications, relatively unknown corporate, governmental, and organizational publications.]

Pogany, Istvan. *The Security Council and the Arab-Israeli Conflict.* New York: St. Martin's Press.

Porch, Douglas. *The Conquest of the Sahara.* New York: Knopf; distributed by Random House. 332 pp. Bibl.; map; index.

Possarnig, Renate. *Gaddafi: Enfant terrible der Weltpolitik.* Hamburg: Hoffman und Compe, 1983. 225 pp. Illus.

Presley, John R. *A Guide to the Saudi Arabian Economy.* London: Macmillan; New York: St. Martin's Press. 256 pp. Maps; figs.; tables.
[An up-to-date account of the Saudi process of economic development for the general reader. Emphasizes the experiences of the last decade and the manner in which oil revenues have been harnessed to the industrialization process. Includes practical business information.]

Qaddafi, Muammar. *Kadhafi, Je suis un opposant a l'échelon mondial: Entretiens avec Hamid Barrada, Marc Kravetz, et Marc Whitaker.* Lausanne: Editions Pierre Marcel Favre. 231 pp.
[In these texts of complete, unedited interviews, the Libyan president

expresses himself on the topics of the Jews and the Arabs, Afghanistan and Poland, Africa, France, Islam, the Kurds, Marxism, terrorism, women, and himself.]

Rabhi, Pierre. *Du Sahara aux Cévennes: Ou la Reconquête du songe.* Preface by André Griffon. Lavilledieu: Editions du Candide, 1983. 238 pp.
[The testimony of a man who came from south of the Sahara and settled as a farmer in Ardèche, where he reconstituted around himself a community similar to those of the Saharan Ksour.]

Rabinovich, Itamar. *The War for Lebanon, 1970–1983.* Ithaca, N.Y.: Cornell University Press. 243 pp. Maps.
[This is a detailed survey of the period, uncovering the tangled web of Lebanese politics and the influence of Hafiz al-Assad.]

Rabinovich, Itamar, and Jehuda Reinharz, eds. *Israel in the Middle East: Documents and Readings on Society, Politics and Foreign Relations, 1948–present.* New York: Oxford University Press. 407 pp. Bibls.; maps; index.
[An anthology of annotated documents from Israeli, American, Arab, and Soviet sources, providing an overview of the most crucial foreign and domestic policy issues facing the state of Israel from 1948 to 1983. About a quarter of the documents have been translated from Hebrew and Arabic for this book.]

Radjavi, Kazem. *La révolution iranienne et les Moudjahidin.* Preface by Maxime Rodinson. Paris: Editions Anthropos, 1983. 251 pp.

Radji, Parviz C. *In the Service of the Peacock Throne: The Diaries of the Shah's Last Ambassador to London.* London: Hamish Hamilton, 1983. 343 pp. Index.
[The author was Iran's ambassador to England during the last two and one-half years of the shah's reign. His personal diary during those years has been reproduced with only minor editing. Although offering no political revelations that have not already appeared in other accounts, the diary expresses the attitudes and reactions, the self-doubt and ambivalence, typical of courtiers in a monarchy on the verge of collapse.]

Ragette, Friedrich, ed. *The Beirut of Tomorrow: Planning for Reconstruction.* Beirut: American University of Beirut; distributed by Syracuse University Press. 142 pp. Illus.; maps.
[The ten papers and discussion in this book result from a January 1983 symposium organized by the American University of Beirut, the Goethe Institute, and the Association of German-Speaking Graduates. Taking place during a brief period of calm and looking toward the future, the symposium illustrates what an exciting challenge the city of Beirut offers to planners if, and when, its formidable intercommunal conflicts can be overcome.]

Rajaee, Farhang. *Islamic Values and World View: Khomeyni on Man, the State, and International Politics.* American Values Projected Abroad; Exxon Ser., vol. 13. Lanham, Md.: University Press of America. 1983. 162 pp. Bibl.
[This volume gives a well-organized and systematic exposition of Khomeini's views.]

al-Rashid, Ibrahim, ed. *Yemen Enters the Modern World: Secret U.S. Documents on the Rise of the Second Power on the Arabian Peninsula.* Documents on the History of Saudi Arabia, vol. 6. Chapel Hill, N.C.: Documentary Publications. 228 pp. Index.
[A reprinting of fifty-eight miscellaneous U.S. State Department memoranda, telegrams, and reports dated from 16 June 1945 to 22 December 1949. Because of the book's narrow focus and lack of supporting commentary, scholars who already are conversant with the period will find many documents of interest, but others will find the book less valuable.]

Razavi, Hossein, and Firouz Vakil. *The Political Environment of Economic Planning in Iran, 1971–1983: From Monarchy to Islamic Republic.* Boulder, Colo.: Westview Press. 194 pp. Bibl.; illus.; index.
[Based on both research and firsthand experience, this book provides a politicoeconomic analysis of the operation of Iran's economy before and after the 1979 revolution. The authors discuss the function and effectiveness of economic planning during the shah's tenure and the institutional problems the revolutionary regime has been facing. They predict the possible consequences of its failure to deal appropriately with these problems and outline prospects for future economic planning.]

Regan, Geoffrey B. *Israel and the Arabs.* Cambridge Introduction to the History of Mankind Topic Book. Cambridge and New York: Cambridge University Press. 48 pp. Illus.

Reich, Bernard. *The United States and Israel: Influence in the Special Relationship.* Studies of Influence in International Relations. New York: Praeger Publishers. 236 pp. Bibl.; index.

Reich, Walter. *A Stranger in My House: Jews and Arabs in the West Bank.* New York: Holt, Rinehart, & Winston. 134 pp. Bibl.; illus.; index.
[A Washington psychiatrist who has written on the Soviet Union and the Mideast provides a slim volume of reporting, based on interviews with Arabs and Jews during his visit to Israel and the West Bank. He sketches viewpoints from both sides. The book's defects lie in Reich's failure to catch Arab attitudes as well as he has Jewish moods and in his unworkable suggestion that the West Bank Arabs might break with the PLO and somehow negotiate with Israel in their own name.]

Reiser, Stewart. *The Politics of Leverage: The National Religious Party of Israel and Its Influence on Foreign Policy.* Harvard Middle East Papers, Modern Series, no. 2. Cambridge, Mass.: Center for Middle Eastern Studies, Harvard University. 90 pp. Gloss.
The nature of coalition government in Israel has given great leverage to small parties with less than 10 percent of the electoral vote, such as the National Religious Party. This paper explores the consequences of the leverage exerted by the NRP on the Arab-Israeli conflict in general and the occupied territories in particular, which resulted from the NRP's shift toward an active, militant foreign policy, leading in 1967 to its participation in a coalition government with the Likud party.

Renglet, Claude. *Israël face à l'Islam.* Roanne, Loire: Editions Horvath, 1983. 250 pp. Illus.
[Discusses the origins of Jewish and Arab nationalism.]

Renz, Alfred. *Morokko*. Munich: Prestel. 463 pp. Illus.; maps.

Richardson, John P. *The West Bank: A Portrait*. Washington, D.C.: Middle East Institute. 221 pp. Illus.; maps; index.
A comprehensive, objective coverage of the nature, history, and likely future of the West Bank, whose special status and role in the Arab-Israeli conflict is reflected in the name itself. Part one covers the historical setting from before World War I to the Hashemite era; part two describes life under occupation; and part three analyzes the area in its international context.

Ricks, Thomas M., ed. and comp. *Critical Perspectives on Modern Persian Literature*. Washington, D.C.: Three Continents Press. 510 pp. Bibl.; illus.; map.
This is an anthology of critical essays on modern Persian literature originally published in English or translated into English from works published in Persian or Russian. The emphasis is on the genres of prose and poetry and on the larger socioliterary context within which the classicists fought the engagé writers from 1919 to 1979. Given the logistical and political difficulties of collecting these essays and the technical difficulties of translating many of them, the often poorly edited and obviously hastily published nature of this collection may be forgiven, for it offers a treasure trove of information about modern Iranian life as reflected in the attitudes of that country's literary elite.

Riech, Andreas. *Unsere Wirtschaft: Eine gekurtze kommentierte Übersetzung des Buches "iqtisaduna" von Muhammad Baqir as-Sadr*. Islamkundliche Untersuchungen, vol. 93. Berlin: Klaus Schwarz Verlag. 747 pp.

Rifaat, Alfia. *Distant View of a Minaret and Other Stories*. Translated by Denys Johnson-Davies. London: Quartet Books. 116 pp.
[This is a collection of fifteen short stories, whose Egyptian author comes from a traditional Muslim family. Her stories focus on the position of women in her society.]

Ristelhueber, Sophie. *Beyrouth photographies*. Paris: Editeur Fernand Hazan. 68 pp. Illus.
[Photos of a Beirut devastated by the war, taken by members of the French Institute of Architecture in Paris in March-April 1984.]

Rodinson, Maxime. *Cult, Ghetto, and State: The Persistence of the Jewish Question*. London: Al Saqi Books, distributed by Zed Press, 1983. 256 pp. Index.
[A collection of essays and articles, which appeared originally in French in various journals or newspapers, on the theme of cultural confrontation and historical experience. The author also reflects upon his own career in Arab studies.]

Ro'i, Yaacov. *The USSR and the Muslim World: Issues in Domestic and Foreign Policy*. London and Boston: Allen & Unwin. 298 pp. Illus.
[Based on papers given at a conference held by the Russian and East European Research Center at Tel Aviv University in December 1980, this volume contains fourteen essays by contributors from Israel, Western Europe, and North America, which treat historical and contemporary aspects of the conference's topic. An integrated summary concludes the work.]

Rosen, Lawrence. *Bargaining for Reality: The Construction of Social Relations in a Muslim Community.* Chicago: University of Chicago Press. 264 pp. Bibl.; illus.; index.

Rosenblatt, Roger. *Children of War.* New York: Anchor Books. 216 pp.

Rouleau, Eric. *Les Palestiniens.* Paris: Editions la Découverte and Le Monde. 240 pp.
[The author, chief reporter for *Le Monde*, has covered the Middle East for nearly twenty years. This work, one of the fruits of his investigations; portrays the Palestinian people in all their variety.]

Rous, Jean. *Habib Bourquiba.* Romarantin-Lanthenay and Paris: Editions Martinsart. 312 pp. Illus.
[A biography of the Tunisian leader that thoroughly analyzes the personality and thought of this symbol of Third World independence. The author, a journalist and writer, was one of the most active pioneers of decolonization.]

Rowley, Gwyn. *Israel into Palestine.* London: Mansell; distributed by H.W. Wilson. 176 pp. Bibl.; maps; index.
[A noted authority on urban and political geography surveys the history of the Arab-Israeli conflict from antiquity to the present, focusing on the role of land for its strategic importance, its religious and psychological dimensions, and its water and other resources. Includes a valuable treatment of events since Camp David and of Israeli policies in Lebanon and in territories occupied in 1967.]

Roy, Jules. *Beyrouth: Viva la muerte.* Paris: Editions Grasset et Fasquelle. 160 pp.
[A book on Lebanon, for which every one feels compassion. Roy raises the question of whether it was not the West, rather than Lebanon, that was in deadly danger.]

Rubenstein, Alvin Z., ed. *The Arab-Israeli Conflict: Perspectives.* New York: Praeger Publishers. 221 pp. Bibl.; maps; index.

Rubenstein, Sondra M. *The Communist Movement in Palestine and Israel: 1919–1984.* Boulder, Colo. Westview Press. 250 pp. Bibl.; index.
[This book traces the origin and development of the communist movement in Palestine and Israel, examining the problems affecting it in the years preceding Israeli statehood, within the context of the Jewish community in Palestine and the international communist movement. He concludes with an overview of the movement today and explains the virtual extinction of party influence on current Israeli politics.]

Rubinstein, Ammon. *The Zionist Dream Revisited: From Herzl to Gush Emunim and Back.* New York: Schocken Books. 204 pp. Index.
The author grapples with the question: "What happened to the Zionist dream?" After an extended review of Zionist thought and its development, Rubinstein concludes that the future of Israel depends "on its will and ability to return to [the] old truths [that] Zionism has built: a home and not a temple, a secular nation and not a sacred tribe, a good neighbor. . .and not a recluse. . .willing to survive alone." However, he wonders if Israel

has fulfilled the Zionist dream of a "state that would liberate the Christian world from anti-Semitism," or has it come to serve "as the ostensible cause for [its] reappearance?" See also Gavron; Oz.

Saada, Al Hadi. *Les lanques et l'école: Bilinguisme inégal dans l'école algérienne.* Bern and Nancy: Editions Universitaires Peter Lang. 258 pp.
[The problems posed by French-Arabic bilingualism in Algeria are treated, and general reflections are made on the subject of bilingualism and schooling.]

El-Sadat, Anwar. *Those I Have Known.* Foreword by Jimmy Carter. New York: Continuum. 140 pp. Illus.

Sa'edi, Gholam-Hossein. *Fear and Trembling.* Translated by Minoo Southgate. Washington, D.C.: Three Continents Press. 121 pp. Bibl.
The author is one of Iran's most prolific, contemporary writers of engagé literature. Southgate's excellent introduction and bibliography place Sa'edi in historical and aesthetic context. The novel itself was published in 1968 and deals in a symbolic, sinister style with issues of social change that face modern Iran through the technique of telling six stories about the inhabitants of a Persian Gulf village—an area about which most Iranians as well as Westerners know little, but about which the author has also written a first-hand anthropological account published in 1966 as *Ahl-i Hava* (People of the wind).

Saint-Prot, Charles. *Les mystères syriens: La politique au Proche-Orient de 1970 à 1984.* Paris: Albin Michel. 217 pp. Illus.; maps.
[An analysis of Syrian policy in Lebanon, of the links that exist between terrorist attempts in France and in Beirut, and of the international terrorist web set up by the Syrian and Iranian services.]

Salem, Isam Kamel. *Islam und Völkerrecht: Das Völkerrecht in der islamischer Weltanshauung.* Berlin: Express-Edition. 260 pp. Bibl.

Salem, Norma. *Habib Bourguiba, Islam, and the Creation of Independent Tunisia.* London and Dover, N.H.: Croom Helm. 270 pp. Bibl.; index.

Saliba, Maurice, comp. *Arabic and Islamic Studies: Doctoral Dissertations and Graduate Theses in English, 1881–1981.* Middle East Bibliographical Serials, no. 2. Antélias, Lebanon: M. Saliba; Paris: Diffusion Synonyme. 219 pp.

———. *Arab Gulf States: Doctoral Dissertations and Graduate Theses in English, French, and German. 1881–1981.* Middle East Bibliographical Serials, no. 1. Antélias, Lebanon: M. Saliba; Paris: Diffusion Synonyme. 171 pp.

Sammut, Carmel. *L'Impérialisme capitaliste français et la nationalisme tunisien, 1881–1941.* Paris: Publisud, 1983. 416 pp.

Sanson, Henri. *Laïcité islamique en Algérie.* Recherches sur les sociétés méditerranéenes. Paris: Editions CNRS, 1983. 176 pp.
[A study in religious sociology which approaches secularity as a social influence affecting Algeria's religious statutes—not only those of the

Islamic community but also those of the minority religious communities, such as the Ibadite and the Catholic.]

Sarpa, John G. *U.S.-Arab Relations: The Commercial Dimension*. Occasional Paper no. 1, National Council on U.S.-Arab Relations. Washington, D.C.: National Council on U.S.-Arab Relations. 23 pp. Bibl.
["Published in conjunction with the National Center for Export-Import Studies, Washington, D.C."]

Scheftelowitz, Erwin E. *Israelisches Handels-und Wirtschaftsrecht: Einschliesslich Arbeits- und Sozialrecht*. Schriftenreihe Recht der internationalen Wirtschaft, vol. 24. Heidelberg: Verlagsgesellschaft Recht und Wirtschaft. 196 pp. Bibl; index.

Schiff, Ze'ev, and Ehud Ya'ari. *Israel's Lebanon War*. Translated by Ina Friedman. New York: Simon & Schuster. 320 pp.
[Lebanon has often been called Israel's Vietnam. When first published in Hebrew last year, this book gave Israelis a factual basis for the malaise that led to the downfall of the Likud government in 1984. With publication in the United States of this inside history, Lebanon also emerges as Israel's Watergate, an entanglement that caused a breakdown of political accountability, an intrigue of manipulation and personal deception at the highest levels of a parliamentary democracy.]

Schmitt, Eberhard, ed. *Türkei*. Vol. 1, *Politick, Ökonomie, Kultus*; vol. 2, *Ein Reisenhandbuch*. Berlin: Express-Edition. 383 pp.; 420 pp. Illus.; maps.

Scholl-Latour, Peter. *Allah ist mit den Standhaften: Begegnungen mit der islamischen Revolution*. 4th ed. Stuttgart: Deutsche Verlags-Anstalt, 1983. 766 pp. Maps.

Schopen, Armin. *Traditionelle Heilmittel in Jemen*. Wiesbaden: Steiner, 1983. 256 pp. Bibl.; map; index.

Schreiner, Martin. *Gesammelte Schriften: Islamische und jüdisch-islamische Studien*. Translated and introduced by Moshe Perlmann. Collectanea, vol. 11. Hildesheim, Zürich, and New York: Olms, 1983. 674 pp.

Schweizer, Gerhard. *Persien, Drehscheibe der Kulturen: Von Zarathustra bis Khomeini*. Düsseldorf and Vienna: Econ, 1983. 320 pp. Bibl.; illus.; maps; index.

Scott, Charles W. *Pieces of the Game: The Human Drama of Americans Held Hostage in Iran*. Atlanta, Ga.: Peachtree Publishers. 350 pp.
[Scott, a colonel in the U.S. Army and a student of the Farsi language and Persian literature, was one of the Americans taken hostage in 1979. During his captivity, he became acquainted with one of his captors and alternates the telling of his own story with episodes from Akbar's life, thus introducing a human dimension into this readable and informative account of an incident too often characterized by misinformation, political abstractions, and cultural stereotypes.]

El-Shagi, El-Shagi, and Martin Raschen. *Arbeitskräfteabwanderung aus*

Entwicklungsländern in die arabischen Ölländer. Forschungsberichte des Bundesministeriums für Wirtschaftliche Zusammenarbeit, vol. 58. Munich, Cologne, and London: Weltforum-Verlag. 185 pp. Bibl.

Shaheen, Jack G. *The TV Arab.* Bowling Green, Ohio: Bowling Green State University Press. 146 pp. Bibl.; index.
Shaheen reviews the images of Arabs presented in U.S. television programs and asks why almost all the images until recently have been negative. He bases his insightful analysis upon an extensive study of and personal experience with the American mass media.

Shahrani, M. Nazif, and Robert L. Canfield, eds. *Revolutions and Rebellions: Anthropological Perspectives.* Institute of International Studies Research Series, no. 57. Berkeley: University of California Institute of International Studies. 394 pp. Bibl.; maps; gloss.; index.
[This volume is the result of a symposium at the 1980 meeting of the American Anthropological Association in Washington, D.C. Thirteen contributors analyze local-level resistance in Afghanistan to the Marxist coup of 1978 and the subsequent Soviet occupation from the cultural/ historical perspectives of the regional, tribal, religious, ethnic, gender, and class groups that make up the heterogeneous Afghan society.]

Sharaf, Shamil. *Die Palästinenser: Geschichte der Entstehung eines nationalen Bewusstseins.* Forschungsberichete, Österreichisches Institut für Internationale Politik, vol. 6. Vienna: W. Braumüller; Laxenburg: Austrian Institute for International Affairs, 1983. 214 pp. Bibl., maps.

El Sheik, F.A. *The Legal Regime of Foreign Private Investment in the Sudan and Saudi Arabia: A Case Study of Developing Countries.* Cambridge Studies in International and Comparative Law. Cambridge and New York: Cambridge University Press, in association with Khartoum University Press. 462 pp. Bibl.; index.
[This detailed treatment of investment law in two Arab states shows how foreign investment is controlled through legislation, treaties, and contracts, and how a developing country might steer its diversified financial capability toward international investment. Because Islamic practices prevail in both countries, the author stresses the contribution of Islamic jurisprudence to the development of international economic rules.]

Shiffer, Shimon. *Opération boule de neige.* Translated by Bertrand Levergeois. Paris: J.C. Lattès. 311 pp. Illus.
[Published in Jerusalem in 1984 under the title *Kadur Shelge,* with the English title *Snow Ball* on the verso.]

Shuval, Judith T. *Newcomers and Colleagues: Soviet Immigrant Physicians in Israel.* Foreword by Mark G. Field. Houston: Cap and Gown Press. 157 pp. Bibl.; illus.; index.

Silver, Eric. *Begin: The Haunted Prophet.* New York: Random House. 278 pp. Bibl.; illus.; index.
[British journalist Silver, who covered Begin's premiership for the *Guardian* and the *Observer,* traces Begin's career from his youth in Eastern Europe, through his immigration and leadership role in the Irgun guerrilla movement that ousted the British from Palestine, to his years as head of the

Israel government. Silver is critical of Begin's ethnocentricity, his invocation of the Holocaust as justification of nearly everything, and his "selective compassion," which, the author feels, made him feel no remorse for the loss of non-Jewish lives.]

Sirriyeh, Hussein. *U.S. Policy in the Gulf 1968–1977: Aftermath of British Withdrawal*. London: Ithaca Press. 297 pp. Bibl.
[Basing his account almost entirely on congressional hearings, the author focuses on the formulation of policy toward the Gulf region in the period between the announcement of British withdrawal and the collapse of the Pahlavi regime.]

Smith, G. Rex, ed. *The Yemens*. World Bibliographical Series, no. 50. Oxford, England, and Santa Barbara, Calif.: Clio Press. 200 pp. Map; index.
[Smith's annotated guide provides a reliable bibliography of the two Yemens for the English-speaking world. All major subjects and reference works are included. The introductory essay provides a historical survey from earliest times to the present.]

Smooha, Sammy. *The Orientation and Politicization of Arab Minorities in Israel*. Rev. ed. Haifa: Jewish-Arab Center, Institute of Middle Eastern Studies, University of Haifa. 225 pp. Tables; index.
[A thorough analysis, based on the first national survey of Jews and Arabs in Israel, of issues in Arab-Jewish relations. Criticizing the dominant Arab radicalization thesis, the author presents politicization as an alternative perspective, consisting of the simultaneous processes of Israelization, factionalization, and radicalization that the Arab minority is undergoing.]

Smooha, Sammy, ed. *Social Research on Arabs in Israel, 1977–1982: A Bibliography*. Haifa: Jewish-Arab Center, Institute of Middle Eastern Studies, University of Haifa. 100 pp.
[This bibliography is a sequel to an earlier volume compiled by Smooha and Ora Cibulski that covered publications for the years 1948–76. The book contains English and Hebrew sections, and is divided into three parts: social science titles on Arabs within Israel's pre-1967 borders; other titles on the same subject; and titles on Palestinians, here defined as Arabs living in Palestine before the creation of Israel or those living in the occupied territories or abroad.]

Al-Sowayegh, Abdulaziz. *Arab Petro-Politics*. New York: St. Martin's Press. 207 pp. Index.
[This concise book contains much useful data on oil and its derivatives. The author explores the interaction among oil companies, consumers, and producers, beginning with a historical survey and then discussing the Palestinian issue, relations with the West, and the role of oil in these relations.]

Spain, James W. *American Diplomacy in Turkey: Memoirs of an Ambassador Extraordinary and Plenipotentiary*. New York: Praeger Publishers. 256 pp. Index.
[Ambassador Spain uses his experiences in Turkey as a basis for describing and analyzing the kinds of things a modern American ambassador must do, with respect both to the foreign official and nonofficial circles in the host

country and to official and nonofficial Americans who have an interest in the host country.]

Stein, Janice Gross, and David Dewitt, eds. *Middle East at the Crossroads: International Forces and External Powers.* Oakville, Ontario, Canada: Mosaic Press; New York: Flatiron Press (Distributor). 233 pp. Bibl.; index.
[This book comprises articles written by participants in the May 1982 conference of the Canadian Professors for Peace in the Middle East.]

Stein, Kenneth W. *The Land Question in Palestine, 1917–1939.* Maps prepared by Karen L. Wysock. Chapel Hill: University of North Carolina Press. 314 pp. Illus.; maps; index.
[Based primarily on archival research, this book investigates how and why Jews acquired land from Arabs in Palestine during the British Mandate. Stein argues that Zionists were able to purchase the core of a national territory for three reasons: they had the capital and single-mindedness of purpose; the Arabs were willing to sell because they were economically impoverished and socially fragmented; and the British were ineffectual in regulating land sales and protecting Arab tenants.]

Stevens, Mary Anne, ed. *The Orientalists—Delacroix to Matisse: The allure of North Africa and the Near East.* New York: Thames & Hudson; Washington D.C.: National Gallery of Art. 235 pp. Illus.; map.
[Catalog of the First Major Exhibition of Orientalist Art in London, held at the Royal Academy in 1984 and then at the National Gallery of Art, Washington. This exhibit catalog traces the development and popularity of Orientalist painting during the nineteenth century with examples; shifts in artistic imagery and analyses of specific painters are included.]

Stone, Frank A. *Academies for Anatolia: A Study of the Rationale, Program, and Impact of the Educational Institutions Sponsored by the American Board in Turkey: 1830–1980.* Lanham, Md.: University Press of America; co-published by arrangement with the I.N. Thut World Education Center, University of Connecticut. 363 pp. Bibl.; illus.; index.

Stookey, Robert W., ed. *The Arabia Peninsula: Zone of Ferment.* Stanford, Calif.: Hoover Institution Press. 151 pp. Maps; index.
[Essays exploring the various societies of the Arabian Peninsula and their influence on international policy.]

Sulaiman, Khalid A. *Modern Arabic Poetry and Palestine.* London: Zed Press. 272 pp. Bibl.; index.
[The author looks at how twentieth-century Arab poetry reflects the most tragic problem the Arab nation has experienced in its contemporary history. He examines how political events have affected the development of poetry in the Middle East and shows that the loss of Palestine did not simply introduce new themes into modern Arab poetry but influenced its very nature, injecting a new poetic tone, a new symbolism, and a new angst that have combined to profoundly transform the essence of this poetry.]

Sullivan, John L., and Michal Shamir, eds. *Political Tolerance in Context: Sup-*

port for *Unpopular Minorities in Israel, New Zealand, and the United States.* Boulder, Colo.: Westview Press. 190 pp.
[Comparing data from Israel, New Zealand, and the United States, this book seeks to identify the universal social and psychological characteristics of political intolerance. The authors provide descriptions of mass publics in the three countries, incorporate individual and contextual factors into their cross-national model of tolerance, and highlight common issues for democratic regimes struggling with the problems of unpopular minorities and how to integrate them into the political process.]

Die syrische Besatzung im Libanon: Analyse eines Völkerrechtsbruches. Schriftenreihe Libanon aktuell, no. 5. Bonn: Osang-Verlag, 1983.

Talib, Kaizer. *Shelter in Saudi Arabia.* London: Academy Editions; New York: St. Martin's Press. 144 pp. Bibl.; illus.; figs.; index.

Tawil, Camille. *Der Nahe Osten-Krisenherd in den 80er und 90er Jahren: Eine libaneschen Stellungnahme.* Schriftenreihe Libanon actuell, no. 1. Bonn: Osang-Verlag, 1983. 42 pp.
[In German and French, with parallel title: *Le Moyen-Orient, foyer de trouble des années 80 et 90.*]

Tignor, Robert L. *State, Private Enterprise, and Economic Change in Egypt. 1918–1952.* Princeton Studies on the Near East. Princeton, N.J.: Princeton University Press. 317 pp. Bibl.; index.
[This study of Egyptian efforts to diversify the country's economy between the end of World War I and the Nasir coup d'état of 1952 focuses on the nascent bourgeoisie and the relationships of its segments to one another. Challenging important aspects of prevailing dependency theory, Tignor shows how native-born entrepreneurs and resident foreigners failed to reach all the goals of their capitalist strategy, but laid the foundation for industrialization and nationalization programs carried out later by the Nasir regime.]

Tripp, Charles, ed. *Regional Security in the Middle East.* Adelphi Library Series. New York: St. Martin's Press. 182 pp. Index.
[The London-based International Institute for Strategic Studies republishes groups of related articles in this series. The six articles here focus on long-term trends and root causes of behavior in the Middle East region.]

Turner, Bryan S. *Capitalism and Class in the Middle East: Theories of Social Change and Economic Development.* London: Heinemann Educational Books; Atlantic Highlands, N.J.: Humanities Press. 229 pp. Bibls.; indexes.

Tworuschka, Monika. *Allah ist gross: Religion, Politik, und Gesellschaft im Islam.* Gütersloher Taschenbücher Siebenstern, no. 1079. Gütersloh: Gütersloher Verlagshaus Mohn, 1983. 111 pp. Bibl.

Üçüncü, Şadi. *Die Stellung der Frau in der Geschichte der Türkei: Ein historischen Überblick von dem alten Türkvölkern bis heute.* Frankfurt: R.G. Fischer. 231 pp. Bibl.

al-Udhari, Abdullah, trans. *Victims of a Map: A Bilingual Anthology of Arabic*

Poetry. London: Al Saqi Books, distributed by Zed Press. 167 pp.
[This collection presents fifteen newly translated poems by three leading contemporary Arab poets: Mahmud Darwish, Samih al Qasim, and Adonis. The volume includes the Arabic texts beside the translation, and a brief biography of each poet. Themes of war, destruction, love, and longing for peace make the book a powerful document of contemporary Arab history.]

UNESCO. *Les relations historiques et socioculturelles entre l'Afrique et le monde arabe de 1935 à nos jours: Documents de travail et compte rendu des débats du colloque tenu à Paris du 25 au 27 juillet 1979.* Histoire générale de l'Afrique: Etudes et documents, vol. 7. Paris: UNESCO. 222 pp.

————. *Social Science Research and Women in the Arab World.* Papers from the Experts' Meeting on Multidisciplinary Research on Women in the Arab World, held in Tunis, May 18–21, 1982. Dover, N.H.: Frances Pinter; Paris: UNESCO. 175 pp. Bibls.
[The validity of much research on Arab women has been questioned because it has been conducted in large part by those foreign to Arab culture. A meeting of Arab women social scientists sponsored by UNESCO's Division of Human Rights and Peace was held in 1982 to rectify this situation. Included in this book are seven studies prepared for that meeting by regional specialists from Algeria, Iraq, Libya, Morocco, Saudi Arabia, Tunisia, and Sudan.]

Unwin, P.T., ed. *Bahrain*. World Bibliographical Series, vol. 49. Oxford, England, and Santa Barbara, Calif.: Clio Press. 265 pp. Map; index.
[A comprehensive English-language bibliography aimed at the general reader and professional. Includes a substantial introduction that provides necessary historical background.]

Vatin, Jean-Claude, ed. *Connaissances du Maghreb: Sciences sociales et colonization.* Paris: Editions du CNRS. 438 pp.
[These essays represent an attempt to rewrite the historical sociology of French Orientalist scholarship. Although the authors represent various disciplines, they present the evolution of the individual social sciences in a unified manner; the approach of each discipline is viewed in terms of its attempts to deal with Maghrebi realities. They conclude that the scientific analysis of colonial North Africa fulfilled two functions: first, it secured a French monopoly over both a territory and a society; second, it provided the French as well as the Maghrebi communities with a system that explained the North African experience.]

Viabilité économique d'un état palestinien indépendent: Document établi pour la Conférence Internationale sur la Question de la Palestine et pour les réunions préparatoires régionales (U.N.E.S.C.O.). Cahier 24. Louvain-la-Neuve, Belgium: Centre d'Etudes et de Recherches sur le Monde Arabe Contemporain. 43 pp.

Vieille, P., N. Eftekhari, B. Ghalioun, M. Gadant, and E. Longuenesse. *Pétrole et société.* Peuples méditerranéens, no. 26. Paris: Institute d'études méditerranéens; Diffusion Chiron. 250 pp.
[Presents the results of socioanthropological research which was financed by the Agence française pour la maîtrise de l'énergie, and which compares Algeria with Norway.]

Viorst, Milton. *UNRWA and Peace in the Middle East*. Special Study 4. Washington, D.C.: Middle East Institute. 63 pp.

The study focuses on the ambiguous, complex, but critical role that the United Nations Relief and Works Agency (UNRWA) plays in the Arab-Israeli drama. It functions as a continuing symbol to the world and to the Palestinian people that they are indeed a people, as a means for providing humanitarian aid to alleviate what originally was thought to be a temporary refugee problem, and as a political tool that can be manipulated either to continue the present zero-sum game between Arab and Israeli leaders or to negotiate a workable settlement of the conflict. Using as his prime example the Reagan administration's change in 1982, first to a position that threatened to cut off all support for the UNRWA as a tool of the PLO, then back to a position that saw the agency as "a practical necessity" for U.S. interests, Viorst combines firsthand knowledge of the agency, its clientele, its detractors, and its partisans with published data to show how the UNRWA acts as an important intervening variable that constrains the actions of all parties involved with it.

Wallach, Jehuda L. ". . .*Und mit der anderen hielten sie die Waffe": Die Kriege Israels*. Koblenz: Bernard und Graefe. 174 pp. Bibl.; map; index.

Warburg, Gabriel R., and Uri M. Kupferschmidt, eds. *Islam, Nationalism and Radicalism in Egypt and the Sudan*. New York: Praeger Publishers. 368 pp.

[Compares the politics of the two states as they are confronted with the forces of Islam, nationalism, and other ideologies in the twentieth century. Based on a conference held at the University of Haifa in 1981, the book contains articles written by experts from the Middle East, Europe, and America.]

Watanabe, Paul Y. *Ethnic Groups, Congress, and American Foreign Policy: The Politics of the Turkish Arms Embargo*. Contributions to Political Science, no. 116. Westport, Conn.: Greenwood Press. 272 pp. Bibl.; index.

Wiebe, Dietrich. *Afghanistan: Ein mittelasiatischen Entwicklungsland im Umbruch*. Stuttgart: Klett. 195 pp. Bibl.; illus.; maps.

Wielandt, Rotraud. *Das erzählerische Frühwerk Mahmūd Taymūrs: Beitrag zu einem Archiv der Modernen Arabischen Literatur*. Beiruter Texte und Studien, vol. 26. Weisbaden: Franz Steiner Verlag, 1983. 434 pp. Bib.; appends.; index.

[The author provides a comprehensive treatment of Taymur's short stories, putting them in both a historical and a theoretical context. Supporting materials—such as an inventory of Taymur's early stories with information about their production and dissemination—are well organized and comprehensive.]

Wiener, Daniel, ed. *Shalom: Israels Friedensbewegung*. Reinbek bei Hamburg: Rowohlt. 183 pp. Bibl.; illus.

Wilson, Rodney. *The Arab World: An International Statistical Directory*. Boulder, Colo.: Westview Press. 256 pp. Illus.; tables.

[This authoritative directory provides up-to-date, comprehensive statistical profiles of seventeen Arab countries. Wilson includes information sources previously unavailable in the West on all major economic indices. Analyzes the shortcomings of various data sources and indicates what further sources should be consulted.]

Wohlers-Scharf, Traute. *Les banques arabes et islamiques: De nouveaux partenaires commerciaux pour les pays en développement.* Paris: Organization for Economic Cooperation and Development. 184 pp.
[A study of the appearance on the international financial scene of these banks concurrently with the spectacular growth during the 1970s of an oil surplus in OPEC countries.]

al-Yassini, Ayman. *The Socialist Transformation of Syria under the Ba'th.* Discussion Paper Series, no. 13. Montreal: Centre for Developing Area Studies, McGill University. 54 pp.

————.*Religion and State in the Kingdom of Saudi Arabia.* Boulder, Colo.: Westview Press. 178 pp. Bibl.; tables; index.,
[The author examines the complex processes by which the traditional relationships among religion, society, and polity in this, the Arab state most closely identified with Islam, are being radically altered in modern times. His study focuses on the critical question of whether the differentiation between religion and state will increase or will be retained by means of some form of accommodation whereby the political elite keeps the forces of modernization under control and the religious elite accepts some elements of change.]

Yodfat, Aryeh Y. *The Soviet Union and Revolutionary Iran.* London: Croom Helm; New York: St. Martin's Press. 168 pp. Bibl.; index.
[This book by a noted Israeli scholar was completed just prior to his death. Its first three chapters are devoted to a thumbnail sketch of U.S.S.R.-Iranian relations from the nineteenth century to 1978; its last five chapters provide a richly documented chronicle of Soviet-Iranian interactions during the last year of the shah's regime and the early years of its revolutionary successor.]

Yoshitu, Michael M. *Caught in the Middle East: Japan's Diplomacy in Transition.* Lexington, Mass.: Lexington Books. 113 pp. Bibl; index.
[Japanese-American relations have been under a severe strain since the oil embargo of 1973 curtailed energy supplies and forced the transformation of Japan's U.S.-centered foreign policy. Based on information from personal interviews with key Japanese decision makers, the author traces the historical development of these policy changes and their contemporary implications. He analyzes the effects of the tenuous U.S. position in the Middle East in relation to situations such as the Iran hostage crisis and the Iran-Iraq war, and he delineates how events have changed the course of Japanese foreign policy.]

Yurtdaş, Barbara. *Wo mein Mann zuhause ist. . . .: Tagebuch einer Übersiedlung in die Türkei.* Reinbek bei Hamburg: Rowohlt. 189 pp.

Serials

Abir, Mordechai. "Saudi Security and Military Endeavor." *Jerusalem Quarterly*, no. 33 (Fall): 79–94.
This is a detailed look at Saudi Arabia's military establishment, with attention to foreign technicians and the lack of a large pool of native Saudi technicians. Abir believes the present government of the Sa'ud family has a wide enough power base to survive short-term threats.

Aburdene, Odeh. "Energy, Investment, and Trade: The U.S. and the Gulf." *Fletcher Forum* 8, no. 2 (Summer): 273–83.
The author clarifies the close economic relationship between the United States and the Gulf oil producers, with much attention to the return of petrodollars to the United States. The importance of the Gulf countries as a market for American goods and services is stressed.

Ansari, Hamied. "Sectarian Conflict in Egypt and the Political Expediency of Religion." *Middle East Journal* 38, no. 3 (Summer): 397–418.
This article deals with the Copts and the Coptic church in Egypt from the 1970s to the present. The author is also concerned with the destablilization of the political system and the effect that new repressive measures may have upon the liberalizing tendencies in Egypt.

Avineri, Shlomo. "Israel's Time of Trouble." *Present Tense* 12 no. 2 (Winter): 16–21.
Briefly develops the theme that the 1967 war was a turning point for Israel because it changed the nature of the public concept of the proper political agenda. Now that concept (which is personified by Begin) is called into question. Avineri, who is professor of political science at the Hebrew University, hopes that "Israel will be wise enough and generous enough to find an accomodation with the Palestinians based on compromise and mutual recognition."

Aziz al-Ahsan, Syed. "Economic Policy and Class Structure in Syria: 1958–1980." *International Journal of Middle East Studies* 16, no. 3 (August): 301–23.
A scholarly and documented approach to the question of how economic policy affects class structure. This article, which includes comparative information about Egypt, details the economic moves in Syria that caused al-Assad "to strike a middle way that enabled him to derive the benefits of both a limited liberal economy and a limited socialist economy." Aziz states that the "class structure has changed substantially as a result of economic policies," but he is weak in relating particular social changes to causative economic changes. An interesting conclusion is that "even after two decades of socialism. . . the regional and religious ties (at least in the realm of politics) are emerging to be more important than class ties."

Balta, Paul. "Oman: La stabilité retrouvée." *Le monde diplomatique* 31, no. 360 (March): 19.
This is a quick review of Oman's history. The recent construction of a highway the length of the country is seen as having strategic and psychological significance.

Benjelloun-Ollivier, Nadia. "Armes et armements au Proche-Orient." *L'Afrique et l'Asie modernes,* no. 141 (Summer): 22–46.

Most of the article dwells on military expenditures in the Middle Eastern states in comparison with their GNPs. Certain new trends are mentioned: the changing nature of war from the typical Israeli blitzkrieg to the fixed-position, large-scale encounters of the Iran-Iraq war, with civilian targets becoming objects of attack, not just enemy military power; the arms suppliers providing more and more state-of-the-art equipment, not just outmoded weaponry; and the ever-greater mobilization of the civilian populace for warfare. Israel, she notes, still far outspends other powers in the area.

Bill, James A. "Resurgent Islam in the Persian Gulf." *Foreign Affairs* 63, no. 1 (Fall): 108–27.

This is a masterful survey, summary, and analysis with recommendations by one who knows the full intricacies of the subject, not just the superficial political aspects of the contemporary Middle East. It should be required reading for all, from students to statesmen. Bill introduces the concept "populist Islam," which is sure to become a catchword of subsequent studies.

"Blacks, Catholics, Protestants, and Jews." *Present Tense* 11, no. 4 (Summer): 4–19.

Consisting of short articles by Ellen Stone, Basil Patterson, Jim Castelli, and A. James Rudin, this is an interesting and thought-provoking popular piece bringing into focus the place of Israel in the United States today. The section by Rudin, for example, makes clear the differences between liberal Protestantism's positions toward Jews and Israel, and the positions of conservative evangelicals of the Jerry Falwell variety.

Chafetz, Ze'ev. "Beirut and the Great Media Cover-Up." *Commentary* 78, no. 3 (September): 20–29.

Chafetz, a Michigan-born former director of Israel's government press office, presents a disturbing indictment of Western journalism that, he argues, succumbed to intimidation and violence from the PLO and the Syrians in Lebanon. As a result, Western journalists failed to report the full and true story of events. This is a highly controversial article.

Chenal, Alain. "Egypte: Des elections sans importance?" *L'Afrique et l'Asie modernes,* no. 142 (Autumn): 14–25.

The article provides one of the few accounts and analyses of the 27 April elections in Egypt to appear in Western sources. In general, Chenal believes that the elections were held fairly, that they were accompanied by a minimum of disorder, and that they served to reinforce the growth of democracy in neighboring states as well as in Egypt. Electoral statistics, in broad categories, are appended.

Cobban, Helena. "Lebanon's Chinese Puzzle." *Foreign Policy,* no. 53 (Winter 1983–84): 34–48.

A casual survey by a well-versed writer who suggests that closer attention be paid to the enormous growth of Beirut and the "political revolutions caused by the rapid urbanization of the Maronites and Shiites."

Cohen, Eliot A. " 'Peace for Galilee': Success or Failure?" *Commentary* 78, no. 5 (November): 24–30.

Cohen starts with severe criticism of American press coverage, accusing it of intense prejudice against Israel during the Peace for Galilee campaign. The article reviews three recent and detailed books about the subject. Written entirely from a pro-Israel viewpoint, the article clearly presents the campaign's failures and sees closer U.S.-Israel cooperation as one of its successes. Cohen, though, ignores the larger, long-term regional consequences of "Sharon's War."

Dawisha, Adeed. "The Motives of Syria's Involvement in Lebanon," *Middle East Journal* 38, no. 2 (Spring): 2 228–36.

Dawisha, one of the most astute students of contemporary Middle Eastern politics, argues that Syria's main aim is to attain and keep primary political influence over Lebanon and to this end has worked to reconcile the conflicting groups. Syria works on the assumption that the United States and Israel are one, and plays up this "alliance" to achieve a leadership role among the Arab states. Hafiz al-Assad's foreign policy also stems from internal political problems that come from the Alawi/Ba'th–Sunni tensions: in order to gain support from the Sunnis (whom he has at times brutally suppressed), he portrays himself as the principal proponent of Arabism.

Therefore al-Assad strives to control the PLO, which is the most prominent rallying point of Arab sentiment today. Those who desire to engineer a settlement in Lebanon must accomodate the desires of Syria. A valuable essay, both for its analysis and for clarity of expression.

Dayan-Herzbrun, Sonia, and Paul Kessler. "Mission à Bir-Zeit." *Le monde diplomatique* 31, no. 364 (July): 1, 14–15.

The authors, French Jews, visited Bir Zeit and al-Najah universities in Israel on behalf of a center at the University of Paris-X that cooperates with Bir Zeit. During their visit, they observed an increasing Israeli presence, and especially a presence of Jewish Israeli university students, in a movement of "solidarity" with the Palestinians. They hope that this movement will have a beneficial effect on Arab higher education in Israel.

Deeb, Marius S. "Lebanon: Prospects for National Reconciliation in the Mid-1980s." *Middle East Journal* 38, no. 2 (Spring): 267–83.

Deeb's well-written article presents much useful information on the leadership of the major groups in Lebanon (Shiites, Sunnis, Druze, Christians). Deeb sees hope in this leadership's "common economic interests, which bind them together, and which make them support a democratic parliamentary system with a free enterprise economic system as its socio-economic foundation."

Delpuech, Bernard. "Un gouvernement toujours sous tutelle." *Le monde diplomatique* 31, no. 366 (September): 22–23.

Mentions the antiresistance measures undertaken by the Afghan government under its Soviet guidance. Violent measures have caused rural populations to flee the country or to move to urban areas; this makes guerrilla operations more difficult in rural areas. The government tries to overcome ethnic rivalries while at the same time developing regional cultures. The government also attempts to secure the favor of the mullahs, and constructs or repairs mosques. Twenty thousand Afghans are now studying in the Soviet Union.

Devlin, John F. "The Political Structure in Syria." *Middle East Review* 17, no. 1 (Fall): 15–21.
This is a brief but competent exposition of the structure of Syria's political power, with some attention devoted to present contenders for leadership in the event of Assad's demise.

Dowty, Alan. "United States Decision-Making in Middle East Crises: 1958, 1970, 1973." *Jerusalem Journal of International Relations* 7, nos. 1–2 (1984): 92–106.
This is a study of the decision-making process and of crisis behavior during the three crises under review. Common attributes in each were the prevalence of a global perspective (i.e., anti–Soviet Union), lack of political-military coordination, and intelligence failure (each crisis came as a suprise to policymakers); nevertheless, in each crisis the immediate American ends were achieved. Dowty does not provide much of a recommendation for future crises, except to urge "regional experts" to improve the quality of their input to the decision makers.

Eizenstat, Stuart. "How Washington Sees Jerusalem." *Moment* 9, no. 3 (March): 21–25.
This thoughtful, well-written article by a high official of the Carter administration reviews "36 years of a special relationship." Some of its interest derives from Eizenstat's emphasis on putting Israel into the overall context of American foreign and domestic interests. Eizenstat thinks that "shared values" are important in explaining the support given to Israel by the United States, more important even than the undoubted political leverage exercised by Jewish pressure groups. He theorizes that the continuation of Israel's identity as a *Jewish* state is essential for the continuation of U.S. popular opinion in favor of Israel.

Entessar, Nadir. "External Involvement in the Persian Gulf Conflict." *Conflict Quarterly* 4, no. 4 (Fall): 41–56.
Concentrates on the military involvement of other countries in the Iran-Iraq war. The author notes the recent U.S. and Soviet support of Iraq and predicts that the war will continue until a new political alignment takes place in Iran (unlikely) or Saddam Hussein falls.

Fischer, Stanley. "Unraveling Israel's Tangled Economy." *Moment* 9, no. 8 (September): 22–24.
A concise, incisive explanation of the causes of Israel's current economic problems (400 percent inflation) and an equally terse prescription: cut government spending by $2 billion a year; freeze wages and prices; face up to consequent unemployment. Fischer, an economist at MIT, argues against "dollarization" and trusts that the new unity government will be politically able to make the hard decisions.

Freedman, Robert O. "Moscow, Damascus and the Lebanese Crisis of 1982–1984." *Middle East Review* 17, no. 1 (Fall): 22–39.
A fact-filled, heavily documented treatment of Soviet Middle East policies.

Freyer, Eckhard. "Zu den Auswirkungen Öleinnahmen auf die Entwicklung Saudi-Arabiens und die Wirtschaft." *Orient* 25 no. 2 (June): 204–22.
A heavily documented essay on the effects of reduced oil revenues on the development of Saudi Arabia. Freyer sees inevitable social repercussions and a departure of foreign technicians. However, the government seems stable and able to survive the present situation.

Galtier, Gerard. "Culture arabe et culture africaine: Comment reconstruire l'Etat tchadien?" *Le monde diplomatique* 31, no. 368 (November): 18–19.
Galtier describes the bases of power drawn upon by Hissen Habré and the composition of those forces opposing him, and traces the interest of Colonel Qaddafi in Chad. The essay has a valuable analysis of the North-South division of Chad.

Gérard, Alain. "Le maréchal Nemeiry face à ses 'démons.' " *Le monde diplomatique* 31, no. 364 (July): 1 10–11.
Gérard provides information about the economic conditions of Sudan and the limited power base of General Numayri. The North-South problem is discussed; the interesting point is made that some spokesmen from the South now oppose the government-imposed separation and call for unity instead. Numayri's Islamicization policies may have paralyzed the opposition, but for how long, wonders Gérard.

Goldstein, Walter. "The War between Iraq and Iran: A War That Can't Be Won or Ended." *Middle East Review* 17, no. 1 (Fall): 41–49, 57.
A survey of the broader issues of the war, with no attention paid to battlefront details. The author adheres to the now common theme that both sides should battle themselves into exhaustion. He mentions lessons learned from the four-year-old conflict and explores the reasons for both the U.S.S.R. and the United States favoring Iraq.

Gregory, Frank. "The Multinational Force—Aid or Obstacle to Conflict Resolution?" *Conflict Studies*, no. 170 (1984): 37 pp.
Although this general study of multinational peacekeeping forces starts with examples as early as 1850, much of the information concerns the Middle East, and specifically the Sinai and Lebanon, with explanations of the successes and failures of those two efforts to maintain peace.

Greilshammer, Ilan. "Failure of the European 'Initiatives' in the Middle East." *Jerusalem Quarterly*, no. 33 (Fall): 40–49.
Traces the past fifteen years of efforts by the European Economic Community (EEC) to influence Middle Eastern states and the Arab-Israeli conflict, and analyzes reasons for the EEC's failure in every instance, compared with the relative "success" of the United States and the U.S.S.R. He isolates seven conditions necessary for any EEC initiative to succeed.

Harkabi, Yehoshafat. "The Kahane Phenomenon." *Moment* 9, no. 10 (November): 21–23.
Written by a former chief of military intelligence who is now a professor of Middle Eastern studies at the Hebrew University, this analysis is remarkable for its candid acknowledgment of the failure of several past and present general Israeli attitudes and policies. Harkabi brings out the danger to Israel that may result from Kahane's election to parliament.

Herbert, Jean-Loup. "La force mobilisatrice d'une spiritualité." *Le monde diplomatique* 31, no. 361 (April): 17–18.

This important article contributes to an understanding of the nature, extent, and determination of the Islamic revolution in Iran. The theme is the infusing of religion into all aspects of Iranian life through indoctrination, or education. Of particular interest is the description of what the author terms *guerre de civilisation* which involves examining the human sciences, such as psychology, sociology, education, law, and economics, and confronting the foundations and structure of Western thought from a rigorous Islamic perspective.

Inbar, Efraim. "Sources of Tension between Israel and the United States." *Conflict Quarterly* 4, no. 2 (Spring): 56–65.

As Israel becomes increasingly dependent on the United States, and as the United States becomes increasingly interested in good relations with Arab states, the likelihood of problems developing between them increases. Inbar, a political scientist at Bar-Ilan University, presents a remarkably clear-sighted, unbiased examination of the "special relationship" and the actual and potential threats to it.

Jalbert, Paul. " 'News Speak' about the Lebanon War." *Journal of Palestine Studies* 14, no. 1 (Fall): 16–35.

A semantic discussion of various types of bias that are revealed in several analyses of news coverage of the Lebanon war. Useful and worth pondering the next time one hears an expert analyze the Middle Eastern scene. Jalbert concludes that the U.S. media (i.e., television) was pro-Israel.

Junqua, Daniel. "L'explosion tunisienne." *Le monde diplomatique* 31, no. 359 (February): 1, 19.

Takes the viewpoint that the bread riots demonstrate the wide gulf that separates the leaders from the rest of Tunisia and reveal the existence of two increasingly antagonistic societies within the country. These two societies correspond to a North-South division of Tunisia. Junqua devotes most of the article to expanding upon the differences between the liberal, Western-oriented North and the more conservative, fundamentalist South. Social justice, claims Junqua, is the prime issue in Tunisia.

Kaplan, Howard. "Abu Nidal: A Terrorists' Terrorist." *Moment* 10, no. 1 (December): 33–37.

Kaplan, in a characteristically brief, but informative article, details the career of Abu Nidal, probably the most implacable foe of Israel. In Kaplan's analysis, Abu Nidal acted on behalf of Iraq in attempting to assassinate Israel's ambassador to Great Britain, Shlomo Argov, thereby providing Begin and Sharon a pretext to invade Lebanon. Abu Nidal is also depicted as intent upon discrediting the PLO and especially Arafat—indeed, any effort toward peace and reconciliation. Kaplan expresses the hope that responsible persons can distinguish between the Abu Nidal types and those among the PLO and other Arab groups that are moderate and may wish to work for a resolution of political problems.

———. "Israel, As Arab Writers See It." *Moment* 9, no. 4 (April): 50–54.

A popular but sensitive treatment of the topic by a novelist and teacher of Arabic literature. Kaplan concentrates on the best recent Arabic fiction, recommending that through fiction one gains "a path to the mind and heart of a people we most often encounter in. . .polemical settings."

Kassir, Samir. "L'élan de la résistance dans le sud du Liban." *Le monde diplomatique* 31, no. 367 (October): 1, 15–16.
Kassir recounts the increasing resistance mounted by the villages of southern Lebanon against the Israeli occupation forces. The detention camps, notably Ansar, are described, and the countermeasures used by Israel are explained. Some attention is devoted to General Lahud and the South Lebanon Army; the Shiite aspect of southern Lebanon is stressed.

———. "L'O.L.P. et les impératifs de la legitimité." *Le monde diplomatique* 31, no. 359 (February): 10–11.
Consists mostly of a long description of the history and organization of the PLO, with emphasis on al-Fatah, Yasir Arafat's organization. The author explores new directions for al-Fatah, now that the PLO is expelled from Lebanon.

Khalidi, Rashid. "The Palestinians in Lebanon: Social Repercussions of Israel's Invasion." *Middle East Journal* 38, no. 2 (Spring): 255–66.
Khalidi, a professor of politics at the American University of Beirut, traces the plight of Palestinian refugees in Lebanon, and blames the United States and Israel for their continued misery.

Klare, Michael T. "Le rôle de l'Union Sovietique dans les ventes d'équipements militaires au tiers-monde." *Le monde diplomatique* 31, no. 361 (April): 9–10.
Klare offers much information on arms sales to the Arab world by the United States and Russia. He concludes, though, that the sale of weapons does not necessarily result in political advantage.

Klüver, Hartmut. "Die 'Brot-Revolten' in Tunesien und Marokko im Winter 1983/84." *Orient* 25, no. 1 (March): 123–30.
Klüver finds that the populations of both countries have an extremely high proportion of people younger than fifteen years. This, plus demographic changes that are massing populations in northern coastal regions, have created a potential for urban disturbances. Unable to be agriculturally self-sufficient, the two countries import food, but as the population increases more than production rises, the governments are short of foreign reserves, which forces them to double the price of bread. In the riots that have resulted, hundreds have been killed in Morocco and Tunisia: Klüver doubts that the governments can continue the high subsidization of food costs.

Kushner, David. "The Turkish-Greek Conflict: Lessons for Israel." *Jerusalem Quarterly*, no. 31 (Spring): 64–77.
Kushner, a professor of modern Turkish history at Haifa University, gives a balanced view of Greek-Turkish relations during the Ottoman and modern periods. From the Cyprus question, he draws the parallel (admitting the dangers in such reasoning) that the best chance for coexistence between Palestinian Arabs and Israel would be a settlement that, while "allowing for free contact. . .would still keep them geographically and politically apart."

Kutschera, Chris. "Nouveaux espoirs pour l'opposition chiite irakienne." *Le monde diplomatique* 31, no. 361 (April): 15–17.

In the late 1950s, the Ayat Allah Muhammad Bakr al-Sadr founded the Da'wah, a Shiite party in Iraq. al-Sadr was executed in 1980, and his loss weakened al-Da'wah vis-à-vis various recently founded and more radical Shiite groups. The Supreme Council for the Islamic Revolution in Iraq, an outgrowth of al-Sadr's teaching, was created 17 November 1982 and is the object of this essay.

Lanne, Bernard. "Les causes profondes de la crise tchadienne." *L'Afrique et l'Asie modernes*, no. 140 (Spring): 3–14.

Lanne concentrates on the causes of Chad's internal strife beginning in 1965, a strife that progressed into a civil war in 1979. He touches on the North-South division, progress in the South, backwardness in the North, education (surprisingly more widespread in the South), Islam and Christianity, and so on. He emphasizes the psychological makeup of the northerners as the deepest cause of the rebellion and brings out the fact that the newly formed Muslim elites did not support the rebellion.

Lavy, Victor. "The Economic Embargo of Egypt by Arab States: Myth and Reality." *Middle East Journal* 38, no. 3 (Summer): 419–32.

The embargo, slapped on Egypt as a reaction to the treaty with Israel, is found to have changed the direction if not the magnitude of trade: Libya, Algeria, and Iraq cut off trade, while Saudi Arabia and Lebanon increased their trade with Egypt. Aid to Egypt, however, was cut off completely. Turkey (not an Arab state) is seen to be the principal beneficiary of the embargo.

Lawson, Fred. "Comment le régime de president El Asad s'emploie à remodeler l'économie syrienne." *Le monde diplomatique* 31, no. 358 (January): 12–13.

Lawson traces a change in state investment from heavy industry to agriculture, along with the development of light industry in small towns. His thesis is that internal political considerations influence the economic policies of Hafiz al-Assad's government.

Mattes, Hanspeter. "Die Grundzüge der libyschen Aussenpolitik: Ein Überblick." *Orient* 25, no. 2 (June): 189–203.

This fact-filled survey takes up the bases and content of Libya's foreign policy. Attention is given to Qaddafi's efforts to achieve unity in the Arab world, and to the confrontation with the United States.

Muir, Jim. "Lebanon: Arena of Conflict, Crucible of Peace." *Middle East Journal* 38, no. 2 (Spring): 204–19.

Muir, a British journalist with long Middle East experience, gives a running account of political conflicts in Lebanon since 1975. He credits Israel's invasion of Lebanon to the desire to forestall moves that would impede the planting of further settlements in the West Bank, to drive a wedge "between the U.S. and the Arabs," to damage "U.S. credibility in Arab eyes," and to undermine "moderate Arab advocates of a peace which would challenge Israel's claim to the occupied territories." Even more specifically, the invasion "was to preempt an impending U.S. peace push" and, by destroying the PLO, to remove the symbol of West Bank Arab unity.

Muir brilliantly explores the complexity of United States, Israeli, and Syrian motives and moves, and sees that an outside agreement by these three must be achieved before an internal settlement can be made. One ray of hope, for Muir, is seen in Lebanon's factions coming to understand that economic necessity may require the unity of the country.

Nettler, Ronald. "Islam vs. Israel." *Commentary* 78, no. 6 (December): 26–30.
A nonscholarly account of fundamentalism, largely in Egypt, and the threat it poses to Israel.

Nezan, Kendal. "La destruction de l'identité culturelle kurde au Turquie." *L'Afrique et l'Asie modernes*, no. 140 (Spring): 51–58.
Written by the director of the Kurdish Institute in Paris, this article is a sad recitation of the measures taken by the Turkish government to destroy Kurdish culture. The Kurds, one of the most important minorities in the Middle East, may number 20 million, of whom 10 million live in Turkey, according to Nezan.

Nicolai, Hermann. "La politisation de la crise sociale libanaise." *L'Afrique et l'Asie modernes*, no. 142 (Autumn): 33–52.
A brief, cogent analysis of the Lebanon problem. Believing the underlying causes of the civil war are social, Nicolai first looks at long-term changes in the economy and at social crises brought forth by these changes. Next the unsettling effect of Palestinian refugees is developed, along with the growth of numerous parties of the disenfranchised and the Kata'ib reaction. Nicolai sees the true problem to be the abuse of power by a multiconfessional minority dominated by the Maronites, rather than a simple inequilibrium of Christian and Muslim power. He sees little hope of success by the present Lebanese cabinet for, with the exception of Nabih Berri, it is composed of representatives of the old order.

Oweiss, Ibrahim M. "The Israeli Economy and Its Military Liability." *American-Arab Affairs*, no. 8 (Spring): 31–40.
Oweiss stresses the adverse economic effects on Israel of its war economy and concludes that only a "long-term redirection of resources from the military to civilian industrial production and agriculture" will best serve Israel, its neighbors, and the United States. The author, a professor of economics at Georgetown University, ignores the external pressures on Israel that make a war economy necessary.

Peterson, J.E. "American Policy in the Gulf and the Sultanate of Oman." *American-Arab Affairs*, no. 8 (Spring): 117–30.
Peterson goes well beyond the requirements of a survey of the political, economic, and military relations of the United States and Oman. His numerous recommendations for American policy reveal a deeper comprehension of the Arab world in general and the Gulf in particular than is found in most articles on political topics.

Quandt, William B. "Reagan's Lebanon Policy: Trial and Error." *Middle East Journal* 38, no. 2 (Spring): 237–54.
Quandt, the doyen of U.S. political analysts dealing with the Middle East, offers a reasoned critique of Reagan's policies. He concludes that the United States should work primarily for political reconciliation in

Lebanon, shift emphasis from the military to the diplomatic front, and concentrate on local and regional concerns rather than on global strategy.

Ramonet, Ignacio. "Maroc: L'heure de tous les risques." *Le monde diplomatique* 31, no. 358 (January): 7–9, 10–11.
Against a background of recent drought and long-term demographic change, Ramonet sets out Morocco's many and severe social, religious, political, financial, and other problems for 1984. He dwells on the lavish expenses of King Hassan II for villas.

Rondot, Philippe. "Le Dhofar: De la guerre au développement." *Le monde diplomatique* 31, no. 360 (March): 21.
Traces the revolts that have occurred in Dhofar since the 1960s. They were finally quelled in 1975 with Jordanian and Iranian assistance.

———. "Oman: Priorité à la defense." *Le monde diplomatique* 31, no. 360 (March): 20.
Relates the efforts and success of Sultan Qabus in building up the military forces of Oman. The heavy reliance on foreigners in the armed services is stressed.

Rondot, Pierre. "Le Grand Maghreb arabe: Projet et perspectives." *L'Afrique et l'Asie modernes*, no. 143 (Winter): 47–60.
Traces the idea of a unity of the North African Arab states of Morocco, Algeria, and Tunisia, and mentions what favors and what opposes such a unity. The rapprochement of Libya and Morocco is examined, and the reactions of Tunisia and Algeria to this diplomatic surprise are brought out.

Rubenberg, Cheryl A. "The Conduct of U.S. Foreign Policy in the Middle East in the 1983–84 Presidential Election Season." *American-Arab Affairs*, no. 9 (Summer): 22–45.
Rubenberg focuses upon "the impact of pro-Israeli groups on the formation and implementation of U.S. Middle East policy" and the influence of these groups on the electoral process. Much evidence is adduced and many sources cited to support the thesis that Jewish voters and money ultimately determine U.S. Middle East policy.

Sadria, Modjtaba. "Cooperation et sécurité dans le Golfe: Un premier rôle pour l'Arabie Saoudite." *Le monde diplomatique* 31, no. 358 (January): 14.
A quick description of the Gulf Cooperation Council.

Schiff, Ze'ev. "Lebanon: Motivations and Interests in Israel's Policy." *Middle East Journal* 38, no. 2 (Spring): 220–27.
Schiff, scholar and editor at *Haaretz*, tersely relates the difficulties faced in Israel's Lebanese venture and sees agreement with Syria to be the only way out. In his opinion, Israeli public opinion is willing to compromise all its objectives in Operation Galilee except the security of Israel's northern border.

Schlicht, Alfred. "Le renouveau de l'Islam et les Coptes." *L'Afrique et l'Asie modernes*, no. 142 (Autumn): 26–32.
A quick survey of relations between Copts and Muslims in Egypt. These

relations have worsened since 1970, and although the situation is quiet under Mubarak Schlicht predicts a period of trouble.

Schoenbaum, David. "The Truth Makes Us Free Though Not Especially Happy." *Present Tense* 11, no. 3 (Spring): 31–35.
The author, professor of modern European history, relates his experiences in teaching a course at Iowa on the "Historical Background of the Arab-Israeli Conflict." Worth reading as an account by an intelligent and compassionate teacher leading his class of Americans (Jews and Arabs) to an understanding of the historical roots of the issue.

Sharabi, Hisham. "Looking Back at AUB; A Memoir." *Jerusalem Quarterly*, no. 30 (Winter): 43–49.
Sharabi, a leading Arab intellectual and teacher at Georgetown University, presents an honest and frankly critical portrayal (truly devastating) of the teaching methods and class content he encountered during his student days at the American University of Beirut. Sharabi also directs pithy comments at his fellow Arab intellectuals at AUB.

Sheffer, Gabriel. "The Uncertain Future of American Jewry-Israel Relations." *Jerusalem Quarterly*, no. 32 (Summer): 66–80.
Sheffer paints in detail the erosion of support by American Jews for Israel. She observes that this is a long-term trend originating well before the invasion of Lebanon and provides statistical information to support her argument. She discusses what would happen if the U.S. government and Israel were to clash head on. She expects widespread acceptance of strong U.S. measures against Israel—but not to the extent of accepting that which would damage the existence or security of Israel.

Sid-Ahmed, Mohamed. "La résurgence du Wafd et les calculs de M. Moubarak." *Le monde diplomatique* 31, no. 362 (May): 24–25.
Traces the history of the Wafd, the oldest political party in Egypt, and tries to account for its continued vitality. He argues that President Mubarak favors a revitalized Wafd as a counterweight to other, less desirable political groupings.

Steinbach, Udo. "Germany's Attitude toward the Middle East." *American-Arab Affairs*, no. 10 (Fall): 33–43.
Steinbach, editor of *Orient*, reviews the evolution of West Germany's Middle East policy, starting with 1970 and the policies of the European Communities. The Federal Republic is following the common European foreign policy that forthrightly recognizes the "legitimate rights of the Palestinians" and the necessity for self-determination. Germany shares the frustration of the total failure of these policies to have positive results. Apart from the Arab-Israeli problem, the security of the Gulf is a new and important element in Germany's (and Europe's) foreign policy considerations, "now that the United States, as a result of political developments in recent years, has lost credibility as a guarantor of security and stability." The Bonn government because of its major influence in the European Communities and because it was never a colonial power in the Middle East, may be called upon to play a greater role in Gulf security. In the meantime, for a number of reasons, relations with Turkey and Iran are carefully pursued. Steinbach's analysis and observations offer a

perspective that is lacking in most of the recent articles on the political problems of the Middle East.

Sterner, Michael. "The Iran-Iraq War." *Foreign Affairs* 63, no. 1 (Fall): 128–43.
Sterner, a former U.S. ambassador to the UAE and Department of State official, provides a well-written and useful overview of the war and related issues of the Persian Gulf. The United States, in Sterner's view, pursues three policy objectives in the Gulf: (1) to maintain shipments to avoid disruption in Western economies; (2) to maintain the security of reasonably friendly governments in the area; and (3) to avoid giving the U.S.S.R. an opportunity to dominate either Iraq or Iran. In the event of an Iranian victory over Iraq, the United States would have to act to oppose Iranian efforts to subvert Gulf governments. An Iranian attack on Saudi Arabia would require U.S. military response, but less violent pressure by Iran would be best met by diplomacy, an aim of which would be to support those in Iran who do not want to export revolution or embark on imperialistic conquest.

Tolotti, Sandrine. "L'Arabie Saoudite, nouveau centre du monde arabe?" *L'Afrique et l'Asie modernes*, no. 143 (Winter): 70–84.
Addresses the question: To what extent can Saudi Arabia influence the present state of affairs in the Arab world? One limiting factor is the country's military weakness. The potential threat of Yemen to Saudi stability is explored, and the dependence of Saudi Arabia on others for virtually everything except oil is emphasized. Oil wealth is obviously the basis of any real influence the Saudis enjoy. The author concludes that "Saudi leadership has substituted pragmatic Arabism for Nasser's ideological pan-Arabism; Arab solidarity, not unity, is their aim."

Vernant, Jacques. "Chypre: Les constantes et la tentative de partition." *L'Afrique et l'Asie modernes*, no. 141 (Spring): 40–49.
Most of the article skillfully recounts the diplomatic history of Cyprus from the nineteenth century to the present, leading up to the establishment of the Turkish Republic of Cyprus. Vernant realizes that no one is going to act to undo the unilateral action of Rauf Denktash—whose solution recalls that proposed by Dean Acheson in 1964. He thinks the only hope lies in integration, not separation, of the two ethnic communities.

Wingerter, Rex. "U.S. Zionist Organizations: Their Tax-Exempt Status Challenged." *Journal of Palestine Studies* 14, no. 1 (Fall): 106–17.
Charitable transfers from the United States to Israel may amount to $1 billion a year. Channeled through six major Zionist organizations, this money appears to be largely tax-exempt charitable deductions. The article describes a lawsuit brought by a combination of Palestinians and American citizens (including Jewish Americans) who protest the use of funds that is allegedly in violation of American law and several public policies.

Yaniv, Avner. "Jews and Arabs on Campus." *Jerusalem Quarterly*, no. 30 (Winter): 29–42.
The author focuses on Haifa University, whose increasingly conservative student body in the late 1970s led to difficulties for Arab students. Yaniv details the problems and the means employed to reduce hostilities between the two groups, which led to the present relatively successful situation of ethnic relations.

Index

South Yemen, 71
Soviet Union: and Gulf region, 90–91, 103; and Libya, 141; and Saudi Arabia, 59, 75, 76–77
Standard of California (SOCAL), 57
Sudan, 141–42
Sudayri Seven, 62–63
Sultan (Saudi minister), 62, 63
Sunnis: in Gulf region, 92, 93, 94; and terrorism, 150, 151, 153
Syria: and Libya, 142–43, 144; and terrorism, 151, 153, 154, 155, 159

Tami, 111, 112
Tehiya party, 116, 121, 122, 125
Terrorism: Armenian, 151–52, 154–57; evolution of, 149–50; Iranian, 158–60; Jewish, in West Bank, 121; Libyan, 143, 158; Palestinian, 157–58; patterns in, 150–51; Shiite, 149, 150, 151–54, 160
Transitional Government of National Unity (GUNT), 142
Tribalism, in Saudi Arabia, 60, 61, 64
Turkey, 155
Turki al-Faysal (Saudi prince), 63

UAE, 88
Umm al-Qaiwain (UAE), 88
United Arab Emirates (UAE), 88
United States: aid to Israel, 118–19; and Gulf region, 91, 103–4; and Libya, 134, 143–44; and Saudi Arabia, 53–60, 74, 76–78
U.S.-Saudi Joint Commission for Economic Cooperation, 56
USSR. See Soviet Union

Vigilantes, Jewish, 121–23

Wahhabism: in Qatar, 87; in Saudi Arabia, 61
Weizman, Ezer, 117, 124
West Bank, 119–21
Western Sahara, 142–43
Women: in Libya, 135–36; in Saudi Arabia, 66, 68

Yahad party, 117, 124

al-Zawi, al-Shaykh al-Tahir, 137
Zayid Al Nahayyan, 88, 101
Zionism. See Labor Zionism

Contributors

John W. Amos II is an associate professor at the Naval Postgraduate School in Monterey, California, where he teaches Middle Eastern politics and international law. He holds a Ph.D. in Political Science from the University of California at Berkeley, and a J.D. from the Monterey College of Law. He has lectured and written extensively on Middle Eastern politics, including two books, *Arab-Israeli Political/Military Relations* (New York: Pergamon Press, 1979) and *Palestinian Resistance: Organization of a Nationalist Movement* (New York: Pergamon Press, 1980).

Mark Tyler Day is an associate librarian in the Reference Department of the Indiana University Library. He has held a variety of library positions in a number of universities, including the University of Riyadh, Saudi Arabia; Princeton University; and the University of New Brunswick, Canada. He recently earned an M.A. in Arabic language and literature from Indiana University and is a candidate for the Ph.D. He earned an M.A. in library science, an M.A.T. in social science, and a B.A. in political science from the University of Chicago. Current research activities include work on computer-assisted bibliographic reference service, the theory and practice of cross-cultural literary translation, and the development of modern literary cultures with their supporting social institutions—such as reading publics, libraries, and the book trade—in Middle Eastern countries. Day is the author of "Contemporary Saudi Writers of Fiction: A Preliminary Bibliography of Published Books, Accompanied by Short Biographical Sketches," *Journal of the College of Arts, University of Riyadh*, 7 (1980): 57–78.

Marius Deeb is a visiting professor at the Center for Contemporary Arab Studies, Georgetown University. He has previously taught at the American University of Beirut, at Indiana University, Bloomington, and at Kent State University, where he was chairman of the Middle East Program. He has been a senior associate member at St. Antony's College, Oxford University, and a senior fellow at Princeton University. Dr. Deeb has published widely in the area of Middle Eastern politics and history. He is the author of *Party Politics in Egypt: The Wafd and Its Rivals, 1919–1939*, St. Antony's Middle East Monographs Series, no. 9 (London, 1979); *The Lebanese Civil War* (New York: Praeger, 1980); and coauthor, with Mary-Jane Deeb, of *Libya since the Revolution: Aspects of Social and Political Development* (New York: Praeger, 1982). He received his B.A. and M.A. from the American University of Beirut, and his Ph.D. from Oxford University.

Mary-Jane Deeb is a Ph.D. candidate at the School of Advanced International Studies of Johns Hopkins University. She received her B.A. and M.A. from the American University in Cairo, where she was also a university fellow. She has been a consultant to the UN Economic Commission for Western Asia (ECWA), UNICEF, USAID, America-Mideast Educational and Training Services Inc. (AMIDEAST), and the Ford Foundation. She has also been a research associate at the Arab Development Institute in Tripoli, Libya. She has carried out a number of research projects, including studies on women, education, drug addiction, vocational training, and small-business enterprises. She is coauthor, with N. Tewel, of the Lebanon Country Profile prepared for USAID's Office of Foreign Disaster Assistance, and, with Marius Deeb, of *Libya since the Revolution: Aspects of Social and Political Development* (New York: Praeger, 1982).

R. Hrair Dekmejian is a professor of political science at the State University of New York at Binghamton and a lecturer in Middle Eastern politics at the Foreign Service Institute, Department of State, Washington, D.C. He is the author of *Islam in Revolution: Fundamentalism in the Arab World* (Syracuse: Syracuse University Press, 1985), *Patterns of Political Leadership* (Albany: State University of New York Press, 1975), and *Egypt under Nasir* (Albany: State University of New York Press, 1971). He has worked as a consultant for USAID, USIA, and other government agencies.

Don Peretz is professor of political science and director of the program in South West Asian and North African Studies (SWANA) at the State University of New York in Binghamton. He is the author of *Israel and the Palestine Arabs* (Washington, D.C.: Middle East Institute, 1958); *The Middle East Today*, 4th ed. (New York: Praeger, 1983); *The Government and Politics of Israel*, 2d ed. (Boulder, Colo.: Westview Press, 1983); and *The Middle East: Selected Readings*, rev. ed. (Boston: Houghton Mifflin, 1973). His articles have appeared in *Foreign Affairs*, *Middle East Journal*, *Wilson Quarterly*, *Jewish Social Studies*, *Christian Century*, *Commonweal*, *Christianity and Crisis*, and other publications. He is coauthor of several books, and his articles have appeared in several published collections.

J. E. Peterson is a Washington-based writer on Middle Eastern Affairs, a research fellow at the Middle East Institute, and an associate scholar at the Foreign Policy Research Institute. He has taught at Bowdoin, William and Mary, Penn, and Portland State, has been a research analyst at the Library of Congress and the Thornton Hooper Fellow in International Security Affairs at the Foreign Policy Research Institute. Among his publications are *Oman in the Twentieth Century* (London: Croom Helm; New York: Barnes & Noble, 1978), *Conflict in the Yemens and Superpower Involvement* (Washington, D.C.: Georgetown University Center for Contemporary Arab Studies, 1981), *Yemen: The Search for a Modern State* (Baltimore: Johns Hopkins University Press, 1982), and, as editor, *The Politics of Middle Eastern Oil* (Washington, D.C.: Middle East Institute, 1983. He has also written more than a dozen articles, has recently completed a book-length annotated bibliography, *Security in the Arabian Peninsula and Gulf States* (forthcoming), and is presently completing a book titled *Defending Arabia*.

David H. Partington was educated at Lehigh University, received an M.A. in European history from Rutgers University, and earned his doctorate in Oriental Studies at Princeton University in 1961. Successively employed by Princeton, Michigan, and Harvard universities, he has been since 1970 the Middle Eastern librarian in the Harvard College Library and an associate of the Harvard Middle East Center. The author of numerous reviews, articles, and studies related to bibliography and Middle Eastern librarianship, and articles on Arabic, Persian, and Turkish literatures in the *Reader's Adviser*, he has served on the board of directors of the Middle East Studies Association, been chairman of the Mid-East Committee of the Association of Research Libraries, and is now an editor of *Mundus Arabicus*, an annual devoted to modern Arabic literary topics. He brings to the editorship of the *Middle East Annual* a broad background in Arabic, Turkish, and Persian studies.

Previous Essays

U.S. Economic Ties with the Gulf Cooperation Council and Egypt
Ragaei El Mallakh

Vol. 3—1983

Islamic Fundamentalism: Historic Mission and Contemporary Mood
John O. Voll

The PLO since Beirut
Philip Mattar

The Soviet Union, Syria, and the Crisis in Lebanon: A Preliminary Analysis
Robert O. Freedman

Chad: Escalation Leads to Impasse
Edouard Bustin

The Middle East in the U.S. Media
Edmund Ghareeb